The Last Who Remember:
Traditional Ireland in the Words of its People

Brian Kaller

With a Foreword by Rod Dreher

The Last Who Remember:
Traditional Ireland in the Words of its People

Brian Kaller

With a Foreword by Rod Dreher

Academica Press
Washington ~ London

Library of Congress Cataloging-in-Publication Data

Names: Kaller, Brian (author)

Title: The last who remember : traditional ireland in the words of its people |
Kaller, Brian.

Description: Washington : Academica Press, 2025. | Includes references.

Identifiers: LCCN 2024952856 | ISBN 9781680535662 (hardcover) |
9781680535686 (paperback) | 9781680535679 (e-book)

Contents

Foreword

Rod Dreher

I first became aware of Brian Kaller through the *Restoring Mayberry* blog he wrote when he lived in rural Ireland. We shared an interest in dissatisfaction with modern life and a curiosity over what people today had lost by turning our backs on the old ways. The difference was that I only wrote about it; Brian Kaller did it. That, and the fact that unlike me, a big-city journalist who jittered from topic to topic, Brian – I call him that, because he later became a friend – has a well of deep patience that allowed him to go deep in the life and lore of Ireland's country people. As I would learn after we met, Brian has a boundless capacity to listen, and to listen well.

The Last Who Remember: Traditional Ireland And Its People is the fruit of two decades of listening to the final Irish generation who experienced an agrarian country that has now disappeared. It is little known in the United States that the kind of modernity that Americans have lived through since at least the end of the Second World War only arrived in Ireland much later. That was an Ireland that was poorer, yes, more insular, and far less technologically advanced. But it was also an Ireland whose material poverty and backwardness compelled its people to become more resilient, more generous, and more humane.

The cheques story Brian tells in these pages is only one example. Between 1966 and 1976, the Irish economic crisis was so severe that the nation's banks closed for a period. In 1970, the bank closure lasted for six months, and then they only re-opened on limited hours. This meant that for a year, most people could neither deposit nor withdraw cash. Nor could they gain access to their bank records.

What did the Irish do? There wasn't enough cash in circulation to maintain the economy, so they wrote cheques as IOUs to their neighbors and to tradesmen. One economist estimated that about five billion Irish pounds had been traded that year in these informal cheques, on which everyone made good when the banks re-opened. It's a miracle, if you think about it, and certainly unimaginable in Ireland or any Western country today.

How did they do it? Because the Irish of that time – well within living memory – dwelled in a high-trust society. Everyone knew everyone else and had faith in them. Those homemade cheques held value, because the Irish people believed that their neighbors would make good on them one day.

Fast-forward to the present day, when community life has all but evaporated in an age of mass migration, social mobility, and the ubiquitous presence of smartphones, which trap everyone in a solipsistic prison of their own choosing. Few people know each other, and nobody knows what the ground rules of social conduct are. Result: the loss of social and personal trust necessary to make society resilient in times of great crisis, economic or otherwise.

The Last Who Remember is filled with stories like that, told by old men and old women who hold within their lived experience the recollection of that time, an era when most Irishmen still did as their ancestors had done: gathered in each other's homes in the evenings and sang songs and told stories passed down through generations. But those people are dying out, and those who still live are often treated as backwards, bitter, and nostalgic for a world that needed to die so modernity could thrive in Ireland. Well, contemporary Ireland is a much worldlier and wealthier place than the Ireland of days gone by, but "progress" has rendered the human qualities of life that used to be held dear by the Irish people, and that made up their social fabric, into tatters. There is so much we take for granted about how to live a civilized life in community – and when it is gone, we wake up in a dark wood, having lost the straight path. It is not just the Irish who are living this tragedy. We all are.

The Last Who Remember is far from a work of mere nostalgia, though. Brian Kaller is a journalist with the soul of a cultural anthropologist. He closely observed the daily life of his adopted country, and took the time to do what so few younger men these days bother to do: talk to the old people, and hear their stories. He didn't do this simply because it fed his soul, though it did. Brian did it because he has long been interested in how societies and cultures build resilience.

Though personally a religious traditionalist, Brian is also deeply engaged in thinking critically about the way modern people abuse and exploit Nature – a cause more often associated with the political left. Brian is no leftist (and not terribly political in any case), but he cares about human ecology as much as he does about the natural world. He uses his knowledge of cultivation of fields and husbandry of forests to understand how people create sustainable communities – and how they allow them to fall to ruin, if only by neglect.

In these pages, Brian Kaller casts his eyes across the Irish past to wake contemporary people up – not only Irishmen, but all who live in modernity – to how bizarrely anti-human this world of wealth, sophistication, and ease has become. We are living and raising our children in a constructed environment unlike any the world has ever known. The social and cultural breakdown of the last half-century has broken so many bonds that emerged since time out of mind among people – props, guardrails, and cultural jigs that allowed them to live meaningful lives together, to bear each other's suffering, and to share each other's joys.

If *The Last Who Remember* were only an elegy for a lost past, it would still be valuable as a tragic record of what we allowed to slip through our soft, clean, well-manicured fingers. Happily, it is also a book about the future. As Brian points out, the neighborly, human-scaled world of the Irish past did not emerge as the gift of a fairy spell. It was something built by real people, over time, to meet their real needs. They made this lost homeland, this haven in a heartless world, under harsh conditions much more dire and oppressive than today. If they could do it, why can't we?

"Hope is memory that desires," said the French novelist Honoré Balzac. Brian Kaller has written a book of memory, to be sure. But if what your read in its pages kindles desire to recover what once was, and what could be again, then *The Last Who Remember* will be a book not just of mourning, but, as the author intends, a book of hope. In that case, there is another Balzac saying that applies: "It is easy to sit up and take notice. What is difficult is getting up and taking action."

Rod Dreher
Budapest, November 2024

Introduction

You make your choices. You stop the car to help the person on the side of the road, and approach them cautiously. You take the job offer in a new city. You think about marriage. Your days are counting down, and sometimes you must accept a challenge, risk everything while you're still young, plunge into an adventure that forces you to become someone new and perhaps better. Sometimes everything goes to plan, and sometimes you find yourself broke with a toddler in a bog in Ireland.

Why Ireland? It was foreign but still English-speaking, and for the first time in centuries its economy was booming. My wife had family land there, and my Irish-American family still kept in touch with cousins there. I had never been far from my native Missouri, but grew up with my family's songs and stories of Ireland, and was curious to see if they matched the reality.

Rather than stay in the dying profession of journalism, I wanted to see if I could build a new life with my own hands. In an increasingly decadent world, I wanted an innocent space where my baby daughter could be a child in peace, where I could read to her by the fire.

So we checked the place out. I got on a plane for the first time I can remember, saw the ocean for the first time, and saw another country for the first time. I made my choices, and we settled into a house in the Bog of Allen.

***

We moved in shortly before Halloween, which I quickly learned is the night for Irish kids to launch fireworks into the dark fields. Where our house was. I also learned that jet-lagged babies have strong opinions about the sound of artillery in the middle of the night.

I also realised that all the postcard photos you see of Ireland were taken in summer, and the island sits at the same latitude as the southern tip of

Alaska. Ocean currents keep the island from freezing, but winter still brought sixteen-hour nights, and with no streetlights in the country or even stars in the perpetual drizzle, everything was treacle-black, slick and corpse-cold.

When we moved in the days were already shrinking to several hours of sunrise and sunset, the orange sun crouching behind the hedges and bar-coding the land with thin shadows. Ironically, it's when I most often needed sunglasses, as the eye-level sun blinded me without illuminating the world. Cars drove with streetlamps on under a dim pewter sky, trees reached like skeletal hands from the grey earth, and puddles stretched across roads until they became impassable.

The roads. All my experience driving was to follow America's vast rivers of concrete, an industrial circulatory system that slices through mountains in straight lines and predictable paths. Everything else on the land -- billboards, shopping plazas, gas stations like neon cathedrals – lines these arteries, so you can get anywhere fast with a car and nowhere without one.

I thought the main difficulty would involve learning to drive on the other side of the road, not realising that I was lucky to have a road with two sides. The road outside our land had only one lane – not one lane each way, but one pothole-riddled obstacle course slightly wider than a car, and you pulled into someone's driveway when another car approached in the distance. On one side was a canal, and one slip would plunge your car into the water.

Even the two-lane roads twisted around fields in tight bends, flanked by high stone walls or hedges. You drove through a winding trench, never able to see far, or when a car or tractor pulled out in front of you. Cars were relatively new here, and nothing had been built with them in mind.

Between the narrow lanes, high hedges, hairpin turns, potholes, floods, slick roads, dim winter light, drizzle and fog, I rarely drove, and then only slowly and white-knuckled, past signs for ridiculously high speed limits that I assumed were posted to cull the population of gullible outsiders. Thankfully there was a regular bus service that took me to the city, although I did have to fight seasickness as the double-decker hurtled around the hairpin turns.

Nor was there much around us to drive to – the nearest "village," three kilometres away, was an intersection with a shop, church and pub. When I did need to get somewhere, in a time before smart phones and GPS, I asked locals for directions, and found that none of the roads had names beyond a map label like "R303" that no one used.

None of the roads had names.

Nor did any of the houses have numbers, as they would be pointless, and there were no postal codes then. You wrote your address as your name and then the name of the local area, and then the county. The postman simply knew everyone and where they would be, and accordingly was much valued as a friend and source of gossip.

A road might be called the "Ballinagappa road" if it went to Ballinagappa, but if you turned around you were on a different road. Or people referred to the "doctor's road," as a doctor used to live there a century ago. I quickly learned where everything used to be throughout the bog.

Curiously, *intersections* sometimes had names like "Bundle of Sticks," but the roads coming from them remained nameless. On my first trip to Dublin someone told me to turn at the "Red Cow," and I asked, hesitantly, if the cow was always in the same place. Larger *houses* sometimes had names, and if you lived in the area everyone assumed you knew the house.

There were a few road signs, but no Irish word sounds remotely like it looks; Irish actors like Saoirse (SIR-sha) Ronan, Ciaran (KEER-an) Hinds or Domhnall (DOUGH-null) Gleeson must wince through many red-carpet mispronunciations. It was a long time before I felt comfortable asking directions through the bog to Newtownmoneenluggagh, Stookalargachuitread or Gubpaudeenshaneneese.

I should explain what a bog is. Bogs are wetlands, where the water table is about as high as the ground and wet weather turns the land to liquid. A flooded land with trees is a *swamp*, one with just grass is a *marsh*, and one fed by a spring is a *fen*. All have flowing, oxygen-rich water that supports microscopic life, and thus feeds insects, frogs, and birds. When we hear that we need to preserve wetlands, it's because so much lives there.

In a bog, though, water collects in hollows of the land and stays there, losing its oxygen until nothing in it decays properly. Farmers here still fish out trees that fell in centuries ago, the wood stained black but still solid. Very occasionally they fish out bodies sacrificed by ancient Druids, cured like leather but their expressions fixed. They fish out giant hunks of butter from prehistoric times, aged like fine cheese and still edible – more on that later.

The surface is mostly shaggy peat moss, layers of new growth covering the old each season. The old growth does not decay, though, so centuries of it compact into an organic mass like soft black cheese. For centuries farmers have drained sections of the bog, sliced out bricks of peat – "turf," locals call it – then dried them over the summer and burned them in the fireplace in winter. What little infrastructure had been built here, like the 200-year-old canal that ran past our house, was built to pull barges of turf to warm the homes of Dublin.

Roads get sparse through the bog, as the saturated ground swells and settles with each rain; a nearby pub began leaning to one side decades ago, and the owners ran with it and advertised it as an attraction, like the Leaning Tower of Pisa. Locals here were used to being cut off from the world.

***

Every leap risks a fall. My marriage started to go bad as soon as we moved here, yet my wife was not willing to leave, or let me take our daughter away, and I would not leave my daughter. So we began a comfortless truce for years, while I spent every spare moment with my daughter. I was grateful to have so much intimate time with my child, which many fathers don't get, but nothing changed the fact that we were alone – or worse than alone – in a cold house in a desolate area of a foreign country during the long darkness, with plans collapsing around me and with no adults to talk to.

Salvation came the next spring from a bent old man in an Irish flat cap working his potato fields, like a scene from another century, and when he saw me wave from the road he shuffled over to where I stood holding my daughter's hand.

"Tis a fine morning," he said by way of introduction, and I heartily lied that it was.

"New to the parish?" he asked. He was Seamus (SHAY-mus) and this was his land – not just in that he owned it, but that he had built up the soil over decades into a fertile plot surrounded by bog. When I told him we had just moved here, he smacked me lightly on the back and asked us to come in the meet the wife.

I put aside my city wariness and followed him with my daughter. We met his wife of fifty years, who gave us tea and scones with jam they made themselves. Most of what I saw in the house, I realised, they made themselves. Seamus had dug turf for most of his life, and it couldn't have made much money, but they didn't seem to lack anything they needed.

When I said I wanted to build a garden myself, they eagerly shared tips – how to stop weeds by boiling a plant called mare's tail, or how to cut and bend willow to make a living wall that stops wind and cattle. When I said I had planted apple trees, they asked me if I was grafting them, and explained what that meant – that I could surgically replace a branch from one tree with one from another, to grow dozens of varieties of apples on a single tree. He dug into the pantry and gave me some of his own to take home.

"These are cookers," he said, holding up an apple, "and save the peels for jam – the flesh under the peel is where all the pectin is, and that's what sets the jam. Save the peels." He had a way of repeating everything that helped you remember. I asked if I should store them in a refrigerator, and he looked puzzled. "No, store them in hay – it keeps them sweet."

He was showing us his garden when my daughter was stung by a nettle – a ubiquitous weed here that leaves painful welts when touched. As I tried to calm my screaming child, Seamus explained how to find dock-leaf nearby and rub it on the sting to make the pain disappear. I looked at him sceptically, but darned if it didn't work, and she stopped almost instantly.

He asked my daughter and I to come back tomorrow, and we did.

One by one, we began to meet the other neighbours – Jim training his pony on the road, Martin driving his polished 1930s roadster, and Nanny Peg tending her gardens. They were delighted to see a child again, running along forest paths and fields that had gone strangely silent in this age of screens, and asked us back again and again. I introduced myself to Angela waiting for the bus, Mary when my daughter played with her grandchildren, Jack through a friend, Ellen on the train, and our priest introduced me to Christy and Peter. Soon we were making daily rounds, and when they were pulling weeds or feeding the animals I asked if we could help.

While I never did get used to the chill or dark winters in Ireland, making friends with neighbours changed everything for us. I would learn they were only the remaining scraps of community, mostly among elderly people, but they made the grim weather bearable, and made roads and cars less necessary.

I became active in the parish and met the other local parents, and saw the dark side of Ireland's new prosperity, as the cost of homes and land had soared and most Irish found life less affordable than before. Fathers – and many of the mothers – had to spend long hours commuting to Dublin, and like so many American parents, didn't see their own children except in the evenings. I would eventually have to do the same, but for now I offered to mind some of their children for income, and soon I was making my rounds through the bog paths to the neighbours with toddlers following me like ducklings.

I got to know the nearby pubs, the opposite pole of Irish life to the churches but just as sacred. The pub was the coffee shop for heartfelt talks, the restaurant for date night, the town meeting hall and concert venue. It was the place for "the craic" (pronounced "crack"), an Irish word that Google insists means "crazy," but in practice can include singing, dancing, joking, storytelling, flirting and general hanging out. Pub owners sometimes doubled as undertakers, and when someone in the village died, the pub sometimes hosted the wake, with family and neighbours drinking and celebrating around the body of their departed loved one.

By the time I moved there in the Celtic Tiger, many of the old pubs had already disappeared or turned into modern bars, with loud music and giant screens, and in the 20 years I lived in Ireland more would follow. Here, though, a few kept on going as they always had, with farm families chatting at the end of the day. One local pub allowed no screens, only the music of local people who brought in their fiddles and accordions and led everyone in song. Another forbade music and allowed only conversation; local lore claimed that the publican threw out Mick Jagger and Keith Richards once. Every pub was its own nation, and the publican the benevolent lord. One of the few drawbacks was the food; I realised why there were Irish pubs around the world but no Irish restaurants.

In American cities police are everywhere, and need to be. Here the local garda (police) station looked like an ordinary house, and had a small sign out front that said "Open Wednesdays and Thursdays. Noon to 2 pm." When pubs had "lock-ins," staying open past legal hours, they shut all the windows and kept a lookout, and celebrants inside quieted down when the garda came by. The garda himself, I learned, made his rounds more to satisfy himself that no one was making too much noise, rather than trying to catch anyone in the act. Laws in the countryside, I learned, were basically suggestions, and upholding them focused less on the letter than on the well-being of neighbours.

If someone caused a disturbance, the neighbours might have a quiet word with them long before getting police involved. That had happened, I was told, with a local "boy racer" who drove too fast and dangerously on the roads; several locals, including the priest, knocked on his door and were ignored. A nearby farmer, however, owned a construction crane, and one morning the boy racer walked out his front door and saw his car sitting in the high branches of a tree. When he called the police, the officer – who understood what had happened – gave him a ticket for illegal parking. The young man took the hint.

I found that local people used to take care of most things themselves, with little need for government. My neighbours described how everyone used to do this, to cut turf or sow seeds or harvest crops or build homes by assembling their neighbours and working as a team.

When I asked my neighbours about getting turf for our fire, Tommy and Liam took me with them to cut it in the bog. With our children playing nearby, we sliced it into black slabs like liquorice and "footed" it, or stacked it to dry, over the summer. When autumn came Tommy came with his tractor and dumped everything I had footed – a winter's worth – in front of our house, and my daughter and I spent our evenings curled up together, reading in front of the warm fire.

When I started work on a garden, neighbours brought me seedlings, cuttings and tractor-loads of manure, a much more welcome gift than it sounds. When I wanted to get chickens, a neighbour helped me put up the fencing in exchange for my help feeding his cows. Country people do this all over, so in some ways it wasn't much different than the rural Missouri I knew well. Missouri, though, doesn't have many medieval castles on the hill, much less neighbours who will happily take you on a trespassing tour (laws = suggestions). And tell you the story of why it was given to Strongbow for defeating Richard the Lionheart.

Conversations with elderly can be interesting anywhere, but an American in their 70s or 80s today came of age in the 1950s, surrounded by televisions and refrigerators, suburbs and highways, drive-in movies and fast food. The churning of fashions makes their world feel quaint, but the elements of modern life were all there.

Because of its unique history, though, Ireland did not join the rest of the West until the late 20th century. Many of my neighbours grew up in the 1950s and 60s without electric lights, without television or cars, without mass media and celebrity pop culture. They drove horse-carts, lived in thatched cottages, grew their own food and raised their own meat, and traded with the neighbours. They lived in the kind of world we associate with a primeval past, or with marginal sects like the Amish.

Conversations over farm gates and on the bus gradually became interviews, as I told them I wanted to collect stories like theirs. Some neighbours left me record them with a camera or microphone, and I asked them questions like: were you ever hungry? Where did you play as children? How did people resolve conflicts? How did they spend the evenings together?

I had been a investigative reporter and was not easily shocked, but I kept stopping them in conversation and asking to go back and explain something that sounded unbelievable – like when my neighbour Christy mentioned the times there was no money.

"You mean jobs were scarce?" I asked. No, he said, there were times the 1960s and 70s that all the banks were closed for months, locking up almost all the cash in the nation. *There was no money.*

"I'm sorry, *what?*" I said. "How ... did people get buy anything to live?"

Well, he explained, most individuals just grew and made things themselves, and when they couldn't, they wrote checks – IOUs to each other. When the banks re-opened, almost no checks bounced. Three million people knew their promises and kept them, and a country without money kept running.

The incredulous moments kept coming. Wait, I asked, people let any stranger sleep in their house in exchange for a story?

You walked miles to school barefoot, but also learned Latin?

The priest held Mass in people's homes, and everyone took turns?

When someone died, you lay out their body on the kitchen table and held a party for them?

I treated these stories with scepticism at first, but I read through old newspaper clippings, listened to radio archives, visited historical societies and read through people's journals from a century ago, and it was true – all of it. Most of Ireland had become a very modern country, but a short distance from Google and Facebook's European headquarters lived some of the last Westerners who remembered a traditional world.

Let's unpack that for a moment. For thousands of human generations, all over the world, most people lived in small groups, whether Irish villages or Old West towns or Amazon tribes or Neanderthals. As different as these groups were in culture or knowledge, they spent most of their days and nights surrounded by loved ones, in a world with few strangers. They roamed freely as children, honing their bodies and brains with games passed down through generations. They shaped wood and fibre and stone and metal into useful things they needed, and learned from parents and older relatives until they became masters of a craft.

They celebrated the turning of the seasons, and the passage of boys into men and girls into women. They lived mostly outdoors and knew their own land, and could find their way by sun and stars. They picked plants and slaughtered animals, turned roots and seeds and organs into food, letting nothing go to waste. In the evenings, around the fire, they sang the stories of their people, tales of love and loss and fear, which carried inside them the knowledge they might need someday. With luck, they died surrounded by children and grandchildren, who sang songs of grief and lovingly prepared their body for the grave.

Only in the last century or two – the most recent 0.05 percent of humanity -- did all these things change. Only in the last few generations have we spent most of our lives indoors, staring at screens, dependent on distant powers for food and water and life, knowing only the songs and stories that the screens sell to us.

I'm not proposing that their lives were idyllic or that all this change has been for the worse. No one had much money, and many lacked electricity during the long nights. Some died of polio or tuberculosis, for which we now have cures. Children wore hand-me-downs or clothes sewn from flour sacks. Nor was the world peaceful in their lifetimes; I met people who lived through the Irish Revolution, the Irish Civil War, the Emergency of World War II, and decades of working hard for little money. I wouldn't want people today to live exactly as they did, even if that were possible. Their lives were remarkable, not because they lived without hardship, but because they maintained a safe, highly literate, high-trust despite – or perhaps because of – all that hardship.

My neighbours, too, remembered those days fondly. Poverty was not a burden for them, they all said, for neighbourhoods were full of people who sang and worked and worshiped and celebrated and grieved together, their joys greater because they were shared, their suffering lessened because it was shared.

I accumulated my own library of interviews. I read more than a hundred diaries and memoirs of Irish who grew up in this agrarian world. I went through historical archives, century-old school-papers, old radio and television interviews, and put them all together -- all told, the words of a few hundred people – to reconstruct a traditional world.

That became this book. Through it I've mostly quoted published memoirs that anyone can check, but almost any quotation backs up what many elderly neighbours told me over and over. The elders quoted were from various backgrounds; some city, some country, some better off than others. Nonetheless, they repeated each other with remarkable precision, and were largely positive about the world of their childhoods, and disappointed in the modern one. As they are the few people in the world who have seen both, I take their testimony seriously. And the book grew in the telling, as Tolkien put it, becoming a story not just of rural Ireland in the mid-20th century, but of all traditional culture, and of what we gained and lost when we went modern.

Bit by bit, as my daughter grew up, we learned to homestead ourselves. We built a garden and got chickens and a beehive. We built and whitewashed a coop. We learned which wild plants and mushrooms we could pick and went through the woods grabbing food everywhere. We made pickles and sauerkraut and jam and wine and vinegar. We learned to preserve eggs in limewater and vegetables in sand, to gather wildflowers and make them into wine. We made our own butter and preserved it by burying it in the bog, where it ages but does not go rancid.

We learned to cut willows and make them into baskets or fences, to cut and shape trees into hedgerows, and to stack the loose stones in Ireland's soil and stack them into walls without mortar. We helped build a home out of cob, a mix of sand, clay and straw. We experimented with making our own charcoal and ink and candles. I learned to forge old metal into knives, shape leather into purses and turn calfskin and paper into books. I learned to shoot a bow and arrow and occasionally got a rabbit for supper. Of course these were hobbies and I continued to take the bus every day to a normal job; I don't claim or desire to live exactly as people in some other era did, but to see what skills they had that could still be fun or useful.

As I learned, my daughter learned, and when chores were done on the homestead I gave her homeschooling lessons, and read to her curled up by the fire – Robert Louis Stevenson and C. S. Lewis, Rudyard Kipling and Laura Ingalls Wilder. A selfish part of me wanted her to remain a child forever and preserve those golden moments in amber. But each moment flickered by like cars outside the window, too swiftly to see in detail. I wanted to throw a hook into the blur and reel in the moments, pore over them, plead with each of them … stay. Please, linger a moment longer.

But children do not wait for us, and as I wrote this she became five, then ten, then fifteen, each age with its battles and casualties, its moments of comfort and joy. I escorted her as long as she let me, as I grew old beside her. I hoped I gave her the freedom and innocence many children no longer experience, and that the lessons lay inside her like seeds awaiting the spring.

Chapter One

Growing Up

Beneath the mundane world you and I inhabit lies the secret barbarian world of children, who follow a separate tradition of solemn rituals, contests and codes of honour, like a Viking horde living underfoot and unnoticed. Our histories record the deeds of adults, but all those adults began as children, and it was in their realm that every future general first learned to lead a team, every potential scientist first turned over stones to delight in the tiny nightmares underneath, and every budding explorer first took a dare to enter the haunted woods.

What we dismiss as "play" is children stretching and pushing their bodies through the boot-camp training they need to survive, and just as tiger cubs practice pouncing and foals running, children act out being heroes and warriors, maidens and mothers. Foals, though, can stand within hours of being born; human children require a decade or more to grow up, the longest of any species, and those years spent playing are the secret to our success.

They were also the birthright of every child, whether in the Amazon or the Arctic, whether in the Stone Age or the suburbs. Twenty-six hundred years ago Zechariah wrote that "the streets will be full of boys and girls playing," and writers recorded almost identical scenes in every culture and era, until historically yesterday.[1]

"The whole village was our playground when we were young," said Bill Bergin, who grew up not far from where I lived. They made up games, ran barefoot through fields, climbed trees and peeked into birds' nests, picked wildflowers and looked under logs, and tramped paths in pursuit of pirates or dragons. They built boxing rings, lit camp-fires, turned scrap

---

[1] Zechariah 8:5.

wood into child-sized cars and raced them down hills. In winter they poured water over frosted hills to make ice-slides. They needed no television nor phones nor adult supervision, but spent every moment immersed in the feral joy of childhood.[2]

Even city children roamed far and freely, for crime and cars were rare, and horses and children are sensible enough to avoid each other. My neighbour Christy remembers Dublin children swinging from ropes tied to lamp-posts, all down the street. When a rope came undone the children found the lamp-lighter, who kindly climbed his ladder and tied it back again.

"When the farmers brought their crops to market, they parked their empty carts and the children were immediately all over them," Paddie Crosbie said. "They made ideal see-saws, and the children played on them for hours until the farmers returned and they all ran." Once a farmer asked him to mind his horse-and-cart while he went into the pub; Crosbie made the mistake of play-shaking the reins, and the horse dutifully took off down the road.[3]

When it rained the roads became rivers, and they made boats and raced them toward the drains. Maureen Boyd remembered armies of children swimming in the canals, diving off the bridges into the then-clean water.[4] On warm summer days horse-drawn carts sprayed water to cool the streets, he remembered, and mobs of children ran alongside under the spray all through the city.

"The street was where it all happened," Patrick Boland said. "Traffic was never a problem – the occasional vehicle, usually horse-drawn, could be heard coming a long way off. My recollections are mostly of summertime, when I could play from early morning when I was rushed out to the street clean and shiny, until late at night when I was dragged into the house filthy dirty... Meal times meant nothing, only that they were an interruption to our games."[5]

---

[2] *Some Time to Kill*, 16.
[3] *Your Dinner's Poured Out*, 43.
[4] *Dublin Voices*, 153.
[5] *Tales from a City Farmyard*, 10.

Yet children were not abandoned, for "children were raised as a street," Christy said, under the watchful eye of all local parents, not just their own. One night one of Boland's childhood friends didn't come home for dinner, and all Dublin was in uproar about the missing child. It turned out his friend had fallen asleep in a hay-cart, and the farmer had driven back to the country that evening before he noticed his stowaway.[6]

Today, children might wander the neighbourhood on Halloween, wearing a store-bought costume and with an adult standing guard over them. In those days, though, the children made their own costumes or bonfires in the fields, and not just on Halloween; John Curren remembers similar rituals on Wren Day (the day after Christmas), on New Year's Eve and St. Bridget's Night (February 2), about once every few weeks through the dark months.[7]

I discovered a Wren Day celebration in the nearby woods, and took my daughter there every winter. Wrens are little birds who remain here through the dark winter, and so were symbols of the season. They were sacred to the ancient Celts – its Irish name, dreolin, means "the Druid bird" – and the day after Christmas, when the days began to lengthen, people would decide whether to kill the embodiment of winter or to respect it.

We and dozens of our neighbours sat with hot tea and chatted as the children played around us, or danced as some of the fathers played instruments and sang Irish folk songs. When it was time for the ceremony, local men appeared dressed as "Wren Boys" – looking rather like Robin Hood's merry men – brought out a statue of a wren, telling the children how the wren was in danger from the "straw boys" who wanted to steal and kill it. Then, the children gasped as they heard "straw boys" moving through the woods in the distance, beating their sticks together and chanting ominously.

Then, a mob of straw boys – other local men dressed from straw head to toe -- ran up behind the wren boys, grabbed the statue of the wren, and ran off with it as the children erupted in gleeful outrage. The wren boys led them on a chase through the woods, followed by a lagging crowd of

---

[6] *Your Dinner's Poured Out*, 102, 153.
[7] *Tides of Change*, 34.

dutiful parents. Eventually the straw boys gave up, and the cheering mob of children carried the statue back in triumph.

The wren boys and the straw boys shook hands, agreed to respect the wren, and placed a small crown on the statue's head, declaring it the King of Birds. Finally, the musicians launched into some rousing folk tunes and many of the parents and their children began Irish dancing. With a nod from me, my girl leaped into the fray and copied the big kids until she was halfway to Riverdancing. It was great fun, but also a ritual hundreds, if not thousands, of years old.

***

Boys played hurling – a national sport of Ireland, like hockey with a ball and no ice – with a rolled-up sock and curved sticks gathered from the trees. They played handball between the brick walls of alleys, my neighbour Sean remembered, sometimes managing three or four balls at a time like a juggler. They played football – what Americans call soccer – in the street with a ball made from crumpled newspapers "and scattered like Houdini when the bobby [policeman] came around the corner," Betty McDermot said. "The police had little to do then."[8]

Sports varied widely from one place to another; in Armagh, Gerry Rafferty remembered, it was "bullets" -- throwing a small metal ball for about three miles in the least number of throws -- and local kids became famous not only for being the best throwers, but the best finders of lost balls. They played marbles with chalkies and glassies and aggies and stonies, he said, and his playmates were locally renowned under names like Hurricane Higgins and Demon Bill.[9]

In Belfast "there were so many children ... of the same age that a group very quickly formed when any were seen playing outside," Marianne Elliott said.[10] They played battle in, battle out, jack jack show the light, spin the top, marbles, hoop the hoop, hop scotch, conkers, kick the can, scut the whip, box the fox, Hop and Cock-a-Rooshy, French, Dab, Folly, and Hole and Tar, jack-stones or scragga. "With games and occupations

---

[8] *No Shoes in Summer*, 167.
[9] *And the Band Played On*, 7.
[10] *Hearthlands*, 82.

that spanned the four seasons, we never had a thought for such phrases as 'I'm bored.'" McDermot said. "We hadn't enough hours in the day for all we wanted to do."[11]

Some idea of the rich library of pastimes can be seen in Norman Douglas' whimsical 1916 overview of the children's games of London, which spent dozens of pages -- most of the book -- just listing them. Not dozens of games, mind you -- *dozens of pages of lists of games.*

The games, chants and rituals were so ubiquitous, and so ignored by busy adults, that they were little remarked upon or recorded, and only now, when they have almost disappeared, can we look back and see how remarkable they were. In the 1950s the husband-and-wife team of Peter and Iona Opie interviewed children on playgrounds around Britain and found that, instead of being silly and spontaneous, children's rhymes and rituals actually preserved historical traditions that mainstream culture had lost.

"Boys continue to crack jokes that [Jonathan] Swift collected from his friends in Queen Anne's time," Opie wrote. "They ask riddles which were posed when Henry VIII was a boy. . . . They learn to cure warts . . . after the manner which Francis Bacon learned when he was young. . . . They rebuke one of their number who seeks back a gift with a couplet known in Shakespeare's day. . . . and they are [telling stories] which were gossip in Elizabethan times." They re-discovered the observation of Queen Anne's physician John Arbuthnot, who said that "nowhere was tradition preserved pure and uncorrupt but amongst school-boys, whose games and plays are delivered down invariably from one generation to another."[12]

This is especially remarkable since most of these rituals were not taught by parents or grandparents, who might have learned them decades earlier, but by other children who could only have known them for a few years. Through more iterations their transmission signal should have decayed further. Instead, the children proved stronger at retaining historical knowledge than most adults.

Some of their superstitions, like blisters as proof of lying, date back at least to the 1500s, and they chanted a rhyme that apparently dates back to

---

[11] *No Shoes in Summer,* 162.
[12] *The Lore and Language of Childhood*, 2.

the era of France's Henry IV around 1600. Country children still wore oak leaves or an acorn in their button-holes on the 29th of May to remember the return of Charles II in 1651 -- and could explain why they did so–at a time when few adults remembered the date.

Keep in mind, also, that almost no one recorded children's games in any era, so anything recorded in the 1500s is probably much older. Oral traditions can endure for thousands or even tens of thousands of years; Australian Aborigines have traditions about the sea level changing that seem to date from the last Ice Age. No one knows if any children's rhymes and games date back so far, but Douglas believed that one chant stretched back to the time of Nero, and the Opies seemed to agree.

Here, too, Ireland held onto this heritage later than most countries, and a national radio recording of a Dublin school-yard in 1977 captured children chanting as they played. They weren't all local or ancient – some cited Shirley Temple, "the girl with the curly hair," and had clearly been popular songs -- but even that showed how well they passed down knowledge, as this was two generations after she had been famous.

Their games and rituals remained very local; "while some children roll eggs at Easter," the Opies wrote, "or nettle the legs of classmates on the 29th of May, or leave little gifts on people's doorsteps on St. Valentine's Day, or act under the delusion that they are above the law on a night in November, other children, sometimes living only the other side of a hill, will have no knowledge of these activities."

The Opies also noted that children spontaneously adopted a "code of oral legislation" -- cultural institutions for testing truthfulness, swearing affirmation, making bets and bargains, and determining the ownership of property–the adult legal code in miniature. These codes universally included a practice absent from adult law, however -- that of asking for respite, or "calling time out," and what today's children reportedly call "pause" from video games.[13]

Children's games teach something else too: fairness. In their raw state children can be cruel and heedless, of course, and need some guidance – that's what parents are for. Since games are voluntary and children can quit if they are unhappy, though, they must learn to negotiate, co-operate,

---

[13] "The Last of the Monsters with Iron Teeth," *Carcinisation*, Oct. 2014.

compromise, take turns, help each other out and put themselves in others' shoes, to determine what is fair and foul. As far back as the 1930s Jean Piaget maintained that we learn to be moral humans through playing as children. One of Christy Kennealey's friends growing up had a speech defect, but Kennealey "understood him perfectly and automatically translated for him," he said. "In a group when we were deciding on how to play, I'd fill in the subtitles ... I never heard anyone from around the place mock him for it, and a stranger never did it twice."[14]

No one needed to be told that playing was good for children, but of course it helps their brain development, their navigation and survival skills, self-confidence, intellectual focus and physical health.[15] It was simply normal – and remains so even in an abnormal world, when entire generations grow up obese and enclosed, like caged animals conditioned to recoil from sunlight.

Olympian athlete Silken Laumann credits such free play with starting her on her path to being a champion. When she became a parent herself, however, she found none of the neighbourhood children played anymore, or remembered how. She created her own courses to teach parents and children how to play tag, hopscotch, capture-the-flag or other such rudimentary pastimes. "Kids used to live outside," she wrote in her book *Child's Play*. "Adventure was a central part of most days, found in the form of a scavenger hunt down a path near home ... a meeting of friends on the first snowy day to sneak our toboggans onto the exhilaratingly steep slopes ..." Today, however, "the streets my children and I walk resemble the ones I grew up on -- snug houses, big old trees and tons of space for adventure -- but there is one critical difference: The streets today are silent."[16]

"Even the idea of a children's game seems to be slipping from our grasp," Neil Postman wrote in 1982. "Hide-and-Seek, which was played in Periclean Athens more than two thousand years ago, has now almost

---

[14] *Maura's Boy,* 25.
[15] See Maynard 2013, Gabbard 1998, Ellis 1984, Hughes 1998, Blair 1989, Bixler 2002.
[16] *Child's Play,* 3.

completely disappeared from the repertoire of self-organized children's amusements. Children's games, in a phrase, are an endangered species."[17]

Nor should anyone be surprised that in the same decades that play has declined, childhood mental illness has skyrocketed, and not because we're seeing disorders we once overlooked. Questionnaires to measure anxiety and depression in teens have been given unchanged since the 1950s, and disorders are five to eight times higher than they once were. The suicide rate for people aged 15 to 24 has doubled, and below 15 has quadrupled. Empathy, as far as can be measured, has plummeted.[18] More children are joining – or are made to join – organized sports, but these train children how to obey authority, not to improvise or negotiate.

To see how recently outdoor play was assumed, look at a map of most American cities; anything built before World War II is typically a grid for easy transport, but post-war suburban streets curl like tossed spaghetti and end in cul-de-sacs in order to do the opposite, to slow and discourage traffic to be "safe for families." Suburbia looks the way it does because it was made to be safe for children to play in the street -- which in 1945 was exactly what they would be doing.

If the returning GIs who first moved into these homes could be transported to the present day, however, they would be puzzled. Aside from the fact that the future never happened -- no flying cars or robot butlers -- the most glaring difference would be the absence of children. To a time traveller it would seem like the beginning of a *Twilight Zone* episode, and they would demand to know what happened–was there a plague? An alien invasion? Are the children grown from pods now? Are they marched to an altar and sacrificed to some dark god? Or is this some horrific science-fiction future where children grow up staring at glowing rectangles, and are drugged when they get restless?

***

Of course children went to school – more on that later – but this too was a daily adventure, especially for country children who walked miles to get there. "If the journey to school took thirty minutes, the coming home

---

[17] *The Disappearance of Childhood,* 4.
[18] "The Play Deficit" by Peter Gray, *Aeon magazine,* 18 Sept 2013.

could take anything up to two hours," Alice Taylor said. She and her friends ran through fields, stretched under the sun and made up stories, checked on birds' nests, and being invited in for tea by the neighbours. "Finally, we arrived sun-soaked and relaxed, with school almost forgotten because it was, after all, only one part of a much larger cycle of education."[19]

Most of the children were barefoot from April to October to make the winter boots last longer, my neighbour Jack remembered, but it wasn't the hardship for them it would seem to us, for the roads were not covered in broken glass and automotive shrapnel as they would be today. Other times they walked the "mass paths" through fields, worn from people walking to church.

They climbed and inspected each tree along the way for nests, my neighbour Angela said, and when they found one with eggs they took responsibility for the chicks. "We minded them," she said. "If I found it, you couldn't touch mine ... we'd leave them there, and keep an eye on them every day" until they hatched, and then on the chicks until they flew away. Along the way they "picked blackberries and robbed someone's orchard," Angela said. When I asked if anyone minded, she said that "one farmer came after us one time with a [pitch]fork one time," she said. "But God help him he was grinning. Ah, they were good days. We enjoyed them."

This, too, seems to have been a universal pastime; I saw a 19th-century gardening book whose list of garden pests included, after beetles and boll weevils, "boys." If your garden is infested with boys, the author noted drily, a dog might be just the thing.

Decades later, most of these elders remembered these walks in loving detail. They "picked wildflowers to bring for the altar, passed herons, frogs, water-hens and a millwheel then in use, a maid putting out their cows after milking and a ploughman urging on his horses," Angela Mitchell said.[20] "I pity the country children of today," Nancy Power said.

---

[19] *To School Through the Fields*, 118.
[20] audio recording, *Local Voices Database*, CD22, T67.

"The journeys to and from school were an education as valuable as any we managed to imbibe at school."[21]

Like free-range play, walking to school was the norm not just in Ireland, but in most countries, and has also vanished rapidly and without comment. A UK survey found that in 1971, 80 percent of third-graders walked to school alone; in only 20 years that figure fell to nine percent, and is now close to zero.[22] As recently as 1979, Chicago public schools sent a checklist to parents describing the things every child had to know to start school, like "Can he travel alone in the neighbourhood (four to eight blocks) to store, school, playground, or to a friend's home?" Schools assumed children as young as six would walk up to eight blocks from home alone. *In Chicago.*[23]

Beyond going to school and back, children once roamed long distances without worry. Christy roamed all over Dublin with his friends without fear of being robbed or attacked, but "it was safe," he said. "It didn't happen in those days – children were free."

A UK study demonstrated the loss of children's freedom over three generations, starting with a typical 10-year-old in 1919 who walked 10 kilometres alone to a favourite fishing spot, and ending with his great-grandson only allowed to walk a few hundred meters.[24] Surveys in several other modernized countries show the same dramatic declines; one study found that one-third of eight-to-12-year-olds never venture more than a hundred meters from their house on their own.[25] In the USA children' roaming declined *90 percent* between 1970 and 1990.[26]

---

[21] *No Shoes in Summer*, 60.

[22] "ONE FALSE MOVE...A Study of Children's Independent Mobility," Policy Studies Institute 1990.

[23] http://www.chicagonow.com/little-kids-big-city/2011/08/is-your-child-ready-for-first-grade-1979-edition.

[24] "How children lost the right to roam in four generations," by D. Derbyshire, *Daily Mail,* 15 June 2007. Available from: www.dailymail.co.uk/news/article-462091/How-children-lost-right-roam-generations.html

[25] *Children's Independent Mobility: A Comparative Study in England and Germany (1971-2010).*

[26] "Nature deficit disorder 'damaging Britain's children,'" BBC News, 30 March 2012.

You can see glimmers of this lost world, strange as it might sound, in the "funny pages" of American newspapers, in comics like *Blondie* or *Family Circus* or *Dennis the Menace*. These comics are now several decades old and have changed remarkably little over the decades, as their simple premises couldn't bend much without breaking, and as their increasingly elderly audiences liked them just fine the way they were. Thus they remained frozen in time, and serve as an underappreciated historical window into the world that children used to inhabit.

In *Family Circus*, one of the standard gags shows the mother of the family sending a child over to the neighbours to borrow something and to "come right home." You know what's coming next: the rest of the panel shows the child's winding route back, hitting the playground, the woods, the creek, his friends' houses and finally home to an exasperated mother. When the strip was created in 1960 this immediately earned a chuckle, as adults saw children do this every day, and remembered being that child.

Today, the scene looks too incomprehensible to be funny; not only would few Americans even know their neighbours, much less borrow from them, but few parents would allow their child to wander the neighbourhood unsupervised, or play in the woods, or wander in and out of other houses. It's what we might as well call a banana-peel joke, something our culture registers as standard joke material even though no one can remember why it was once supposed to be funny.

Yet children still long to roam; one US survey found that 31 percent of children would prefer to cycle to school but only three percent were allowed to.[27] There are legitimate reasons not to let children roam, of course. The tiny country roads have been replaced by rivers of traffic, often covered in broken glass and automotive shrapnel. The one or two cars a day that Angela saw has become thousands per minute, all driven by people unaccustomed to pedestrians and distracted by mobile phones. UK public safety campaigns publicising driver distraction did lead to a decline in road deaths, but the campaigns were entirely focused at parents to make them afraid of cars, not on drivers to watch out for children.[28]

---

[27] Worpole 2003.
[28] *ONE FALSE MOVE... A Study of Children's Independent Mobility.* 1990.

Letting children roam might actually be illegal where you are, and even if it isn't, someone might still call the police. Mothers have been thrown in jail for letting their children go to the park alone, and two-thirds of Americans polled want a law prohibiting children nine and under from being unsupervised; 43 percent said the same for all children under 12.[29] At that age some Irish children were journeying from town to town hiring themselves out as farm-hands.

In the USA as in most Western countries, children went to the market, or stayed with cousins for the weekend, all on their own. They rode bicycles, took buses, hopped boxcars, and hitch-hiked. It was so normal that Young Men's Christian Associations – today's YMCAs – were originally created partly to give such young wanderers a wholesome place to stay overnight. The novel *Catcher in the Rye* scandalised people in 1951 for profanity that most kindergartners know today; what strikes modern students as bizarre is that a teenager simply hops on a bus and travels to a different part of the country, alone and without fear.

* * *

Running barefoot through fields and climbing trees also meant that my elderly neighbours learned to treat the natural world with respect, rather than seeing it as something to be stripped bare for money, or as the Edenic exhibit of so many environmentalists. "Growing up surrounded by trees coloured our lives," Taylor said. "My father was a planter of trees and gave nature free rein ... [he] instilled a deep respect for trees in us, telling us that it takes a tree many, many years to grow, but a fool can cut it down in five minutes. He also believed that a person who planted a tree was far less likely to chop one down."[30]

When a tree needed to be cut, Marrie Walsh remembered, "we would tell the tree the reason for cutting it down. Then we would run around to the other trees and tell them not to cry. My father and brothers would mark the first cut with the hatchet, then rub soap on the cross-cut blade and start sawing. We would watch from a distance to see which way the tree would

---

[29] "Poll: 68 Percent of Americans Don't Think 9-Year-Olds Should Play at the Park Unsupervised," *Reason.com*, August 19, 2014.
[30] *Books from the Attic*, 79.

fall." When her father fastened the horse to the tree and set off dragging it home for wood, she said, "some of us perched in the branches, swaying hither and thither as we tried to balance ... by this time we would have collected several children from houses along the way, all wanting a ride on our tree."[31]

Like all children until yesterday, they spent their formative years *in* the world and not seeing it out a window or through a screen. Just as Angela watched the birds' nests, so Tony Carr fished the rivers, Taylor and her siblings watched the swallows come every spring to nest in the barns, and Rose Smith and her friends dammed the streams to create temporary swimming pools.[32]

Even in the Burren land on the west coast, where centuries of erosion washed away the thin soil and carved a rippling moonscape of pale hills, Dersie Leonard wrote fondly of her childhood, saying she and her friends had "lakes and rivers ... bog and rocks, not to mention fairy rings and forts – in fact everything a person could wish for."[33]

"With seven children in the family we were raised free as birds, growing up in a world of simplicity untouched by outside influences," Taylor said. "Our farm was our world and nature as an educator gave free rein to our imaginations; unconsciously we absorbed the natural order of things and observed the facts of life unfolding daily before our eyes. We were free to be children and to grow up at our own pace in a quiet place close to the earth."[34]

City children might seem far removed from Nature, but in Ireland, at least, even inner cities had parks, woods, gardens and cow pastures, and every school and hospital used to be surrounded by rows of vegetables to feed those inside. In Belfast, "... many streams still oozed from the floor of the forest ... where we spent many summers climbing trees, making woodland dens and decking them with the bluebells, violets, primroses, forget-me-nots and sweet-smelling delicately pink wild roses that grew in abundance in the early summer," Marianne Elliott recalled. "It made for a

---

[31] *An Irish Country Childhood*, 9.
[32] *Growing Up With Ireland*, 236.
[33] *No Shoes in Summer*, 13.
[34] *To School Through the Fields*, 10.

magical dell-like landscape ... ponds full of tadpoles and wild irises; rivulets to be bridged with driftwood and stones, marking out imaginary territories."[35]

Woods allow children places to create their own dens, tree-houses and forts, where they collect their own treasures and form secret societies. We're all cavemen under the surface, and something in us needs to live that way for a while as children. The most meagre "vacant" lot can for children become a secret and dangerous place full of old gods and buried treasure, of canyons to be leapt across, a place to smell a campfire or feel a ladybird on one's arm. Time can stand still for a child, and the primal moments we felt in stillness and storm are what stay with us when our bodies wizen and everything else fades.

Nature is not always pretty and harmless, as in the panda branding of eco-products; it can also be the "waste howling wilderness" of Deuteronomy, or where Gilgamesh went to fight monsters. It could be a place of testing, as when Christ was tested by Satan. It can provide a clean challenge, as when Ishmael flees civilisation to return to the sea. It offers a chance for men to create, to explore, to risk – passions we might today medicate away. It is where generations of monks ripped off the world, layer by layer, until only God remained.

One of my first memories – I couldn't have been more than four – was of fishing with my grandfather in a rowboat on a warm summer lake. We were catching bluegill, and I remember feeling them squirm in my hands before we threw them back.

Then we were caught in a surprise shower, and I remember watching with alarm as the shores in the distance were replaced by grey curtains of rain. To my child's eyes we seemed to be adrift and blind, with water collecting around us in the boat. My grandfather calmly rowed us back to shore; he was a man, and capable.

As Richard Louv pointed out, most of us who love Nature today can trace it back to some transcendent experience like this; feeling the tingle of distant lightning, or the smell of rain, or the cries of animals in the darkness, or the sight of a breeze rippling an ocean of green barley, or helping a sheep give bloody birth.

---

[35] *Hearthlands,* 19.

"My father was constantly chanting the refrain 'Wrong Nature and we will pay a terrible price,' and it is only now that I realise what he meant," Taylor said. "We have neglected the planting of trees and we have built on bogs and flood-plains, damaging our natural habitat and affecting our bird life. Great trees are the lungs of the Earth, cleansing the air and drinking surplus water, and while doing all this are still majestic and beautiful."[36]

Anyone who loves the outdoors as adults fell in love with it in childhood.[37] Most scientists begin their passion through contact with Nature, and Edith Cobb researched 300 autobiographies and concluded that almost all creative people have an awakening in their childhood in Nature. People say that children are natural scientists, but scientists are the people who never stopped being children.[38]

Today, however, few children run with magnifying glasses through the woods; in one generation British children went from half its children playing in wild places to one in ten, and in the USA kids with outdoor hobbies fell by half. We also struggle to get kids interested in the sciences, and the usual explanation is that the children don't have enough "information," which we think comes through screens. But children today already spend most of their lives in front of screens; they grow up gorging on images and data with no meaning to them, creating a mental obesity that should not be mistaken for wisdom.

Ironically, we now push for children to become eco-conscious at the same time that we shut them away from any real experience with the natural world. Many young activists who care deeply about the environment know it only in the abstract. Louv, author of *Last Child in the Woods,* describes ecologists who have never seen the communities they model, which is like a heart surgeon never having seen an actual heart.[39]

As Anthony Esolen points out, try asking children today "how do you clear trees and stumps from a field? How do you handle a mattock? What is an ice saw? How do you know if the ice on a pond is thick enough for skating? How do you cut blocks of ice for use in the summer? How do you

---

[36] *Books from the Attic,* 78.
[37] Wells, 2006.
[38] Pyle 2002.
[39] *Last Child in the Woods,* 225.

keep them from melting? What do you do with the eyes of potatoes if you want to plant them? How do you make sourdough bread? Does that mushroom growing out of the side of a tree, looking like a beefsteak, good to eat? What is that bright red star in the night sky that does not keep the same place among the constellations? If you wanted to find Jupiter in the sky, where would you generally look? Why on Cape Cod is the sun never directly over your head? What makes the day so short in winter? ... I have asked my freshman honours students at college where in the sky the sun will be in the middle of the afternoon in September.... They don't know. They are strangers to the world ..."[40]

If few of us know the animals and plants around us, fewer still could say how much they have declined, as we don't realise how much there used to be. This isn't simply speculation; Lizzie Jones at the University of London compared the population records of various bird species back several decades, and then asked more than 900 people of all ages to estimate the populations now versus when they were teenagers. Since the younger you are, the fewer years have passed, you'd think the youngest participants would have the best estimates. In fact, the opposite was true – perhaps because older people used to know the natural world better than we do today, or perhaps because they could see more of a change in their longer lifetimes.

Daniel Pauly at the University of British Columbia called this "shifting baseline syndrome," where everyone thinks of the "normal" baseline as whatever they grew up with; he cites photos of fishermen in Florida over decades, who posed equally proudly with ever-shrinking catches.[41]

***

Keep in mind that for all humans until yesterday, nighttime illumination was moon and stars and fire. It's difficult for most of us to imagine, as we have never experienced true night; we grew up surrounded by electronic devices, streetlights, headlights, floodlights and that one neighbour whose Christmas decorations can be seen from orbit. We

---

[40] *Out of the Ashes*, 26.
[41] "Young people can't remember how much more wildlife there used to be," *New Scientist*, 11 December 2019.

picture people before electricity behaving as we would in a power outage, banging our shins against coffee tables as we fumble around.

Living without electricity, though, wasn't like that for them, or for any premodern people. For one thing, most people worked outside, and came in when it was dark. Even when it got dark, people didn't stop; paintings from a few hundred years ago show people reading newspapers, chatting and generally celebrating, all to candles or oil lamps.

It was "a gentler time when many chores were timed to the light of day," said Rhoda Twombley, who lived in the last place to be electrified in Ireland, in 2000. "...it was as if the world stood still ... it was a pleasure to sit on the bench outside the front gate, senses heightened, to look out of the water and listen to waves gently splashing ashore ... The stars shone, impossibly close and radiant, and we might be treated to an occasional shooting star and a glimpse of the Aurora Borealis ... You could not feel any more surrounded by Nature: far from being lonely, the feeling of being at one with our island, our little space in the universe, was life affirming ..."[42]

When Eileen Casey's husband was young, she said, his father took him fishing at dusk, and "there was just enough natural light to get them through the woods onto the lakeshore," she said. "Father and son worked by instinct and senses. Ears were finely tuned for the sudden splash or ripple of water. Oftentimes, campfires on the shore threw up a blaze of colour and it must have seemed so simple and close to nature, the world of father and son."[43]

Before electricity, humans never experienced light after sunset in the intensity we do now. Our electric lights are both brighter and bluer than candles and campfires, and more likely to disrupt the mental and hormonal cycles tuned to daylight. Our eyes evolved to adjust from very bright to very dark, and our brains to not notice; if you've ever had to adjust camera film or video for day or night, you know the change looks more extreme on video than it looked to you. For that reason, though, we are terrible at sensing when we have too much, and in modern cities we might get literally hundreds of times more than we need.

---

[42] *Then There Was Light,* 36.
[43] *Then There was Light,* 57.

Like almost all living things, we are deeply tuned to the sun's cycle; many people suffer from insomnia at home but see it vanish on camping trips, as the sun and moon re-regulate our bodies and minds.[44] Even a slight reduction in our sleep can ruin our day, and a few days without sleep is literal torture. The less sleep you get, the more likely you are to get infections, heart attacks, even breast cancer. Too little sleep also causes mental disorders, which have skyrocketed in the decades we've had electric lights. For people with neurological issues like autism, extreme lights cause stress or panic attacks, and for epileptics our often flashing city lights are a constant danger.[45]

We assume that everyone would want electricity given the chance, but when electric lines spread into the country, officials "found that some houses did not want electricity, even cheap electricity set up for free," said Luke McGuinness.[46] Joe Kearney's grandfather, for example, was "comfortably at ease with the waxy smell of paraffin, of the guttering glow of candles and the soft-focus of firelight ... conducive to summoning up old ghosts and past events.... The flickering shadow play on the uneven bruising of the old walls kindled his imagination every bit as much as the wall paintings on the caves in Lasceaux, France had done for prehistoric man ... It was preferable for him to remember people and places of his past, not as bright and sharp, but wavering and blurred around the edges."[47] Even later farmers used it only seasonally in the winter – several months would go by without flicking the light switch.[48]

"The pace of life was slow for those who grew up with oil lamps and candles," wrote Alice Taylor. "Candle-light was kind, however, to ageing faces, cobwebs and bad housekeeping, its soft, flickering glow casting gentle shadows over many a blemish, human and otherwise."[49] These days, by contrast, as Ann Gardinier said, "if you step outside your house on a winter's night, you can't see the dark anymore."[50] When country

---

[44] *A Hunter-Gatherer's Guide to the 21st Century,* 100.
[45] Soucise, 2017.
[46] *Then There Was Light,* 82.
[47] *Then There Was Light,* 54.
[48] *Then There Was Light,* 108.
[49] *Quench the Lamp,* 109.
[50] *The House Remembers,* 102.

people did get electric lights, the harsh light "poked nosey brightness into previously darkened corners of my neighbours' lives. It somehow seemed to make them shy of one another as if they had been rendered naked publicly," Kearney wrote.[51]

Many rural people anticipated that about electric lights even before getting them. Mattie Lennon recalled that "one elderly farmer, blessed with two daughters of marriageable age but not film-star looks, was saying he had to find husbands for them before the electric light came in."[52]

It also means that few children grow up knowing the stars, which figure so powerfully in every religion and mythology ever created, and which inspired the first mathematics and science. Almost no one has any idea how to navigate by starlight in the manner of Polynesians and pioneers, Bedouins and Boy Scouts.

We depend entirely on GPS signals from orbiting satellites to get anywhere, and when those satellites bang into an orbiting piece of gravel, are hacked by a hostile power, or simply degrade, we no longer remember the simple ways our ancestors used to fix their location. Every year brings more sophisticated computer-generated imagery from space, but as with all things scientific, they have grown hopelessly distant from our lives. Physics professor Gene Tracy recalled attending a lecture on an X-ray source in a distant galaxy measured by equipment on a suborbital rocket ... but when a student asked where in the sky the galaxy was, the lecturer was flummoxed. He genuinely didn't know; he had never thought to look up where you would point to it.

Even if modern city-dwellers wanted to study the constellations, most can't see them because of the urban glare. Tracy wrote that in 1994, after an earthquake cut power to most of Los Angeles, the Griffith Observatory received phone calls from spooked residents asking about "the strange sky." What those callers were seeing were stars, perhaps for the first time.[53]

***

---

[51] *Then There Was Light*, 53.
[52] *Then There Was Light*, 94.
[53] "Sky Readers," *Aeon*, 23 Dec 2015.

The noise of the modern world was also absent from their lives – although cities like Dublin, of course, were filled with the sounds of people on the street chatting, of sidewalk musicians and clopping horses. There were no loudspeakers, however, even if people had the electricity to run them. Roads had little traffic outside of horse carts, construction crews used no jackhammers, gardeners no leaf-blowers. The ear-buds worn by most people on the street today had not been invented, but there was less cacophony for them to block out.

Most natural settings have little noise, so humans did not evolve to deal with much; 70 decibels has been suggested as a healthy maximum, and more than 85 creates permanent damage. Modern city-dwellers get far more than 85 decibels every day; when she measured noise levels in Washington, DC, Julia Belluz found the metro screamed at an average of 92 and a maximum of 116 decibels.

The decibel scale is logarithmic, by the way, so 80 decibels is not slightly more than 70 decibels, as you might think, but 10 times louder. A 110-decibel roar is 10,000 times louder. Just as with light, though, our brains unconsciously adjust until we no longer notice how loud it is.[54]

Unsurprisingly, modern people are losing their hearing at ever-earlier ages; one in four Americans have hearing loss, making it the country's third most chronic health problem behind cancer and diabetes. A 1997 study of the elderly found that hearing loss doubled in the 30 years between 1964 and 1994, and we are almost 30 years further on from that.[55] Developmental psychologist Lorraine Maxwell, who found that excessive noise warps children's attention and memory, and makes them withdraw from talking with peers. Yet she also found that, when they are accustomed to working with noise, they cannot work without it; the quality of their work deteriorates. When children learned to passively accept "uncontrollable noise" in the background, they show a "learned helplessness" to changing the world around them.[56]

---

[54] "The noise all around us that's destroying our hearing, explained," *Vox,* June 4, 2018.
[55] Wallhagen 1997.
[56] Maxwell 2000.

Since I eventually paid for our life in the country by working a modern job in the city, I spent nine hours a day in an office and three on the bus to and from our land. One day I measured how much of that time I spent without loudspeakers blaring in the background. It was zero. Virtually every public and corporate space in the modern world – elevators, stores, lobbies, offices, doctor's offices and gas stations – has overhead speakers and a piped-in sound system, often at levels I find deafening.

The only way to avoid the deluge of sound, for most of us, is to buy headphones, but that means that all the bus passengers who once chatted now sit in enforced isolation. And if everyone – including the growing legions of the half-deaf – listens to headphones, we get bleed-over from the people around us, forcing us to crank up the volume more in a perpetual arms race.[57]

Silence has become a privilege of the wealthy; airports now have special silent areas for the upper classes where the roar of the airplanes and other passengers are muffled. The Ultima Thule Lodge in Alaska is so remote that digital devices can't get a signal; its rooms start at $1,700 per night, with a three-night minimum. They have to pay more money than some of my elder friends made in an entire year, all to get what most humans everywhere until recently enjoyed for free.

* * *

When I say my neighbours were allowed to be children, they were not free to do whatever they wanted – on the contrary, most elders reported being treated more strictly, and held to higher standards, than children today. Children could roam with peers, but when they spoke to adults they were expected to have manners. "Obedience was the name of the game and you respected your seniors," Kevin Duffy said.[58]

When children came home, they had responsibilities, and "what your parents told you to do, you did," Jack said. Paddie Crosbie was sent to the local shop for groceries, Patty Bolger was left to mind her younger siblings, Jack had to milk the cows and start the fire every day, while other

---

[57] "The Sound of Solitude," *The Atlantic Monthly*, April 2012.
[58] *Fifty Years Behind the Counter,* 19.

elders remembered sweeping the yard, trimming the hedges, pulping turnips for the cows, pulling potatoes or whitewashing the house.[59]

Village children in those days rarely had to worry about strangers, for everyone knew everyone else. Nor could children get away with much either, not with so many eyes on them, connected to people who talked to their parents every day. When John Curran and his friends dressed in costume and went door to door, all the neighbours kept an eye on them, and if "a complaint was lodged for unacceptable behaviour ... then our father's shaving strap that hung on the side of the dresser was brought into action."[60]

It might seem contradictory that parents "were disciplinarians, yet we had total freedom to run around," as Tom Shaw said. The answer, though, is that children need to explore and play, but also need the security of boundaries and consistency. When my daughter and I travelled and she slept in a strange room, she wanted to know I would be there when she woke up. Childhood is itself a time of such profound change that children need stability everywhere – the same parents, neighbours, friends and surroundings, and almost all children had that, in almost every culture, until yesterday. My neighbours were allowed to be free in a way that most young people today are not, but they were also guided and disciplined in a way that most young people today are not.

There was no push to make children into tough, jaded adults, as in our modern culture. "When I was a child (in the 1920s-30s) we never heard of pollution, environment or sex, which takes over all our lives on TV news of every day."[61] No one then believed that children knew best. No one would allow a child to become a political activist, or to see stories involving sex and brutality, or to make their own decisions about surgeries and medications.

Modern people mock their forbears as "repressed," assuming they must have been comically ignorant of sexual matters. On the contrary, they were wiser than most of us, and followed a code of social trust in which people would no more discuss private matters in public than they would

---

[59] *Your Dinner's Poured Out,* 145.
[60] *Tides of Change,* 34.
[61] *No Shoes in Summer,* 46.

strip naked. "In those days childhood innocence was sacrosanct," Curran said.[62]

It wasn't just the absence of certain adult temptations, but the presence of certain values. "People took religion seriously," my neighbour Peter said. "And that would have meant that, from the point of view of Catholics, being really concerned with their eternal destiny, and being really concerned not to make grave sins." "There was a whole atmosphere of Christianity, they were taught faith," Christy said. "They were taught the prayers. Very few kids today would know how to say a Hail Mary – they wouldn't know. When we were kids, we knew all the hymns, and there was a whole ethos, a quality of life ..."

The result was a world unthinkable today, a world in which parents could relax. "It was much more a children's world, for few people remember anyone who would harm a child, nor were there any media around that could corrupt them," Tommy Ryan said on Irish radio. "Children ran everywhere freely and safely ... There was less hurry to get out of childhood and into adolescence."[63] Everyone to the horizon was family; as Francie Murray said, "it was possible for us youth to visit people in their homes over a two or three mile radius at any time of day or night, and always be guaranteed a welcome."

One great unmentioned casualty of the modern breakdown of trust is the close friendships that children often had with local adults. To become their own person children need multiple role models beyond their parents, and my neighbours had them by the dozens. My neighbour Peter described his friendship with the woman across the road who shared her vegetables, and Bill Bergen remembered spending hours watching his village blacksmith work.[64]

You can see this in most novels or diaries written before the last few generations; in his diary in the 1800s William Howitt wrote fondly of how much of his childhood was spent being mentored by kindly adults all around. "We haunted the joiner's [woodworkers'] shop, chipping and boring, and endangering our toes and fingers; at another, the smith's forge

---

[62] *Tides of Change,* 23.
[63] "Up the Church," RTE documentary.
[64] *Tales from a City Farmyard,* 108.

was our attraction ... Many a day of a cold winter did I pass by the pleasant blaze of this forge, delighting in its cheerful light, and in all the curious operations going on, such as making chains, and sharpening ploughshares, and so on; and many a day, of a cold winter too, did I sit cross-legged on the board of a good-natured tailor, making pincushions of a red and yellow strips of cloth ..."[65]

You can see it in American movies from the black-and-white era, in the friendship between a lonely man and a neighbourhood boy in *Mr. Winkle Goes to War,* or in the friendship between the children and local townspeople in *To Kill a Mockingbird.* Here too, American comic strips preserve a window to the past; a neighbourhood boy wanders in and out of Dagwood's house, as does Dennis the Menace with his neighbours, all scenes that are inexplicable now.

Today, if a local man were to spend a lot of time with a child, parents would be likely to call the police. I have mentioned to people that such friendships used to be common and seen them smirk say they know what was "really going on." The idea that any such man must be raping a child is the first thing that occurs to them.

All these combined influences meant that children "were taught more in a year than a lot of children these days are taught in a decade," my neighbour Mary told me. "And you know what? When we met for a reunion decades later, they all arrived in nice cars and happy families – they had all done really well in life. The kids I see now, whose memories of childhood are all of television and video games, I don't think they'll do as well."

Many of my elderly neighbours feel estranged from their own grandchildren, who grew up in an alien culture even a few doors down the road. The decline began when television burned through childhood, and that screen has now multiplied into a billion hand-held ones. When children everywhere carry all the world's pornography in their pocket, as well as electronic games psychologically designed to addict people as powerfully as any opioid, few future leaders will organise their mates, and few budding scientists will turn over any logs. Moreover, children today grow up under effective house arrest, as local ordinances, paranoid

---

[65] *The Boy's Country-Book*, 12.

neighbours and police conspire to prohibit children from venturing far outside. They grow up learning no lessons, organising no peers, and exploring no territory not in a screen.

They are also increasingly sick. In no human culture that ever existed were legions of adolescent girls cutting their arms, or binding their chests, or throwing up in secret, or murdering themselves. In no culture that has ever existed on Earth, in no era, until ours. Until yesterday.

As they age today's generations continue to live indoors, their clothes and tastes remaining juvenile. Their bodies will plump and their hair will grey, but they will never be adults, because they have never truly been children.

Chapter Two

Keeping Animals

By the time my daughter was seven we felt ready for animals, and we put up a chicken fence and hammered a coop together. Rather than buying paint from a store, I learned how to mix water with lime powder – more on that later – and make whitewash. I tried to show her how to paint the walls, but soon gave up and let her exult in her more Jackson-Pollack-inspired technique.

When their home was ready, we picked up the chickens from a nearby farm and brought them home in a box, my daughter cuddling and reassuring them all the way. It took only a day's play for her to give them all names, learn their personalities, and advise me on which ones to watch out for.

"Look at the scratch Marge gave me!" she said one day, holding out her hand.

That's impressive, I said. Marge and Trudy are the troublemakers, aren't they?

"It's Marge doing it!" my daughter said. "Trudy's not really bad at heart – Marge just drags her along and gets her in trouble. Trudy's like Peter Lorre in *Arsenic and Old Lace*."

One of our chicks late-bloomed into a rooster, who ... raised questions for a child. All day. Not consensually. He also darted out of the chicken run whenever we opened the door a crack, rather than just staying where the food and sex were, leading to a frantic chase around the property. The first time I grabbed him, I thought I could simply let him go over the fence, and he would flutter gently to the ground like the bird he was. Instead, he dropped like a bowling ball into the mud and crowed angrily at us all day from behind the fence.

One night one of ours went missing, and we scoured the nearby woods for an hour and found nothing. Just as we were giving up, I noticed a hole next to the coop that led to a tunnel, and poking down it with a broomstick we heard a "BWAK!" The hen apparently started scratching the ground and didn't stop until she was underground, and then panicked when she remembered she was a bird. I eventually fished her out, and my daughter cheered and embraced the prodigal idiot.

Chickens were well worth the trouble, though, as they gave us pest control, lawn-mowing, garbage disposal, fertiliser, entertainment, and their business ends doled out daily concentrated protein. They did seem determined to lay that protein everywhere but the coop, though, so on Easter morning my daughter found twice as many eggs as I hid.

We tried ducks as well, less successfully. Of course they needed water, and the canal that ran past our property offered that and plenty of food; the only problem was how to get them to come back to our house and lay eggs.

Our neighbours – settled Travellers, like Irish gypsies -- had done this, training their ducks to think of their coop as the place to sleep and lay. Their ducks waddled down the road to the canal every morning, fed themselves, and waddled back in the evenings to lay their eggs for my neighbours' breakfast table. They never strayed; I used to tell delivery drivers to "turn right at the ducks."

My daughter and I tried to follow their careful instructions, luring the ducks a little further out every day with food and then luring them back every evening. We did this for weeks, hoping we were building an understanding with the birds. Once in the canal, however, they made a beeline for the far bank and stayed there, laughing at us in the distance.

My daughter looked dejected, but I put my arm around her and reassured her that they are home now, where they want to be, and we'll see them every day. I'm sure they'll be all right.

"But I worry about them out there, Daddy," she said solemnly. She leaned close. *"They're really dim.* And that's by *duck* standards."

I realised she was growing up as few of her peers were but as all most of our ancestors had, with a practical and loving relationship with animals. Before we began using machines for everything, animals were the literal horsepower that carried us, the teeth that guarded us, the wings and legs that helped us hunt and fish, the oldest and most faithful of companions, lovingly nursed to life and health. They were also, without contradiction, meat and milk and eggs and blood and life for ourselves and our children.

As we walked the back roads we saw white-haired Jim training his colt, Martin walking his cows from one field to another, William bleary-eyed after staying up all night with a sick calf. I was always struck by how respectful, how affectionate they were toward their animals, understanding but never sentimentalising their nature.

When I asked Martin about his bull large as a bison in the nearby field, he smiled and said, "Ah, Duke – he's a good lad. Sometimes, when I get close, he lifts me up by the horns and sets me down again, just to remind me he could." He had spent almost every day of his eight decades around bulls, and was no more perturbed than we would be around cars, which kill 100,000 times more people every year.

Many modern people treat cats and dogs as the babies they will never have, and I see first-time riders try to control horses as they do dead machines. Animals, though, are beings with their own personalities and goals, if not the words to express them. "Animals shall not be measured by Man," wrote Henry Beston in his memoir *The Outermost House.* "In a world older and more complete than ours, they move finished and complete, gifted with extensions of the senses we have lost or never attained, living by voices we shall never hear. They are not brethren, they are not underlings, they are other nations, caught with ourselves in the net of life and time, fellow prisoners of the splendour and travail of the Earth."

We can love animals more deeply than we do other people, and they can reciprocate. "There was a great bond between my father and Grey Fann [his draft horse], a mutual trust," Martin Morrissey. "... he took better care of Grey Fann than he took of himself. In return she was a willing worker who gave her best at all times ... he often said, 'Look after your horse and she will never let you down. Only people let you down.'" When his father died, the horse seemed to grieve, and passed only a short time later.[66]

---

[66] *Land of My Cradle Days,* 148.

In the Ireland my neighbours knew, horses not only pulled ploughs through the soil, but carts to town, barges down the canals and streetcars through Dublin. They required and supported an infrastructure of craftsmen -- smiths to make horseshoes, farriers to put them on the horse, leather-workers to make straps, carpenters and wheel-wrights who can build carts, carters to drive them, auctioneers at the annual horse fairs, stable-hands and veterinarians. As horses gave way to tractors, that economy collapsed.

"The old forge, the blacksmith, Willie O'Hanlon, and the farm horse all departed centre stage at about the same time," said Bill Bergin, who lived near me in County Kildare. "A grand old way of life ceased to exist. No longer would you hear the sound "Woah" or "Hike" coming from the fields as strong men who worked these beautiful animals at ploughing or haymaking. No more do they roll belly-up in the pasture as they relax after a long hard day cutting corn. Instead there is just the throb of engines and the smell of exhaust fumes."[67]

Many elders learned as children to tend animals many times their size, learning to be nursemaids, police and impromptu surgeons. Cows and sheep overeat and drink and develop bloat, Alice Taylor said, and once she found her cow "prone on the ground with a swollen bellow, his tongue hanging out and his eyes rolling in his head. Quick action was needed and my father pulled out his penknife and lanced the exact spot in the white-head's belly. It receded like a balloon deflating and within minutes he was back on his legs. He had gone almost past the point of no return and I viewed his recovery as if he were Lazarus rising from the dead. My father took on a new dimension in my eyes."[68]

My neighbours also had to be midwives, to monitor when their lamb or calf was due, help deliver, coax milk from the mother and stay with her all night -- and until electricity came in, to do all this by touch in darkness. Patrick Boland remembered sitting with his pig all night helping it give birth – which he looked forward to, as he got to skip school. Farmers trusted a man who knew animals; when he was stringing electricity cables

---

[67] *Some Time to Kill,* 14.
[68] *To School Through the Fields,* 27.

across Ireland, John Fitzpatrick got a farmer to agree to let them cross his land when Fitzpatrick rolled up his sleeves and helped deliver a calf.[69]

"It's very hard work but it's enjoyable work, interesting work," Frances McCaughan said. "It's hard to explain to anybody the joy you get out of your sheep lambing ... although you're up from all hours of the morning, to all hours of the night. You just get a certain satisfaction from going out there and seeing a ewe standing licking her lamb .... It just brings home to you Mother Nature."[70] No one in Ireland is far from a farmer – in family or miles – and as modern as Ireland has become, there is still a television event called *Lambing – Live!*

Farmers also how to soothe their animals, as Tony Carr said his neighbour Dennis did when transporting a truckload of calves and stopping to drink in a local pub. As the farmers sang together in the pub, the calves outside got restless and began to moo, waking up the neighbours. When a local woman called the pub to complain, Dennis apologised and said he'd fix it immediately. He ordered a bottle of milk from the bar, walked outside and climbed on the cattle trailer, and sprinkled the milk over the calves. "Immediately they began licking each other and quieted down completely," Carr said. "Dennis returned to his stool at the bar, ordered a pint of Guinness and began singing 'The Fields Near Shanagolden,' a Cork song he loved well."[71]

Some farmers migrated once a year to follow the herds, Walter Love said. Local farmers migrated from the croplands in the valleys to the grassy hills to graze their cattle for the summer, and "they built ... huts for themselves and their wives and families," he said. "And if they had bees they brought them with them to make heather honey."[72] Amazing as it sounds, cattle were driven to market in Dublin "by cowboys on bicycles, men with overcoats and hats, furiously pedalling this way and that, whacking the cattle with their sticks and shouting at them," Gene Kerrigan said.[73]

---

[69] *Then There was Light*, 66.
[70] Frances McCaughan interview, Antrim History Archive.
[71] *Some Time to Kill*, 133.
[72] *Times of Our Lives*, 29.
[73] *Another Country*, 95.

Every morning and evening, "milking time was singing time; it was debating time if your fellows ... felt so inclined, or it could just be dreaming time," Taylor said.[74] Milk from the cows went into home-made butter churns, and as churning is exhausting work, each family member took a turn – and any visitors who appeared at the door. "When electricity came in and a few wives got washing machines, a few poured the milk in and used the washing machine to churn it into butter," Kevin Duffy said.[75]

Some villages had a creamery that served all the farms around, saving the farmers time and effort, but also making it the place to exchange gossip, stories, news and free legal advice, Ann Gardinier said. The farmer came home from the creamery "to a welcoming cup of tea and a wife agog with curiosity for all the latest news ... We could never imagine that such a vital facet of country life, with all the attendant fun and social interaction, would, like so many other things, become a victim of progress," she said.[76]

***

Even in the middle of the city, people had their own farmyard animals. My neighbour Christy said that across Dublin many back gardens housed a pig, and many had cows and hens. "I wish to stress again the 'farm' atmosphere of our whole district," wrote Paddy Crosbie.[77] "The only unusual things about the farmyard which joined onto the house in which I was born are that it was in ... Dublin, and there was no farm to go with it," wrote Patrick Boland in his autobiography *Tales From a City Farmyard*.

Feeding backyard animals also gave boys a useful job that kept them out of trouble. Boland described how much of his spare time was spent looking after the pigs, a venture that really took off after they discovered what hotels for the wealthy were throwing out. "The swill they fed their pigs was collected door to door, and mostly consisted of potato peelings, cabbage parts. But the swill from the Clarence Hotel was different – massive steaks with only a few forkfuls taken off, giant turkeys with just

---

[74] *To School Through the Fields*, 121.
[75] *50 Years Behind the Counter*, 75.
[76] *The House Remembers*, 62.
[77] *Your Dinner's Poured Out*, 67.

the breasts missing" – "I tell you, our pigs ate better than some families in the neighbourhood."[78]

Modern suburbanites might be alarmed at the idea of having livestock in their yards, but that's what yards were for originally, when people expected to provide for themselves. As Ireland modernised, my neighbour Christy told me, new laws forced urban families to get rid of their animals, citing public hygiene. Yet when they had animals, he said, "they were getting organic meat, and you were getting it fresh. You knew the pig and where it came from; it wasn't from Argentina or anything like that, it was from your own neighbourhood."

Backyard animals not only gave each household meat for the year and money for selling the extra meat, but also rid the community of rubbish; "float cars were a common sight in the streets as boys or young men went from house to house looking for slop for the pigs," Paddie Crosbie said.[79]

All societies can get rid of food waste in one of two sane ways. Firstly, they could compost it and convert it back into soil again. Secondly, they could re-use scraps and parts of food we can't eat, and feed them to animals to convert it into meat. Or, they can take the insane choice our modern society makes: to wrap it in plastic and throw it into a pit, leaching chemicals for centuries to come.

*** *

My daughter and I never got around to anything larger than chickens – no goats or pigs – but we did learn to keep something smaller: bees. Our relationship with bees goes back so far that it has affected the evolution of third-party species. The honeyguide bird of Africa leads humans to hives so they can get the honey, which they share with the bird – something that must have been worked out over millions of years, before we were truly human. Many ancient societies kept bees, apparently developing the relationship separately in places around the world. Through the centuries that monasteries kept learning alive in Ireland, no self-respecting monastery would be without bees for mead and candle-wax.

---

[78] *Tales from a City Farmyard*, 73.
[79] *Your Dinner's Poured Out!* 44.

For most of that time, though, they were kept in simple containers like skeps, essentially baskets that had to be broken and the hive destroyed any time the honey was harvested. In 1852, though, a Pennsylvania vicar invented the beehive that is still used today – a wooden box with sliding frames inside that the bees can use to make honeycombs, without sealing the frames together. Each frame could be pulled out and checked, the bees inspected for disease and progress, and the honey extracted, all with only a brief disruption to the hive.

Not only do they give us honey and wax, but they are very helpful in pollinating our plants as well, the reproductive solution for living things that must procreate but cannot move. Flowers grow for their benefit, not us, and beautiful as they are to us, have colours and patterns only bees can see. Most gardeners around here grow plants not only for food and beauty, but to advertise like a neon sign to pollinators.

I found beekeepers in our area and asked if I could watch and learn, bought books on beekeeping, and slowly accumulated the gear, my daughter putting pennies in a jar that said "bee stuff." We got an empty hive box, which all the books told us to put somewhere warm and dry --- books not written for someone who lives in a bog in Ireland. We got the bee suit, a one-piece thing that seemed to consist mostly of zippers. We got the smoker to sedate them and the wax slides to get them started. Actually handling a hive of bees and putting them in the box, though, remained an intimidating prospect.

Eventually I found an old beekeeper who had a "nuc" (pronounced nuke), a new mini-swarm with a queen, a new beekeeper's starter kit. When I walked up to him he cheerfully plopped into my arms a wooden box, secured all around with duct tape and with a wire mesh at the top, and right under the mesh, a swarm of bees pulsing like a single animal inside.

Through the next few days of rain I sprayed sugar-water through the mesh of the shoebox to keep them fed, until the sun came out and I was ready to don the suit, smoke the bees and put them in the hive, smoothly as all the books said.

I learned several things that day. I learned to make sure all the zippers are tight on the bee suit, or the elderly neighbours will see a strange, white-clad figure dancing the hokey-pokey in the distance. I also learned to make sure the smoker was still lit before letting the bees out. And to make sure you have a lighter on you to re-start it. As my daughter ran toward me with matches, I shouted out of my bee suit *"NO! Don't come near me! I'm covered in bees!"*

In the end, though, we got them in --- without a single sting, even from the bee that got in the suit. Soon they were filling up the combs, and I occasionally brought one in for my daughter to stare at in awe. We held them to the light, and they shone in different colours like a stained-glass window – the faint yellow cells with honey made from apple blossoms, the darker honey from hawthorn, the faint green from lime flowers, the dark purple of heather. As each flower bloomed, the bees filled the cells row by row, like typing a letter.

***

Living in the country means being surrounded by other animals besides yours, of course, and many of them will take your crops and livestock if they can. Rabbits, squirrels, deer and pigeons will eat your crops, if you don't defend them, and foxes, stoats and hawks will take your chickens. All farm families had to hunt, for protection and for daily food in a poor country.

Most men took their sons hunting, my neighbour Jack told me, and "there were always plenty of rabbits, and if there weren't there was a pheasant or anything else that came up." Even Dublin women caught rabbits from the park and eels from the then-clean river, Mary Waldron said. "Every morning Father would wander off with my brothers and they would catch fish and shoot rabbits. How we loved rabbit stew and griddle cake and buns cooked over an open fire."[80] My neighbour Peter remembered shooting pigeons and baking them in a pie, like the nursery rhyme.

"On a Sunday morning after early mass, men and youths would meet and go hunting across the moors and bogs, not for sport but for the pot," Maire Walsh wrote. "There were grouse, partridge, pheasant, rabbits and

---

[80] *No Shoes in Summer,* 186.

hares; also wild duck and geese, and woe betide anyone who killed out of season."[81]

Boys without a gun were forced to get creative; Francie Murray and John Curran both remembered snaring rabbits by tying wire around one entrance to its warren while trying to scare it at the other. "If the rabbit's leg or any part of its body made contact with the wire it immediately squeezed very tightly," and the rabbit was caught and dispatched, Curran said. "The carcass was then hawked from door to door in the village and offered for sale for two shillings."[82]

Virtually all traditional peoples respected the animals they ate, which seems bizarre to modern people who eat animals raised in torment. At the same time, many cultures put limits on what they can kill and eat, and when, and how. "There was a strict country code which, in later years, as tourists came, was ignored," Walsh said. "Farmers eventually forbade all trespassing on their property in order to protect the wildlife."[83]

Fishing was also part of most people's lives. Ireland can see rain on *two-thirds* of days, and all that water must go somewhere, so the land is covered in streams, waterfalls, rivers and small lakes, or "loughs," clear and ice-cold and thick with fish. Most were gashes in the land scooped out by the Ice Ages and flooded as they melted, and fishermen still bring up bones of woolly rhinos and mammoths.

Each lake has its own ancient legends of fairies and pucks, giants and gods; Mary Carberry told stories of the drowned city at the bottom of Lough Gur, or of the banshee that haunts the lake but consoled the dying. Some have the charming names of Ireland's indigenous language: Tascumshin, Poulaphouca, Inchiquin, Nafooey, Acoose, Shindilla, Keshcarrigan and Cloonacleigha. Others have the terse syllables of the familiar: Tay, Derg, Scur, Beg, Bane, Rinn, Finn, Gill, Talt, Ree, Fee, Doo, Lene, Gur, Fern, Dan, Skean, Conn, Clea.

Each one supported hundreds of local families with trout and pike, crayfish and ducks. Men and children fished from the shore, from docks or by paddling out in basket-boats called coracles – more on them later.

---

[81] *Irish Country Childhood*, 7.
[82] *Tides of Change*, 76.
[83] *Irish Country Childhood*, 7.

Many were local farmers who brought home a fish supper here and there, but for others it was a way of life; Teddy Delaney described how his father spent all his spare time on boats and "spoke of everything in nautical terms – bow and stern, forrad and aft. Life itself was a matter of gaffs, straugh-hauling and feathering your oar."[84]

"I have always thought that fishermen have more spirituality than the rest of us," Carr said. "Maybe this is because they were much mentioned in the gospels. After all, most of the apostles were fishermen, the symbol of the new church was a fish and at least two of Jesus' miracles concerned fish. But the sport lends itself greatly to relaxation. Here you are sitting on a riverbank; there's nobody near; all fuss seems to melt away; you can just sit back, relax and commune with nature... God is in his heaven and a contentment seeps into you which non-anglers never experience."[85]

Most people learned as children to be good with a rod and line, usually making it themselves from sticks and string, but Peter and others "tickled" trout out of the water. "It's an old way of poaching trout ... if you put your hands under the water you could feel them ... and then [I] grabbed it by the gills, and pulled it out, you had your supper."

Walsh and her childhood friends used a bag and a bit of lime powder – made from limestone, as we will see later – to create a trap for fish. "When the small rivers ran shallow in hot weather, we would build a courigh, or barrier, with stones and clauber – damp pieces of grassy earth from the river bank – to stay the flow of water," she said. "We would put lime into a sack, then secure the sack between the stones with the bag mouth opening into the flow of water. When the water volume built up, fish unwittingly became trapped in the bag. The lime stunned them and we would take the trout home to be fried in home-made butter."[86]

They grew up learning from their older relatives how to read the signs around them, a change in air or a gathering of insects over the water, and learn the fishes' patterns. Carr remembers fishing in the Liffey with his second cousin, and his cousin looked at the water and said, "There should be rise shortly."

---

[84] *Where We Sported and Played*, 37.
[85] *Some Time to Kill*, 46.
[86] *Irish Country Childhood*, 6.

"I hadn't a clue what he meant ..." Carr said. "I was soon to find out. It was a lovely stretch of placid deep water that extended maybe fifty yards before sliding gently around a lined tree bank. Swarms of flies were hovering and pitching, dancing and swooping all along the breadth of the river, the sunlight glinted a brown orange on this sequined tapestry. There was a gentle plop as a trout leapt. Then there was another. Now another trout leapt. This was a big one. It was like a drummer playing a solo. First a little beat. Then the rhythm increased. By now trout were popping up all over the surface. Like the drummer they were gathering momentum all the time. Hundreds of trout were gorging themselves in a frenzy of gluttony...

Was this happening all along the Liffey? What a sight. And could it also be happening along the [Rivers] Boyne, Nore, Barrow, Suir and Slaney? Why not? Good God, this is a great country."[87]

At the same time, Taylor said, locals had strict rules about poaching. "Once, when a generous neighbour gave us a present of a poached salmon, [my father] lined us all up around the kitchen table to and proceeded to open up the fish," she said. "As the eggs poured out he explained about the huge loss of fish life due to the poaching of this one salmon. In my father's word nature possessed a balance and man had no right to upset that balance to satisfy his own greed; killing this fish was going against the laws of Nature."[88]

Overfishing and industrial waste, Carr said, mean that "sadly, these streams, brooks, and rivers are no longer blessed with such bounty. The fish population has declined rapidly in my lifetime. Pollution is rampant. The magical word "progress" may be the most misused word in the English language."[89]

Ireland is also networked with canals, dug in the 1700s so barges could ship peat from bogs to city fireplaces. Yet they opened to rivers on one end and the sea on the other, and fill up with their own stock of fish. They were shallower and busier than rivers, with so many barges going past, yet Carr said this actually brought more fish.

---

[87] *Some Time to Kill*, 48.
[88] *To School Through the Fields*, 9.
[89] *Some Time to Kill*, 49.

"When the barges chugged along they disturbed the soil or whatever lay on the bed of the canal," he said. "Little fresh-water molluscs and worms became available to the trout. The trout thrived and increased in number. Pike ate many of the trout ... A symbiotic relationship evolved between the barges, the little worms and snails, the trout and the pike. And then, some unseen bureaucrat in an office in Dublin decided to change the system. It was no longer viable to use the canals for transport. The heady days of the canal ceased. And so did the fish."

Carr blamed sewage and silage have ruined Ireland's waterways – more on silage later. "Who is to blame?" he asked. "The answer is simple. We all are responsible for this long concerted attack upon Nature. At the mouth of every river in the country there stands a town ... The sewage being generated is a major pollutant. Industries are also at fault. These generally rely upon some chemicals in the manufacturing of their products. That is, if they are not actively engaged in producing chemicals themselves...."

Carr said that not only did he no longer see trout "rise" in the river, as his cousin had shown him as children, but he increasingly no longer saw the land life he used to. "How long is it since you've seen a frog?" he asked. "How long is it since you've seen a grasshopper or a "hairy molly?" Have you noticed the scarcity of primroses and cowslips? ... True patriotism begins at your own kitchen sink."[90]

Many of the older people say industrial fish farming has spread diseases that have decimated the wild fish in the lakes. "Now all these lakes are almost bereft of [trout]," Kevin Duffy said. "The very odd angler that ventures out would be lucky to take one or two small trout in a day..."[91]

The same is true even of the vast sea around Ireland. Once many coastal villages supported themselves by fishing, as well as catching crabs and lobsters. Women pickled the fish the men caught, or dried them "all over the roofs of the thatch cottages in fishing villages, where they were dried hard by the sun and, perhaps, the smoke coming from inside,"

---

[90] *Some Time to Kill,* 49 – 50.
[91] *Fifty Years Behind the Counter,* 108.

Christopher Moore said. "The silver scales glistened in the sun and they were called 'chimney angels.'"[92]

Such lives are rare as fish these days. As recently as the 1960s fishermen off Newfoundland, for example, were catching 1.6 million tonnes a year; 30 years later that number had dropped by up to 99 per cent in places.[93] We fished the sea almost barren.

"We used to lose fishing nets all the time as they became overfilled -- not any more," said one fisherman on Irish radio as far back as 1977. "The big trawlers simply vacuum the ocean and nothing ever goes back ... There should be a good and continuing future in fishing, but there isn't now."[94]

"It would sadden the person who had experience of that work if he were to visit the harbour today," Conchur O'Siochain wrote around the same time. "All bustle of the activity that was then utterly gone, and nothing to be seen but the cold and empty quays."[95]

Once men, women and children scoured the Irish shore for mosses, seaweeds and shellfish to eat, and when the ocean pulled away from the land, "there wasn't a rock that hadn't a woman, a child or a youngster gathering limpets, shellfish, winkles or some such thing," O'Croghan wrote. Even the schools revolved around the foraging calendar, he wrote -- his teacher "would leave the boys off from school when the tides were answering. This usually happened about three times a month, but this was only when the weather was suitable, and if there were an 'R' in the month, which is when shellfish are in season. Carageen [a type of edible seaweed] ... could be gathered practically anywhere on the island at low tide."

Carageen was sold to pharmacists as medicine, was dried and mixed with milk to feed calves, and was eaten as a soup or dessert. "This cooking tradition was passed down from mother to daughter, but, alas, today, is no longer growing on the beaches of Scattery," Tomas O'Croghan said. "... unless the beach was kept clean by gathering the carrageen ... annually, [another type of] seaweed grows over the carrageen to replace it."[96]

---

[92] *Around the Farm Gate,* 72.
[93] Smedbol, 2002.
[94] "Alive, Alive O," RTE Radio Documentary, 1977.
[95] *Man from Cape Clear,* 33.
[96] *Memories of an Islander,* 17.

***

If you could boil our global problems down to seven words, they might be these: *we don't see where stuff comes from.* We grow up staring at screens without ever seeing the coal plants that power them, speed down motorways without ever visiting the oil derricks that fuel them, and eat mountains of meat a year without having to grab a live animal or smell blood. Like most things in our lives, meat just magically appears, brought by strangers.

That last example hit home for modern Irish several years ago, after the government tested frozen burgers from a major supplier and found that some of the alleged beef was actually horsemeat.[97] Of course, horsemeat is not harmful, and little different than cow, as evidenced by the fact that no one can tell which one they ate. Nor is it illegal; rather, the emotional punch – and inevitable punch-lines – that came from the idea of eating Black Beauty obscured more important details, like the fact that governments and stores can't tell where much of the meat came from. This is an especially sore point in the UK, which had already dealt with outbreaks of hoof-and-mouth and mad cow disease. Restaurants and stores here proudly advertise their "Irish beef," not only to support local farmers but to distance themselves from such disasters. Now, it turned out, it might not have been Irish or beef.[98]

We accept buying meat from strangers for the same reasons we buy everything else in our lives from strangers these days; because we trust that someone, somewhere, knows what they are doing. On the rare occasions we associate the food on our plates with actual animals, we tend to assume they must have come from some kind of farm, like the overall-and-pitchfork images of preschool toys. We don't picture the vast mechanised factories of reality, or supply chains so long and cobwebby that we can't find out what kind of animal it used to be, or in what part of the world.

---

[97] "Horsemeat scandal: the essential guide," *The Guardian*, 15 Feb 2013.
[98] "A decade on: How the horsemeat scandal changed the way the world thinks of food safety," *Irish Times*, 7 Jan 2023.

Consider how strange this would seem to most of our ancestors. For most of them meat was life; while most foods could be grown or picked, meat was the Leibig's Minimum that forced our primate ancestors to become predators. Their craving for meat transformed the landscape, wiping out the planet's large animals as thoroughly as an asteroid impact did the dinosaurs, and we now know Neanderthals or Clovis people by their meat-getting technologies. It was the main reason we domesticated animals, and that spurred empires and conquests – the Sanskrit word for "war," I'm told, means "a desire for cows," and the ancient Irish epic the *Tain Bo Cuailnge* involves a nationwide war over a single breeding bull. The very word "meat" meant "food" in Old English, so inextricable were the two.

Yet such concentrated nutrition comes with risks; many of our human diseases come from animals, from the Stone Age up to (perhaps) the COVID-19 pandemic, and domestication brought humans and animals into close daily contact. When Europeans first encountered the Americas and Australia, they brought ten thousand years of accumulated diseases to which they had built up immunity but the natives had not, accidentally wiping out 95 per cent of the native population in the largest mass death in human history. Meat means life and death, so many of our religions bind us with meat taboos -- Jews and Muslims ban pig meat, Hindus cow meat, and Catholics all meat on Fridays through Lent. Our rituals invoke the body and blood of the Word made flesh.

Because meat was so precious, most of our ancestors drew on more variety than we do: frogs and snails, pigeons and ducks, liver and pancreas. Old women in Dublin talked about making the cheapest meats – sheep's heads and cow's heads – into stew, or buying rabbits for pennies, or giving the children the heart and liver as a treat, or munching on pig's feet in the cinema. On farms men killed one of their pigs every fall to feed them over winter, all the local wives gathered to turn it into sausage and bacon, Francis Quinn said, and "there was none of the pig went to waste."[99]

Most people today could never endure such honesty about what we are eating. "The implications of having a pig in the window, head and all,

---

[99] Antrim archives.

could not be done nowadays," said butcher Eugene Kierans. "People cannot tolerate the idea of what they are eating, yet they can turn on the telly and watch people getting blown up... I find it most peculiar."[100]

In rural Ireland, most villages also have a butcher, and mine now features a sign about how he buys only from the local farmers. He actually gives me more meat than I ask for, knowing that I like the bones and cast-off meats for soups. Everyone here used to get their meat from people like him, if they didn't slaughter it themselves; it was only recently that the globalised supermarkets, with their shelves of cheap frozen meat and opportunities for fraud, began to proliferate. In my native USA, though, one would have to rebuild the entire infrastructure – local farmers to local shops within walking distance to homes – from scratch.

But if we want to know our where our meat comes from, we will need to revive backyard chickens, vacant-lot pigs and cows, and people who know how to make the most of them. And we need more people like my farmer friend, who I met bleary-eyed from staying up all night with a calf. He gives his animals a better life than any they would have seen in the wild, infinitely better than on a factory farm, before making sure their life ends quickly and painlessly. His small scale makes the butcher more expensive, but that's as it should be. Meat needs to again become hard work to get and precious to eat, so that we again put some sacral value in the lives we take.

---

[100] "A Butcher's Tale," RTE documentary, 2009.

Chapter Three

Foraging

Behind you stands an army of ghosts, the ancestors whose blood flows through you right now. They all lived wildly different lives in different climates and cultures – a Cro-Magnon here, a Viking over there – but every one was tough enough to survive long enough to have descendants. They lived outdoors and fed themselves, they chased boar and rabbits through woods, they spotted the fruits and leaves that would keep them alive amid a sea of poison, herded and trained giant grumpy animals many times their strength, and over thousands of years they took scraggly weeds and transformed them into lush crops. Your ancestors were – if I may put it this way – total bad-asses.

If you'll forgive me for saying so, you probably aren't. It's okay – neither am I. In a few generations we have become the most dependent creatures ever to exist outside of zoos. Almost every modern person – even activists who campaign for notional "freedoms" -- are helpless as babies without our global financial and food system, with anarchy a few missed meals away.

So when elderly Irish tell me they grew up without electricity or cars, or worked for a fraction of today's wages, or spent years with no money at all, we picture them as miserable as we would be without these things. Yet elder after elder said the opposite; people were safer, happier and healthier.

How did they do it? The same way all humans had, in every culture and every generation until us: they grew food, they hunted, they fished, they knew delicious berries and mushrooms from deadly ones. They gave their animals a good life and a clean death. They stocked food for winter by drying, curing, pickling, salting, burying, canning, brewing, fermenting, and making milk into cheese, fruit into jams, vegetables into wines, and grains into beers.

"Our farm was like a little colony, self-contained, where everyone worked hard and all were contented and happy," Mary Fogarty said. "Besides the fields, the farmhouse and its good out-buildings, there was a quarry, a kiln for burning lime, a sandpit, a turf bog and the productive eel-weir ... Everything we ate and drank came from the farm except tea and coffee and J.J. (whiskey), which was kept for visitors and medicine."[101]

"There was a great sense of independence in those days – people, they weren't dependent on supermarkets," Mick Waddell said. "I can remember at home a couple of cows, our own butter, our own milk, plenty of potatoes and vegetables from the garden. Mother spent much of the summer making jam, and baking bread ..."[102]

"Our food came from the fields all around us," said Alice Taylor. "The spring planting led to the autumn harvest ... Our meat came from the pigs rooting in the haggard, and the chickens, ducks and geese wandering around the farmyard. Potatoes and vegetables dug up in the morning were on the table for our midday dinner. The milk from the morning milking was in use soon afterwards and indeed we often sampled it when it was still warm from the cows."[103]

"Nobody had money, but they had farms and they had enough to eat," Kathleen McAlister said. "We never suffered any malnutrition or nothing, because my father, och, he was a great man right enough. He had every vegetable under the sun, as well as potatoes and our own pigs. You killed the pigs and you had your own bacon ... you had soup out of shinbone; the stuff that was really good for you, and we didn't realise it, you know. And you had your own butter, you know, on the farm. We never wanted, never."[104]

They let nothing go to waste; the cloth flour bags became clothes and sheets, food waste went to pigs, the wood from trees became furniture, the

---

[101] *The Farm by Lough Gur,* 20.
[102] "Pilots, Lighters and Horse-Drawn Ships," RTE documentary, 2016.
[103] *Books from the Attic,* 52.
[104] Antrim Archives.

dried peat moss from the bog became fuel to keep the house warm over the winter. "Sure we never went to the shop except for tea and sugar, and my father would buy a big bag of flour," Rose Smith said. "When that would be gone, the bag was taken in, washed, put out on the grass to bleach, and when we had four of them, they would be sewn together and we would have sheets. I was reared on flour bag sheets. It was linen, the best of linen sheets in the end."[105]

Even during World War II, when many imported goods were cut off from neutral Ireland, "other than having to eat brown bread and having no fruit other than native apples and pears, plums, blackberries and so on, we got plenty of good food, and felt sorry for people in England who had strict rationing," Buckley said.[106]

Even Hugh Brody's brutally unsentimental take on rural Ireland, *Inishkillane*, noted that "as long as families were able to grow potatoes, keep a cow, bake bread, and cut turf ... [they] required a bare minimum of commerce with outside economies ... a peasant farmer placed his family, its integrity and independence, at the apex of his values."[107]

Such people, independent but part of a community, are the ideal people to practice democracy, as in Thomas Jefferson's ideal of a "nation of farmers." Ireland, likewise, was in its early days "a republic without leaders, though not without leadership," wrote Irish journalist John Waters. "All the men and women who belonged to it drew their power and their majesty from the skills they had honed in themselves, and the mastery ... that it gave them."[108]

***

Many of the elders I talked to built their own houses, using materials all around. They built with wattle-and-daub, cob, with squares of turf, with stones, bricks or planks of wood, using whatever they had; everyone knew a carpenter or mason, John Curran remembered, and "they pooled their

---

[105] *Growing Up With Ireland*, 233.
[106] *No Shoes in Summer*, 106.
[107] *Inishkillane*, 3.
[108] *Give Us Back the Bad Roads*, 182.

resources, and houses, farm buildings, and stonewalls were constructed when required."[109]

Some of those building materials could be superior to what we use today. In County Clare I once helped sculpt a house out of cob, a wet mix of sand, clay and straw that holds together like concrete, and can be far more durable. The house began with stone walls that went up to waist height, as cob needs to be raised above the damp. Then we heaped the wet cob mix on top of the stone walls one lump at a time – "cob" is from an Old English word for "lump" – and then trod them down in our bare feet. Bit by bit, the walls got higher, until we could lay a roof on top.

After the walls are given a plaster finish, the house can look just like any other, but made at a fraction of the cost, as it uses the simplest and cheapest material on Earth -- earth itself. Despite this, they can last hundreds of years; Sir Walter Raleigh's palatial mansion was built of cob, and still stands after 500 years. Cob houses can be cheap to heat as well, as their thick walls absorb heat over the day and release it slowly at night.

Cob, like wattle-and-daub or other traditional techniques, has disadvantages; in this rainy country it needs an overhang or wooden cladding so its clay walls do not erode over time. At the same time, such techniques solve a lot of problems; unlike modern construction they use no chemicals, create no pollution, and generate no toxic waste. And, of course, they are dirt cheap.

Roofs, also, could be made from materials all around. "Ninety-five percent of the houses at that time were thatched, and I can tell you they were warm comfortable houses," John Lydon remembered. "The fireplace was almost as wide as the house, and there was always a huge turf-fire blazing in the centre, which drove heat all over the kitchen."[110]

The straw from a thatched roof was free from the fields; some roofs even had scarecrows to keep birds from stealing bits for their nests. Local saplings were cut, bent and tucked into place to secure the straw so tightly that the fiercest winds couldn't dislodge it. Nor, in this damp climate, was it a fire hazard. The roofs lasted several years until moss started growing

---

[109] *Tides of Change*, 12.
[110] *Joy of My Boyhood Years*, 98.

over the straw, staining the rain green as it streaked down the white sides of the cottages.

Thatchers were "usually lithe and agile to facilitate climbing on roofs that were often fragile," Joe Keane said. The thatcher "chose his materials with great care to ensure durability against harsh winters. The thatched roofs of Irish cottages were aesthetically pleasing and ecologically sustainable."[111]

"The old-time thatchers could turn their skills with straw to other areas, and one of these was apparently the weaving of mattresses which were said to be of such quality that they would last for years: some of them had even mastered the difficult art of making 'bee skeps' out of straw," Maurice McAleese said. "When a thatcher succeeded in weaving a skep he could consider himself as being at the head of his trade."[112]

Unlike in most of the USA, where everything is a car's drive away, people then had everything they needed in a single village or neighbourhood, and when they needed to go further, they could safely hitchhike. "If I was going to the centre of town I'd just jump on the back of a lorry passing by," Paddy Mooney said.[113]

They also rode trains, as Ireland had twice as many train lines a century ago than it does now. Even now it's impressive to an American; similarly-sized Missouri has only a seventh as much track as Ireland. Also, the trains here cost me around $10 instead of $200, and there are about twenty a day rather than one. They were clean and well-attended, and arrived within a minute of their scheduled time rather than being (as I experienced on Amtrak) eight hours late.

Ireland also has several times more bus lines than trains. For months at a time I never needed a car to travel to my job in Dublin; I just cycled to the bus stop a few miles away, stashed my bicycle in a neighbour's barn next to the cows, hopped on the double-decker bus, and came back the same way in the evenings.

Many local farmers here still run a taxi service on the side, and you can call them day or night to get picked up from the pub. In small, informal

---

[111] *Around the Farm Gate*, 138.
[112] *Back Through the Fields*, 64.
[113] *Dublin Tenement Life*, 99.

communities, bus and taxi services often blur together, as the bus driver might sit and relax in the middle of the village until they have passengers, or make an extra leg of their journey to drop off an old lady at her door.

"We didn't use cars at all, but we had the advantage that there was a man called Amby Meehan who provided transportation for the area," Bob Bernen said. "It was great to see one man, with a car and a mini-bus, transporting perhaps 500 people, and doing it well, in a way that no public system could have equalled ... And if there was someone who couldn't afford the fare, Amby was always willing to take them without charge."[114]

More than any other method, though, Irish in those days used bicycles, in the city and country alike; Jack's company gave out bicycles to new employees so they could get to work and back. "In the mid-thirties and forties having a bicycle of your own meant freedom to come and go just as much as a car means to the people of today," Colm Moloney said. "During the war years there was no petrol for cars or late-night buses so there was no other way to get about. The center of the City used to be just one big mass of bicycles being taken care of by men and boys who made jobs for themselves doing that while the owners were off at a theatre, a dance or a film."[115]

***

Even with all its green fields, Ireland still has patches of forest and bog that teem with edible berries and nuts, weeds and seeds, roots and shoots. Our ancestors lived and multiplied for millions of generations, after all, before agriculture was invented, and every morsel of food they ate was wild – and even when people began farming, they didn't stop foraging. "We made use of most things that grew wild around our area, and learned from older people about country lore," Maire Walsh said.[116]

To those who grew up in a sterilised landscape of manicured lawns and ornamental shrubs, munching on wild plants sounds disgusting and dangerous. In my native USA much of the countryside has little food, as they are covered with monocultures edible for only a brief window each

---

[114] *Tales from the Blue Stacks.*
[115] *Dublin Tenement Life*, 99.
[116] *Irish Country Childhood, 8.*

year. Paradoxically, by turning most meadows and forests into farmland, we have destroyed much of the food that could sustain us in a crisis.

Once I learned to forage, though, almost every month brought new delicacies. March brought hawthorn buds and shoots I ate as salad, and in April the first nettles appeared. May was salad season, as the linden tree outside my window erupted in young leaves fresh as lettuce, eaten in a bowl with fat hen, Good King Henry, daisies, clover and – best of all – tangy sorrel from the forest floor. Every June the hedges erupted in elderflowers, which we made into pancakes or wine, and then the first berries emerged.

"In summertime nature provided us with our own sweet-counter ... gooseberries, currants and, in the early morning dew, some speckled fields of mushrooms," Morrissey said.[117] By autumn, Walsh said, "the countryside offered us all kinds of delicacies: blackberries, bilberries, wild raspberries, sloes and haws."[118] "We had never heard of foraging, but we were foragers!" Taylor said.[119]

Many of the flowers can be eaten as well, or used to make wine, jam or tea. When I was building the cob house we stopped for tea, and as we walked back to the shelter, some of my co-workers began picking certain plants around them as they walked and chatted. By the time we arrived at the kitchen their arms were full, and they quickly rinsed the plants, dropped them into a pitcher, poured boiling water over them, and in a few minutes had free herbal tea.

Even the most poisonous plants had their uses. The bracken ferns that cover the hillsides here formed the bottom layer of a thatched roof, its toxins creating a natural barrier against pests. For the same reason Malachi Horan used it for bedding, and "no beast, nor man either, took the cold from lying in that."[120]

Modern culture urges us to eliminate precisely those plants that could be useful. Take, for example, dandelions, a great source of vitamins that, unlike many wild plants, are easily identifiable by any schoolchild. The

---

[117] *Land of My Cradle Days*, p. 8.
[118] *Irish Country Childhood, 19.*
[119] *Books From the Attic*, 50.
[120] *Malachi Horan Remembers*, 79.

whole plant is technically edible, but only the new leaves are good to eat raw, before they take on their jagged shape ("lion's tooth" or in French, dent-de-lion). The yellow flowers can be made into fritters or wine and the roots can be roasted and ground into a substitute for coffee – I've done all of these, with excellent results. Yet most of us spray poison on our dandelions and cultivate useless grass, now America's most common crop.

Our phobia of the natural might seem slightly more justified with something like mushrooms, which do have fatally poisonous varieties. Compare that risk, however, to your risk of dying from car accidents, which kill 40,000 people each year in the USA alone. Food poisoning made 48 million Americans ill last year, of whom 3,000 died – people who accidentally ate an undercooked fast-food burger or gone-off Chinese. Eating wild mushrooms account for an average of fewer than three deaths per year on average.[121] Most of us, moreover, eat wild mushrooms all the time, from restaurants or jars at the store, so we obviously believe they can be selected safely. Most of us simply trust anonymous strangers more than we trust ourselves to learn.

Ireland has about 3,000 species of mushrooms, and about 25 are deadly poisonous, mushroom expert Bill O'Dea told me. Only about 50, however, are deemed "edible," while the other 2,925 are "inedible," not lethal but could taste terrible or make you sick. Even these, however, are not all off limits: one "inedible" mushroom is spicy like a hot pepper, and in Italy is dried and ground like cayenne. Our garden grew two types of crops every year: the green plants, and under their leaves a crop of "ink" mushrooms that are classified as "inedible," but are harmless and tasty so long as you never consume them with alcohol, as a chemical in them combines with alcohol in the stomach into something toxic.

Irish children hunted them like Easter eggs "in late July and August, when they could be found growing in the pastures of the countryside," said Tony Carr. "People would get up at all hours of the morning to pick them. Anyone who came home with a string of mushrooms was welcomed back like the prodigal son."[122]

---

[121] Brandenburg 2018.
[122] *Some time to Kill*, p. 87.

"Some fields were mushroom fields and others were not, and we knew where to look, but so did all the neighbouring children," said Alice Taylor. "Where mushrooms were concerned it was a free-for-all with farm boundaries of no consequence."[123] "You'd bring them home and roast them on the fire," my neighbour Angela told me. "You'd put your fire on the hearth, and you'd pull out a few coals and you'd put the mushrooms on the top with a bit of butter ... Those were good times."

They also used to be a profitable seasonal business for children who lived near restaurants or hotels. "Armed with one-gallon cans the search commenced," John Curran remembered. "The early bird catches the worm and it was important to get started before the competition and have a first run at the flush."[124]

When an old Irishman taught me how to identify mushrooms, I didn't need to memorise 3,000 species – just a few common, safe and unmistakable species. You learn to check out certain things by rote: Is it mushroom-shaped? Does it have gills under the umbrella part? Does the stem break off cleanly or into fibres? By learning such basic rules anyone can quickly narrow down the species; my then-nine-year-old could find a large mushroom, casually snap the stem, pinch the cap, declare it an inedible Lactarius and move on.

Mushrooms might be hard to find at first, but they are just the "fruits," as it were, of vast networks of threads weaving through the soil under our feet like fibres in a mattress. We think of the living world as consisting of plants and animals, part of a life cycle dimly remembered from old textbooks. Fungi are the forgotten member of the Trinity, recycling the world quietly under our feet.

Traditional peoples did not have our scientific data, but they understood some of this. I know an old man who bought some poor land in County Clare and turned it into a lush forest in just a few decades. When I asked him how, he explained that he prunes his trees each year and buries the branches, feeding the mycellium that create the soil. His entire system depends on his relationship to fungi, and like all the other living things on his land, he treats them with respect.

---

[123] *To School Through the Fields*, 54.
[124] *Tides of Change*, 75.

***

We found fewer mushrooms in the bog, as little decays in its anoxic waters, but bogs yielded other wonders. Walsh remembered watching with fascination as the summer sun dried the bog and exposed the skeletons of ancient trees buried in its depths, "like sentries with their jagged stumps bleached white and ghostly, as if trying to reveal the glory that was once theirs before they were indiscriminately burned down," she said. "Their roots resembled long, bony fingers reaching out to touch and console each other in remembrance of their majestic past. In the moonlight they looked like shrouded spectres rising from the bog, trying to convey their former greatness, when they covered the land and held in their arms the birds of the air and harboured the many wild animals which roamed without hindrance through the Ireland of old."[125]

The centuries of compacted moss from the bog created dozens of metres of peat, as mentioned earlier, and "[t]urf cutting and saving was one of the most important jobs for each and every homesteader," said John Lyons. With no electricity or natural gas, turf "baked the bread, boiled the spuds and meat for the dinner, boiled the water for the tea and all the washing in general, and it provided heat for all the family during the cold winter nights."[126]

Turf harvesting deserves a larger place in history; the tiny Dutch Republic, which pioneered so many scientific breakthroughs, democratic institutions and voyages of discovery in the 1600s, was powered by its own peat bogs.[127] The British, for their part, criss-crossed Ireland with canals, not as nautical shortcuts like the Panama or Suez canals, but to take barges of turf from the bogs to their urban fireplaces. They overtook the Dutch as a superpower when the latter's bogs were spent, and the British learned to capitalise on their supplies of an even more concentrated fuel, coal.

Despite this, most turf-harvesting was done by local farmers, and "there would always be a mad rush in the spring to get to the bog early for

---

[125] *Irish Country Childhood*, 19.

[126] *Joy of my Boyhood Years*, 102.

[127] "Medieval Smokestacks: Fossil Fuels in Pre-industrial Times," *Low Tech Magazine*, 29 Sept 2011.

the sheer honour of it, because that meant you were indeed an industrious farmer – to have all your seeds and potatoes in before your neighbours, and to be down to the bog to cut turf ," said Josie Gray.[128] Each farmer gathered a gang of local men -- in Irish, a *meithal* (pronounced mee-hall) -- and spent the day slicing turf for the next winter.

"After cutting our own turf, we had to cut for the neighbours who had helped us to cut ours," John Lyons said. "It was called comharing [pronounced *cooring*]. The same applied to the cutting of the corn, the threshing, the saving of the hay, and the weeding of the beet, mangolds and turnips. We helped each other at every job, and although the work was hard, we didn't feel the day going, with all the company, because most of them were great characters."[129] "Everything was shared and there was no humiliation in it," said my friend Ellen. The distant ringing of the Angelus bell signalled the lunch break, Francie Murray said, and the men had a picnic, "meals vastly superior to ones obtained from the fanciest restaurant in town."[130]

"The six-man meithal remained together until each person's turf was cut and to ensure that fairness prevailed the cutters worked on a different bog each day," Curran said. "To avoid transferring the implements too often they were buried in the bog, and all the turf in that area was cut. 'All for one and one for all' was the favoured basis on which the meithal worked, nobody received any money and all that was required was strong, willing and able bodies." When the men were done, John Curran said, each "stood his friends a drink after work and occasionally more turf was cut in the bar than in the bog."[131]

Some areas had turf-cutting festivals; Stephen Rynne said his drew thousands of people. It came complete with a barge down the canal with a band playing on it, as well as speeches, music, dancing, hurling matches and an appearance by the then-president of Ireland.[132]

A few of my neighbours still harvested their own turf, and I joined them, slicing the soft black matter into bricks and "footing" them –

---

[128] *Barnacle Soup*, 64.
[129] *Joy of my Boyhood Years*, 102.
[130] *Them Golden Fields I Trod*, 53.
[131] *Tides of Change*, 93.
[132] *Green Fields*, 171.

stacking two one way, two the other – so air could flow between and dry them. We might be some of the last people to do so, as personal turf-cutting is being banned in bog after bog. Ostensibly this is to preserve them as natural wetlands – which is important – but the national energy corporation still harvests on a massive scale, using machines larger than houses that scour the land barren, while banning local families from harvesting their own modest plots.

In the autumn my neighbours and I returned to the stacks of turf, now dried and ready for the fireplace. Some local farmers waved as they passed on their tractors, pulling a cage with all their children inside – an alarming sight out of context. The reason for the cage became apparent when I saw them drive back; the cage was filled with turf for the winter and all the children clung to the outside of the cage, as the tractor slowly puttered down the country roads.

***

Most suburbanites don't live near bogs and could not try these skills themselves, but most could create their own hedgerows or copses. By hedgerow I don't mean typical suburban hedges, often invasive and poisonous species planted for show. I mean a method of harvesting tonnes of wood to the acre without killing a tree, a trick that should be better known in this eco-conscious era.

When certain deciduous trees are cut cleanly, either at the base (coppicing) or higher up in the branches (pollarding), their roots don't die, but put their energy into new shoots. In a few years – or just a year with willows -- the still-healthy tree is ready to be cut again. In a stand of coppiced trees, called a copse, wood can be harvested every year for centuries.

Local people coppiced the slim shoots of willows – "sallies" -- annually to weave into wicker, the woven wood we associate with baskets. Wicker, though, can be used to make sheds, boats, fences, dams, and animal traps, and covered in plaster to create "wattle and daub" buildings.

Basket-weavers here harvest the shoots every St. Bridget's Day from massive old trunks that have never been mature trees, but simply send new shoots every year. Early humans harvested plants for basketry as well as food, and anthropologist M. K. Anderson even proposed that the first agriculture might have been to grow basketry crops, not food crops.[133]

Willow can even be woven while it is still alive and rooted in the ground, and Irish used this to bend and weave rows of willows together into a living wicker-wall – a hedgerow. Farmers could plant a row of saplings and, the next winter, cut each stem part-way through just above the ground, and bend the sapling without killing it. Each sapling could then be woven around the others, like knitting yarn. In spring the still-healthy trees send shoots upward, and the following winter those shoots would be cut and woven the same way. Each winter the wall of still-living wood grew higher and thicker, while other vines, shrubs and weeds grew in the crevices, until the land was surrounded by a solid wall of vegetation. It required no money and only about a day of work each year ... and patience.

Hedgerows improve over modern fences in several ways. When we humans farm we create fields of single crops, and since each plant removes different ratios of nutrients from the soil, the fields need to be continually fertilised. If you've ever wondered why forests and other wild places require no truckloads of fertilisers, it's because the variety of plants and animals fill in each other's nutritional gaps. Hedgerows balance our single-crop fields, creating a river of wild diversity that soaks up our excesses and keeps soil from eroding.

They stop Ireland's high winds, create a home for animals that eat our pests, and offer a trellis for useful climbers. The give cropland here a third dimension, a vertical salad bar of shoots and berries growing between the sallies. Also, willow and other plants literally suck toxins out of the soil and hyper-accumulate them in their tissues, so they clean the soil as they grow.[134]

Modern people often picture nature as an untouched jungle far away, rarely as their own backyards. Yet as ecologist Doug Tallamy put it, if we preserved every scrap of natural forest, it wouldn't be enough to save the world's endangered species.[135] Hedgerows, however, would create foods

---

[133] Anderson 1999.
[134] Landberg 2022.
[135] For example, in "Meet the Ecologist Who Wants You to Unleash the Wild on Your Backyard," *Smithsonian Magazine*, April 2020.

for migrating birds or butterflies that span a continent, a network of wild highways up and down the country.

Hedgerows grow less common in the thin soil of western Ireland, but there too farmers used what they had, stones in the soil left by the Ice Age. The result is one of Ireland's most iconic images, seen in so many postcards, of fields lines with stone walls. These are not bricks shaped and lain with mortar; these rocks are irregular and loose, with nothing to hold them together. If you know what you're doing – and these farmers did – you can pick rocks of the right size and shapes to fill the spaces formed by the ones around it so they hold together of their own weight, like the segments of a stone archway. They look as unstable as a card pyramid, yet many have lasted centuries.

This, too, could be surprisingly applicable for Americans, as degrading infrastructure results in a lot of rubble all around. For American property owners, as for Irish farmers, former pieces of concrete could be stacked into walls to create raised beds or keep in chickens or livestock. Rather than bring all these to a landfill, as we do now, we could make American suburbs look as organic and picturesque as the Irish countryside that tourists travel thousands of miles to visit.

Chapter Four

Farming

We picture Ancient Romans as senators and centurions, Japanese as samurai, Vikings as seafaring warriors – all images from popular culture, mostly of the leader and his soldiers. What almost no one pictures, and no history book or movie portrays, is what most people actually were: farmers. Until we began using fossil fuels a century or two ago, around 95 percent of all people were farmers in any civilisation, and it was they who fed name you know. The details varied by climate, but the yearly cycle of their lives, their prayers and stories, remained much the same across the world, for thousands of years.

In all that time, farmers have never been cool. Teenagers rarely threaten to become farmers to shock their parents. They have no Pride parades or groupies. In our media they rarely appear except as comical rubes. Real farmers in any era, though, had to be meteorologists, botanists, soil and pest experts, hydrologists, repairmen and veterinarians, long before these fields were named and codified. The wrong spot on a plant, bellow from an animal or shift in the wind could change everything, so they had to know the land and sky as you know your body.

Most ploughed the same fields as their fathers and grandfathers before them, going back longer than records. The word plough derives from *plegan*, to take responsibility for, and that describes what farmers did; they were a *husband* to the land in the old sense of a protector, and their craft is still called "husbandry."

"Every evening my father would walk these fields, checking the animals and seeing that everything was as it should be," Alice Taylor wrote. "It was not actually necessary to do this every day but he enjoyed walking the fields – you were never alone in them, with the farm animals and wildlife all around you."

As one elder told me, farming reminds a man who's boss, and it's not Man. Whatever the era or culture, farmers tend to be God-fearing, and Bible verses are thick with references to sowers and grain, vines and trees, sheep and goats – all metaphors that everyone understood until yesterday. "There was a lovely practice known as blessing the crops: these were days of supplication when God was asked to bless the harvest," Taylor wrote. "The farmer went to every field with a bottle of holy water, and he sprinkled the water and said whatever prayers he thought suitable, giving special attention to fields in which crops were planted. I accompanied my father and mother as they did this, and I felt a great sense of harmony, of man, God and nature in complete unity."[136]

That unity meant following the demands of each season as the year turned, so farmers in every culture created detailed calendars of the sun and stars, and our holidays are what remain of their markers. In a land where winter nights here stretch on for up to sixteen hours, the first longer day was cause for celebration, and for that purpose, before the Egyptians built the pyramids, the Stone Age people of Ireland built the monument of Newgrange. When the first dawn of the solstice hit the structure its light poured through a special opening into an inner chamber -- think of the map room scene from *Raiders of the Lost Ark*– where worshippers could celebrate the return of light and life to the world. Today, we call it Christmas.

The longest day in June used to also be a celebration -- Midsummer, as in Shakespeare's *A Midsummer Night's Dream*. Midway between the maximum day and night came the equinoxes when the day and night were balanced; the spring equinox was around St. Patrick's Day, still the day my neighbours plant their potatoes. The Sunday after the first full moon after the equinox is Easter, celebrated with rabbits, eggs and other symbols of new life. The fall equinox was Michaelmas, when villagers made pilgrimages to holy wells, or marched to the seaside to commemorate the end of fishing season.

Halfway between each of these milestones were four more, creating a calendar of eight holidays six weeks apart. Midway between Midsummer and the fall equinox was Lughnasa, a night of dancing around bonfires.

---

[136] *To School Through the Fields,* 142.

Midway between the fall equinox and the winter solstice -- New Year's Eve on the old Celtic calendars -- was what we now call Halloween.

Halfway between Christmas and St. Patrick's Day was the feast of St. Bridget -- Ireland's second-biggest saint after Patrick – when children wove reeds into Bridget's crosses to hang in their homes. Midway between spring and summer was May Day, until recently one of the biggest holidays of the year across the Western world. Around where I lived the local children used to dance around a Maypole in a ritual hundreds if not thousands of years old. The field is still there, with the hole used to put the Maypole in the ground, and the old people who danced there as children still live nearby. Their grandchildren – my daughter's schoolmates – knew nothing of this custom. They hadn't merely stopped practicing it; *they had never heard of it.*

This schedule dictated the chores of the farming year. On Brigid's Day farmers began to prepare the land for this year's crops, and basket-weavers pollarded their willows. They planted the potatoes on St. Patrick's Day, cut the turf in May, sold livestock in June, fished for lobster in July, made hay in August, harvested oats in September, root vegetables in October, and potatoes around Halloween.

The season began in spring, when Mark McGaugh remembered taking the horses from the stables to the local blacksmith – whose father and grandfather were the village smiths before him – to shoe the horses before putting them in front of the plough. "The aroma still lingers of the moment when the smithy first tested the red-hot steel to the horses' hooves to ascertain if it was a correct fitting," he said. The plough needed to be painted, sharpened and oiled, and set at the right depth for the crop, and seed needed to be ready.

When the plough and horse were ready and relatives had come by to help, he said, "the pristine lea field would be scored with the precision of a surgical knife. As the curlews [birds] soared in ever increasing numbers on the exposed subsoil, the very heavens seemed to cry and lament. The solitary figure of the farmer against the enormity of the cumulus sky presented an awesome spectacle. Presently the unspoiled green field would be transformed into a canvas of burnt umber."[137] When the

---

[137] *Around the Farm Gate*, 135.

ploughman passed everyone said "God Bless You," Mary Fogarty recalled, and on his journey back always responded with "And you too."[138]

Where they would grow grains like wheat and barley, she said, everyone in the family walked across the ploughed field wearing bags of grain around their waist, scooping up a handful and flinging it in a circle around them. Such actions were once so familiar that people described new technology with farming metaphors; when radio was invented, the signals circled out the same way, so they were said to be "broadcast."

"It was a joyful sight; a biblical scene," Walsh said. "Man sowing the seed, throwing hope into the air, hoping that when it fell that the God-given Earth and combination of the elements would yield a good harvest in due course."[139]

* * *

When farmers heard the cry of the corncrake – a bird that lived in hayfields – it was a signal that the hay was ready to be cut, she said. Hay fed the animals over the winter – as opposed to straw, which is the leftover stalks of grain crops and is used for bedding – so everyone needed to get the most out of the harvest. The priest said a prayer at Mass for sunshine. Fogarty's mother added a special addition to the rosary. Men from all the neighbouring farms walked the country roads to assemble in a single field and work as a *meithal* -- a team, as you recall.

They formed a row of men at one end of a field, my neighbour Angela said, each holding a scythe, and walked across the field together, twisting their bodies to and fro to swing the blades, slicing the hay short and singing as they worked. Together they cut one man's field, then walked to the next and the next, their many hands making light work.

Most people today recognise scythes only as that thing the Grim Reaper holds, but they are one of mankind's most ancient and venerable tools, unchanged from Ancient Egypt to a few generations ago. In Ireland their use was so widespread that as recently as the 1970s, one family specialised solely in carving whetstones to sharpen scythes.[140]

---

[138] *The Farm by Lough Gur,* 38.
[139] *Irish Country Childhood,* 122.
[140] "Fermanagh Country," RTE documentary, Episode 33 of the "Hands" series.

Scythes are a great example of a simple human tool that we replaced with more complex ones to dubious benefit. Lawnmowers cost hundreds dollars, take fuel and repair, and must be replaced every several years. Scythes can cut almost as quickly, require no fuel or repair, and can last for centuries. They don't cut as close or evenly, so could not create the manicured look that homeowners' associations often demand. In an economic crisis, though, scythes could be widely embraced again ... if only people knew what they were and how to use them.

Once the hay in each field was cut, "the hayfield would be a hive of activity and friendly banter, as the new mown hay was tossed and turned, caressed by the breeze and dried by the warm sun," Francie Murray said. In time the hay was bundled into sheaves, the sheaves bundled into stooks, and finally piled into haystacks, covered with a roof of woven reeds to keep the rain off. [141]

When the job was done they all had a picnic, and "there was a relaxed feeling, as we sat down to enjoy a well-earned rest ... father maintained that tea always tasted better in the hayfield." At the end of the day all the men gathered in the house, were well fed on bacon and cabbage and potatoes, and stayed up and told ghost stories. [142][143]

"The methods people used were time-tested, refined over centuries" to work with Nature and not against it, my neighbour Peter said. The old ways vanished as Ireland modernised, though -- cheaper technology allowed farmers to spend all day on "a 10,000-pound tractor and never speak to anyone," as my neighbour Ellen put it.

Plastic sheeting allowed farmers to wrap the grass and create silage – basically grass sauerkraut, which Peter called "the end of traditional agriculture in Ireland. Because silage has done immense environmental damage. The reason why is they can take two or three cuts of silage per year. It means that the flowers that grow in the grass never get a chance to flower or seed ... That impacts pollinators, because the bees depend on the flowers." He said that the effluent from silage drains into the waterways

---

[141] *No Shoes in Summer*, 111.

[142] *Them Golden Fields I Trod*, 68.

[143] *No Shoes*, 96.

"like pouring vinegar into a river" – and killed the fish as Tony Carr described earlier.

Many elders complained that they can no longer hear the sounds of their childhood around them, like the birds whose calls marked the passage of seasons. Recalling the larks that rose from her neighbour's house, Francie Murray said that "the experience that I describe is a privilege that is denied to the youth of today. The skylark is long since extinct, his demise brought on by modern technology on the farm. The lark built his nest on the open ground in the meadows of the countryside where there is little or no protection from big machinery, fertilisers and sprays which are a feature of present-day farming."[144]

Peter remembered his boyhood "going out with a net and scooping, and the hundreds of different types of insects in the meadow. And it's gone. And what silage has done is turn that five-acre meadow into a desert." It also meant the end of everything that fed on the insects, including the corncrake, whose song all the elders knew but that I, walking these same fields, have never heard.

* * *

A few months after the hay was cut, the grasses that fed humans – wheat, barley and oats – were cut and dried in a similar way, but they had to be threshed to separate their edible seeds, leaving straw that became bedding for animals. Threshing was perhaps the climax of the farm calendar, Francie Murray said, and her teacher let them off school to help. "Threshing time was always a happy and joyous event and in every townland it was the accepted custom that neighbours would give a hand with the work," Kevin Duffy said. "It was a community affair and there was no monetary payment for services supplied."[145]

This was the only time Murray's family used a machine, a tractor-pulled thresher that went from farm to farm. Even so, fuel-powered machines were just coming to Ireland; Alex McKendry remembered threshers powered by horses walking in a circle, and his job was to keep them going. Others remembered threshing by hand, beating the stalks with

---

[144] *Them Golden Fields I Trod,* 17.
[145] *Fifty Years Behind the Counter,* 43.

a flail to get the seeds off and then winnowing them – flipping plates of them into the air to let the wind blow the dry husks away.

The harvest was when "the farmer could see the fruits of his labour in the field," Duffy said. "It was the day of reckoning. Then he could see down to the last bag the amount of seed oats or wheat his crop had yielded. Up to then, it was all guesswork."

If every day was work around harvest time, every evening was a celebration. "There was a dance in every house on the night of the arrival of the thresher," Lyons said. "It was called the 'machine dance' and the men who would be working for twelve hours drawing straw and heavy bags of corn would keep on dancing reels, sets and hornpipes until two in the morning and be up again at seven to start work."[146] With so many young men and women gathering to dance, "there was much playful banter and innuendo," Murray said, and "many a match was made at these threshing dances."[147]

Finally, after the work was complete, "the meithal headed for home, the men with their pitchforks slung over their shoulders," Murray said. "My parents sat over the dying embers of the fire, recounting the day's events."[148]

***

In the days before plastic, farmers also grew flax – 'lint,' they called it – to make linen cloth and canvas, string and rope. It was "a money-making crop because there was very little work with it," said Davy McCrory, but that was just to grow it. Turning it into linen was a long and complicated process that involved uprooting the plants, removing the seeds ("rippling"), soaking them ("retting") in a bath ("dam") until the outer husk rots, drying them again, smacking the stalks to remove the rest of the husk ("scotching"), and combing them ("heckling"). The end result was long yellow fibres of flax that became linen cloth and canvas, and a lot of short loose ones called "tow" – the reason long blonde hair is called "flaxen" and blonde children are called "towheads."

---

[146] *Joy of My Boyhood Years*, 57.
[147] *Them Golden Fields I Trod*, 115.
[148] *Them Golden Fields I Trod*, 117.

Flax had to be pulled out of the ground rather than cut, and here too neighbours assembled to help. "You went to the neighbour to their pulling and they come to you, so that you had eight or nine men to attend and to pull it, all in one day," said Annie McKillop. Then the plants went into the dam to be soaked so all but the fibres rotted away, and "oh the smell was wild altogether," Francis Quinn said.[149]

Women handled the scotching and heckling, said Martin Keaveny, "but scotching wasn't all work for them! They did a bit of match-making as well, planning who would make suitable partners. There was a party atmosphere and a singsong." It also seems to have been an opportunity for community organising; flax workers had a reputation for being political independents who talked back to public speakers, something we still call "heckling."[150]

"It was the custom for the farmer whose flax was being dressed to call at the mill with a bottle of whiskey, for all the workers to share a drop on breaks," Maurice McAleese said. "If this custom was not upheld, that farmer could count on his flax being treated with less care than the rest."[151]

***

At the core of everyone's self-sufficiency, though, were the gardens that surrounded every home. "In our day, Brian, you didn't go to the shop for your mushrooms," my neighbour Angela told me. "You didn't go for your cabbage, or your turnips, there was none of that. Everybody sowed their gardens – potatoes, carrots, peas, everything ..." If one of the neighbours ran out of food, "and if we had some left, you could come and get ours. That's the way we lived."

City children didn't always have room for gardens, of course, but many gardeners in Ireland in the UK turned local vacant plots into allotments; Christy Kennealey's father turned a bit of spare land into a garden and came at the weekends "to tease the black earth into bubble-leaved cabbage, foxy carrots, onions and rhubarb."[152] Front or back yards

---

[149] Antrim Archives.
[150] *Growing Up with Ireland*, 24.
[151] *Back Through the Fields*, 112.
[152] *Maura's Boy*, 60.

also became gardens, the "tableaux of self-sustainability of the post-war generation," Marianne Elliot said. "My father took particular pride in his large marrows and would share tips over the fence with our neighbour."[153]

Gardens were not simply for family homes, however; in those days most hospitals were surrounded by gardens that fed the patients, and most schools had gardens to feed the students.[154] "We at the school had to be self-sufficient," said John Quinn, who attended a boarding school in the 1950s. "We grew our own vegetables, and raised our own meat. Students got a week off each year to pick the potatoes."[155]

Today, of course, those same hospitals and schools are still surrounded by what we now call "green space," but like the yards of suburban homes, they are simply used to grow flat, dull lawns. Cash-strapped hospitals and schools, churches and families all spend money to maintain grass with no purpose, and also spend money on shipping food from thousands of miles away. As in most areas of life, our modern culture has taken a perfect cycle and chopped it into several toxic problems.

The modern world does this with most natural cycles. Suburban estates have spread across Ireland, each with a yard, yet the country now imports most of its food. People pay to grow grass and to mow it short, while also keeping out animals that want to eat the grass. They pay for toxic chemicals to fertilise the lawn, and pay to have their food scraps and animal waste – compost that enriches the soil -- transported away in trucks. We have a lot of gardening that needs to be done, and unemployed people with nothing to do.

Yet we could feed ourselves again. Gardens could flourish in front yards, backyards, on roofs and in parking lots and vacant lots. They could be set along playgrounds and schoolyards, offering free healthy snacks, and encourage children to learn where their food comes from. They could be wedged onto roadsides and street medians – not to grow food, but to suck up car fumes and make the surrounding air cleaner. Berry vines could climb up every building wall, not only yielding food but shading the building and reducing air conditioning bills.

---

[153] *Hearthland,* 1.
[154] "City gardens," RTE documentary.
[155] "Ballyfin - A boarding school memory," RTE documentary.

We know we can feed ourselves because we did once, even in the modern era; when the UK and USA entered World War II popular media pushed growing and preserving food, with Hollywood celebrities and Superman growing backyard "Victory Gardens." What couldn't be grown in a backyard could often be grown nearby; New Jersey's now-ridiculous-sounding motto, "The Garden State," refers to the thousands of market gardens that fed New York City into the 1960s. Ecologist David Holmgren looked at cities in his native Australia, and estimated that with their green space – not just backyards, but parks and golf courses – turned to food production, they could become not just self-sufficient, but food *exporters*.

To do this, though, we would need to revive the practices of these far-northerly islands, where Victorians raised gardening to a high science. The old estates that dot the Irish landscape still have the stone remains of this forgotten technology: melon houses and mushroom dark-houses, heat-retaining walls, espalier trees and greenhouses. Now my daughter plays with her friends in their ruins, and no one remembers their purpose.

We don't think of these things as "technology," but they are among our civilisation's most important developments, for the simple reason that they will still work when every smart phone has crumbled.

***

Farmers then had to know their soil and build it up for future generations, without the pesticides and chemicals we rely on today. We rarely think about our soil, and more rarely still with any reverence; we scrape it off our shoes, scrub it out of our clothes, and pave over it. Yet every spoonful of it is a micro-jungle of fungi, insects, worms and micro-organisms, working away like elves under our feet. They are the resurrection machines that transform the dead into new life, creating the soil that feed plants that feed us. They aren't as cute as pandas, but in all honesty, every panda could keel over tomorrow and the world would go on. If the soil critters die, so do you.

And the world has a lot less soil than you imagine. Only about 29 percent of the Earth's surface is covered by land, and 88 percent of that is desert, mountains, swamps or something else that can't grow crops. As endless as farmland can seem when driving through Iowa, it is 2.5 percent of the planet's surface. What's more, the fertile layer of topsoil sits only a metre thick on average; sink into it like water and it would only come up to your waist. That thin planetary skin, found only in a few patches, supports eight billion people and counting.

Most soils around the world are sick and failing, losing their fertility and water-aborbing abilities as chemicals kill off the life in it and modern machinery compacts it, transforming into what one farmer called "powder, brown dust. It's dead. There's no worms, no life in it."[156] It's also washing away – one percent per year, according to geologist David Montgomery at the University of Washington, and a centimetre of topsoil can take centuries to build up again. In the USA three and a half tons of soil *per person* washes away every year.[157]

The Irish felt the consequences of erosion firsthand, when the conquering British felled its trees and Ireland went from being one of Europe's most forested countries to its most deforested. Timber exports went from 170,000 cubic feet per year in the mid-1700s to nearly zero in 1770 as all but a few bits of forests were cleared. With no roots to hold the soil in place, vast areas now see the bones of the earth stick through the starved skin. This erosion helped cause the Great Famine of the mid-1800s, as the areas most eroded were also the areas hardest hit.[158]

History tells many similar stories; by the 300s BC in Ancient Greece, Plato wrote, the land was no longer producing. "...there are remaining only the bones of the wasted body," he wrote. "All the richer and softer parts of the soil having fallen away, and the mere skeleton of the land being left."[159]

But soil can also be created. J.M. Synge, on a visit to the inhabitants of the barren Aran Islands, observed that they literally created soil by building a rock wall around a bit of land, and gradually filling it with sand and seaweed from the beaches, and waiting for the seaweed to compost.[160]

---

[156] "Only 60 Years of Farming Left If Soil Degradation Continues," *Scientific American*, Dec. 5, 2014.

[157] "The lowdown on topsoil: It's disappearing," *Seattle Post-Intelligencer*, 21 June 2008.

[158] McGregor 1989.

[159] Plato, *Critias*.

[160] J.M Synge, *The Aran Islands*, 1907.

Malachi Horan's father took a field covered in furze – the spiny bush that covers the wild places here – and piled soil on them so they rotted down. John Curran and Martin Morrissey remembered spreading manure on the fields every winter or going to the sea for wagonloads of sand and seaweed.[161] Building a field out of this took years, but farmers think ahead.

Manure was also vitally important. In modern times we have a deep revulsion to thinking about manure, and flush it away quickly to avoid even having to see it. To all humans before us, though, it was a resource; many cities had 'night-soil' men who gathered up the waste from every home, and for 4,000 years the Chinese had an elaborate network of roads and canals to get that waste to farmland. Medieval Europeans had a less organised system, but contrary to popular belief, they didn't necessarily fling the contents of their chamber-pots into the streets either; medieval London actually had many ordinances for keeping streets clean, and people were severely punished for breaking them.

Farmers in some parts of the world built birdhouses to attract flocks, purely so that they would leave tonnes of fertiliser behind.[162] When Europeans discovered large deposits of guano – bird droppings -- on Pacific Islands, they mined and brought home cargo ships full of the stuff, competed for rights to guano islands, and nations even went to war over these poo mountains. Outside of old Irish houses I have seen "dovecotes," stone walls divided into a grid of squares, like office mail slots, all to keep pigeons and doves. Pigeons could be used for many purposes – racing, messages, falconry -- but guano was certainly a benefit.

In Dublin, Patrick Boland grew up taking care of pigs in his back lot, and trading not only the meat, but the manure, with the farmers nearby. "The farmers who took away the dung .... sometimes threw in the odd bag of potatoes, turnips, or cabbage along with their usual payment of straw," he said. "All in all, we didn't do too badly."[163] Even today in Dublin, I see local gardeners bicycle to visit the few remaining horse businesses, returning with a bag of fertiliser hanging from each handlebar.

---

[161] *Tides of Change*, 97.
[162] Bekleyen 2009.
[163] *Tales from a City Farmyard.*

Composting manure can generate a foul odour or attract pests, of course, and takes time. The solution – one of the more underappreciated discoveries of the 20ᵗʰ century – was a method of composting that eliminates most of these problems at once. Called hot composting, or the Berkeley method, it involves getting just the right ratio of nitrogen-rich waste (manure, fresh lawn clippings) to carbon-rich materials (paper, sawdust, dried lawn clipppings), and turning it frequently with a pitchfork to oxygenate it. By getting the mix right you are farming specific kinds of bacteria -- not the kind that generate a foul odour, but that generate heat. It's also many times faster – rather than waiting a year or two for your compost to become soil, the process takes only several weeks.

The compost in this method gets as hot as 60C – 140 Fahrenheit – hot enough to drive away pests and to kill off most weed seeds and diseases. It can also be used to heat water pipes or homes. I have tested this myself, taking a very hot shower on a very cold morning in the middle of a field in Ireland, hooked up to no explosive fuel and to no electrical wires, all the heat generated by invisible bacteria.

Manure restores elements like nitrogen and phosphorous, which today we get from modern industry – nitrogen from fossil fuels, and phosphorus from mines that are predicted to run dry eventually.[164] We still have manure, but instead of using it we create a vast and expensive infrastructure to take it far from our homes to sewage plants, or to septic tanks that require tonnes of cement and yearly drainings. Modern industrial hog farms create vast lagoons of manure that nearby residents never see but always smell, and which contaminate groundwater.

Tony Carr, who used to live near me in County Kildare, said wastewater effluent from sewage and silage, have ruined Ireland's waterways. "Who is to blame?" he asked. "The answer is simple. We all are responsible for this long concerted attack upon Nature. At the mouth of every river in the country there stands a town ... The sewage being generated is a major pollutant. Industries are also at fault. These generally rely upon some chemicals in the manufacturing of their products. That is, if they are not actively engaged in producing chemicals themselves...."

---

[164] "A rock and a hard place: Peak phosphorus and the threat to our food security," paper by The Soil Association, 2010. See also Cordell 2009.

Carr said that not only did he no longer see trout "rise" in the river, as his cousin had shown him as children, but he increasingly no longer saw the land life he used to. "How long is it since you've seen a frog?" he asked. "How long is it since you've seen a grasshopper or a "hairy molly?" Have you noticed the scarcity of primroses and cowslips? ... True patriotism begins at your own kitchen sink."[165]

***

Farmers can use chemicals in ways that don't damage the soil, however. Here in the countryside I occasionally find a stone cylinder, as much as several metres high and wide, open at the top and with a small door at the base. Some resemble medieval fortresses that also dot the landscape here -- but no one built fortresses so narrow, or half-buried in the side of a hill. In fact, they are kilns for lime burning, a now-forgotten industry that sustained many Irish communities.

"Lime" here means neither the citrus fruit nor the tree, but a white powder derived from limestone. For at least 7,000 years humans created lime in kilns, as they might have hardened pottery or smelted ore, and used the material for dozens of purposes now largely replaced by fossil-fuel by-products.

Limestone is mainly coral and shells of long-extinct sea creatures, squeezed over aeons into a solid mass of calcium carbonate, or $CaCO_3$. When burned hot enough it vents carbon dioxide (CO_2), leaving behind the volatile calcium oxide (CaO) – quicklime. Then, when combined with water (H_2O) the quicklime became lime powder (calcium hydroxide or $Ca(OH)_2$) and could be put to many uses.

Romans combined lime with volcanic ash to create concrete that was superior in many ways to ours – far less energy-intensive than modern methods, and its pillars have lasted two thousand years *in seawater*. Lime and water made whitewash, a white paint without the unpronounceable stew of toxic ingredients in modern paints. Lime could disinfect water, and

---

[165] *Some Time to Kill*, 50.

I have used it to preserve eggs for months. Tanners used it to remove hair from hides, gardeners to repel slugs and snails, printers to bleach paper.[166]

Even corrosive quicklime had many uses. It created an early, high-intensity lamp for the stage – the original limelight. It was also shovelled into graves to decompose bodies more quickly, as Oscar Wilde described from prison. It made a rather fearsome weapon; when Irish revolutionary Charles Parnell spoke at a political rally in 1891, someone in the crowd threw quicklime at his face, and "had not [he] shut his eyes in time, he would undoubtedly have been blinded," his wife Katherine later wrote.

But it was valued most for farming. Some 40 per cent of the arable land in the world is too acidic for many plants to grow, but lime temporarily "sweetens" or neutralised the soil, increasing crop yields by as much as fourfold. This made lime so valuable that for hundreds of years, lime supported a vast and vital network of village industry -- quarries to mine the limestone, carts and barges to transport it, and specialists to monitor the burning. In the late 1700s, according to one survey, County Cork alone was said to contain an amazing 23,000 kilns, or one every 80 acres.[167]

Farmers brought cartloads of quicklime straight from the kiln and scattered it right onto the fields, and the next rain both hydrated it into lime and soaked it into the ground. The process only sweetened the land for several years, though, so the kilns were kept in steady business.

Kilns were often built into hillsides to allow people to easily transport coal and lime to the open top, or mouth, and were tapered down so that gravity fed the fuel down to an opening at the base. The kiln had to be filled carefully, with precisely measured layers of limestone and coal, charcoal or turf. It was exhausting work, making them "thirsty as a lime-burner" as the saying went. Once the kiln was lit there was no going back; the lime-burners had to maintain a watch over the kiln for the next three or four days, sleeping nearby.

---

[166] Elsen 2005, Jackson 2013. Also, "Roman Seawater Concrete Holds the Secret to Cutting Carbon Emissions," *News from Berkeley Lab*, 4 June 2013.
[167] *The Ancient and Present State of the County and City of Cork*, by C. Smith, 1815 edition.

With their furnace-like heat, poison vapours, alchemical transformations and vital importance to survival, it was perhaps inevitable that farmers associated kilns with all kinds of magic and ritual. It was around kilns that young people performed Halloween rituals to find out who they would marry. Kilns were places where people saw ghosts and were said to have made deals with the devil.[168]

Perhaps to ward off such influences, the lime burners started with their own ritual, which they explained on Irish radio. "You took a bottle with you that morning ... of holy water," one said, and before the kiln was fired up "you just sprinkled it on top the stones, and made the Sign of the Cross, for you were burning ... the bones of the Earth."[169]

***

When I tell people today about their self-sufficient forbears, the usual answer is that they all ate terrible rotten food, and spent most of their lives starving before dying at 30. Let's take those in reverse order, starting with lifespan.

More infants died in the past, and while we are lucky to be spared that horror, it skews the curve; in many times and places, young adults could expect to live as long as they do today. A book of the Bible written perhaps 25 centuries ago said that humans live "threescore years and ten," or 70 years, and that tracks with many traditional peoples around the world. Of those who survived infancy, 1850-era British men – mostly working-class -- lived to be 75 on average; life expectancy today for working-class British men today is only 72.[170]

Nor were people starving in most times and places. Nineteenth-century British weren't all begging for gruel, but usually enjoyed diets "vastly superior to that generally consumed today, one substantially in advance of current public health recommendations."[171] They ate more fruit and vegetables than most First-Worlders today, as well as nuts and organ

---

[168] *Irish Witchcraft and Demonology*, by St. John D. Seymour, 1913.
[169] "Burning the Bones of the Earth," RTE radio documentary, 1981.
[170] Clayton 2009. See also "The Modern Diet Is a Biosecurity Threat," *Palladium*, June 4, 2022.
[171] Rowbotham 2008.

meats high in micronutrients – most of the things fitness instructors recommend today, and they ate up to twice as much as we do. Similar examples come from many traditional societies; they lived more vigorous lives, so needed extra calories to survive -- and they did, because you're reading this. As writer Chad Mulligan put it, starving people don't build cathedrals.[172]

Of course there have been severe famines in history, most famously Ireland – more on that later. Yet that resulted from the British seizing the land for plantations to export food to Britain, while the small farmers were forced to rely on the one crop with enough calories to feed them. When that crop caught a disease, there was nothing to fall back on, and what might have been unfortunate but survivable turned into a mass death.

Another truism of modern life is that all food until yesterday was bland and disgusting. Just as people today insist that all earlier generations were less free, less healthy, less educated and less tolerant than we are, they insist that food must have been a daily ordeal, tolerable only because they were too ignorant to realise how miserable they were.

Sometimes people cite the often-repeated stories of bakers padding out bread ingredients with ash and bone and lead. As historian Frederick Filby demonstrated almost a century ago, however, those stories – 18th-century clickbait– could not possibly have been true. Filby tried baking bread with the alleged ingredients and found that it almost never became anything resembling bread, and were often more expensive to make than the real thing anyway. Also, food manufacturers put dubious substances into our food now, as we will see later.[173]

Also, the examples many people give – say, of their grandparents' olive loaf or fruit jello -- are not traditional foods at all, but were early examples of processed factory-made food that have simply fallen out of fashion, or marked as unforgivably working-class. Other people point out that old cookbooks never call for much seasoning, and are bland if you cook the dishes as described. But old recipes tended to give the basics of

---

[172] "Modern Diets are Killing Us," HipCrime Vocab blog, Sept. 22, 2022.
[173] *A History Of Food Adulteration And Analysis*, by Frederick Filby, as cited in *At Home: A Short History of Private Life* by Bill Bryson, Vintage; Reprint edition (October 4, 2011).

preparing a dish, with the assumption that people would add whatever herbs and "seasonings" were, well, in season.

Most traditional peoples eat far more variety than we do; English farmers recorded eating pigeons, rabbits, pheasants and geese; vegetables like cardoons, chicory and scorzonera; and fruits like damsons and medlars. These weren't inferior foods that people ate out of desperation -- I can personally attest that most of these taste amazing – but they have been largely forgotten. Some were abandoned because of changing fashions, others because they did not fit our modern mass-production systems – medlars, for example, need to be picked when they are just slightly over-ripe, and cannot sit on a shelf for weeks.

I admit that Irish food took some getting used to, but when you work outside all day, you work up an appetite. Suddenly, food tastes great by itself, and doesn't need a lot of added chemicals. "It was wholesome food, plain and simple, and the golden rule was 'get it into you and it will do you good.'" John Curran said.[174] They were also grateful for the food they had worked hard to earn; they had overseen the plants from seed to crop, and the animals from birth to knife. We have no such connection to the hog factory workers or the genetic laboratories where the corn was designed, or the Godzilla-sized machines that harvest it. We have mountains of food, but it appears before us without context, removed from our capacity for gratitude.

In addition, meals were communal, and the company was as important as the food. Some of my most cherished memories are of Thanksgiving or Christmas at my grandparents' small house with aunts and uncles laughing and chatting as they prepared the meals together, set up the tables and finally packed together snugly to eat and share stories. Looking back, my grandmother wasn't a Michelin chef and we weren't restaurant critics, but no one cared.

"They were great old days," John Lyons said. "There was not much money around, but we had happiness and joy in our hearts, and every neighbour's house was the same as your own. You could walk in any time of day or night. The kettle was always on the boil, the tea was made, you sat down and you were handed a mug of tea with plenty of sugar and a

---

[174] *Tides of Change*, 49.

yellow square hot off the griddle, with lashings of butter – a delicious feed. My mouth waters with longing when I think of it."[175]

***

In the 1930s, an American dentist named Weston Price closed his practice and embarked on a remarkable eight-year tour of the world's remaining traditional peoples: Scottish islanders, Swiss villagers, Native Americans; Polynesians; Australian Aborigines; New Calendonians, and more than 30 African tribes. His goal was to get to the bottom of something that had bothered him for years; in the decades he had been practicing dentistry, the quality of people's teeth had deteriorated alarmingly, with no explanation. His findings, published in 1939 in his book *Nutrition and Physical Degeneration*, were startling: every ethnic group on Earth that ate a traditional diet – *any* traditional diet, whether mostly fish or meat or vegetables, prepared almost any way, in almost any climate – had a robust health that Americans and Europeans had lost.[176]

In what must have been delicate and diplomatic conversations, he persuaded tribal peoples around the world to let him look at their teeth, and he documented what he found in exhaustive detail. Tooth decay, which affects nine out of ten Americans today, touched almost no traditional peoples. More recent research backs up Price's findings; most animals and humans in the wild, despite never brushing their teeth or getting braces, rarely experience any of the conditions we pay dentists thousands every year to correct.[177]

The cause is not just sugar, but processed foods that require little chewing; our jaws get so little exercise when we are children that they literally grow small and misshapen in our mouths, our wisdom teeth lack the room they should need, the other teeth come in crooked. It might even be causing sleep apnea, a condition in which we stop breathing briefly as we sleep, and thus a lot of unexplained deaths.

---

[175] *Joy of my Boyhood Years,* 113.
[176] "The Modern Diet Is a Biosecurity Threat," *Palladium*, June 4, 2022.
[177] "Why We Have So Many Problems with Our Teeth," *Scientific American*, 1 April 2020.

The same is true of many other diseases we accept as part of life. We assume everyone gets acne as teenagers, but tribal peoples like the Ache of Paraguay don't seem to.[178] As the Tsimane get older their brains appear not to atrophy as quickly as ours do, and they have the lowest levels of heart disease ever recorded.[179] Nor do we have to travel to a jungle tribe for examples. Heart disease, for example, were rare the USA in the late 1800s, even though a fifth of the population was over 50.[180]

Of course some undoubtedly died of other, now-curable diseases before they got heart disease, and fewer cases might have been detected. Of course we have made many advances since then, for which we should be grateful. Price's conclusion, however, has since been backed up by others, remains: Billions of us live with heart, breathing, weight, kidney and possibly mental conditions that were rare among our ancestors. None of us remember when it was otherwise, so we accept it as normal, and assume our ancestors must have simply suffered.

The transition from traditional local food to mass processed food happened over decades, and which decades varied widely from place to place. Through the twentieth century, though, wherever processed foods – white flour, sugar, canned goods – took over from local traditional foods, everyone's health declined. "It was the birth of the mass modern diet: high in ultra-processed carbohydrates, sugar, and fats, and deficient in many of the phytonutrients and micronutrients that defined traditional diets," Chad Mulligan wrote.[181]

Here too, Ireland was several decades behind, healthier because it had to produce most of its own food. During World War II, neutral Ireland had to use coarse whole flour to make bread, Boland said, "but it was probably healthier food than any we've had since."[182] "We knew exactly where our food came from," Francie Murray said. "If you found a cake of bread, like my mother used to make, nowadays it would be in an organic food shop and would cost a fortune!"[183]

---

[178] Cordain 2002.
[179] Irimia 2021.
[180] "How Americans Got Red Meat Wrong," The Atlantic, June 2, 2014.
[181] "Modern Diets are Killing Us," HipCrime Vocab blog, Sept. 22, 2022.
[182] *Tales from a City Farmyard*, 195.
[183] *Them Golden Fields I Trod*, 88.

Modern agribusiness transports food thousands of miles, so has focused on a few varieties for easy transport and size rather than nutrition or flavour. As a result grocery store vegetables have been getting less and less nutritious over time.[184] One study examined wild apples to store varieties, and found that the wild ones all contained more phytonutrients – in one case, 478 times more.[185]

We ignore the marrow, organs and blood that are the most nutritious, but are less profitable to package and transport. We take the nutritious bran out of bread and pasteurize the beneficial bacteria out of milk. We think of peasants eating the same gruel every day, but it was often they who ate the more nutritious food, and more of it, in more variety.

Most of what Americans eat today is corn (maize); dairy products and beef are from corn-fed cows, pork from corn-fed pigs, chicken nuggets from corn-fed chickens held together with corn starch and corn flour, and fried in corn oil. Any sweetness in food is usually corn syrup. The parts that aren't corn are mostly wheat and a few other ingredients with similar stories.

Much of this food, in its natural state, tastes like nothing – bland sludge. As Eric Schlosser pointed out in his excellent book *Fast Food Nation*, the powerful flavours we experience come from an infusion of chemicals isolated in the last century or so. Walk down the aisle of a supermarket and look at the ingredients of almost any food and you'll see the words "natural flavour" or "artificial flavour" in just about every list of ingredients. "Natural" and "artificial," by the way, refers to a minor difference in how it's made, but either way, it ends up the same chemical.

What humans call "taste" is actually mostly smell, and these companies literally create the flavours of chips, bread, breakfast cereals, pet foods, ice creams, candy, toothpastes, mouthwashes, medicines, wines, juices, and beers, as well as the smells of perfumes, deodorants, soaps, furniture polishes, detergents and shaving creams.

"Adding methyl-2-peridylketone makes something taste like popcorn," Schlosser wrote. "Adding ethyl-3-hydroxybutonoate makes it taste like marshmallow. The possibilities are almost limitless. Without

---

[184] 2007 report by the Organic Center, 28-29.
[185] Stushnoff 2003.

affecting the appearance or nutritional value, processed foods could even be made with aroma chemicals such as hexanal (the smell of freshly cut grass) or 3-methyl butanoic acid (the smell of body odour)."[186]

Smell is intimately linked to memory, and most of our tastes are established in childhood; memories of going to McDonald's as a child turn into lifelong devotions to those same flavours. Americans spend more on fast food than college – and we spend a lot on college – not because it's the best use of our money, but because most of us were raised with an addiction. And the size of their meals has trebled since the 1950s.[187] No wonder 74 percent of Americans are overweight.[188]

Russian engineer-turned-survivalist Dmitri Orlov noted that modern Westerners have been raised inside a bubble of artificially designed sensory experiences, from plastic surfaces to unnatural tastes, conditioned from a young age to buy the same unhealthy quasi-foods over and over, leaving us with – in his perception – a sickly odour that we must cover with ever-heavier doses of deodorants and perfumes. So conditioned, he said, we recoil in horror when confronted with anything natural, whether a piece of boiled organ meat or the smell of a healthy human body.[189]

As the 20th century continued, processed food spread across the world, and wherever it spread, the effects were the same. The countries with the highest rates of obesity are in the South Pacific, which now neglect nutrient-rich local staples like coconut or breadfruit in favour of processed foods. The New Caledonians that Price once studied are now two-thirds overweight or obese.[190]

Many of us are afflicted with conditions that were once rare: Crohn's disease, diabetes, ulcerative colitis, rheumatoid arthritis, and mental illnesses.[191] Sperm counts in men have been falling for decades, along with

---

[186] Eric Schlosser, *Fast Food Nation*, as excerpted in *The Atlantic Monthly*, Jan 17, 2001.
[187] "CDC Shows Burger Size Has Tripled in Last 50 Years," *ABC News*, 24 May 2012.
[188] "About 74 percent of adults in the U.S. are overweight, according to the CDC," *Washington Post*, 18 Dec 2020.
[189] *Reinventing Collapse: The Soviet Experience and American Prospects,* 103.
[190] Corsenac 2017.
[191] "The Modern Diet Is a Biosecurity Threat," *Palladium*, June 4, 2022.

the number of men with such low sperm levels that they require fertility treatment to reproduce.[192]

Boys and girls are going into puberty earlier, for reasons we cannot fully explain -- something particularly hard on girls, who are developing sexual bodies in a sex-obsessed culture while they still have the brains of children.[193] Media articles about this phenomenon often say that puberty took place later for our ancestors because they must have had worse nutrition.

As in every other area of life, we define our modern experience as normal and insist that everything that came before us must have been worse.

---

[192] "Poor quality Western diet kills sperm count and lowers male testosterone, study says," CNN, 25 Feb 2020.
[193] For example, see Pop 2021.

Chapter Five

Crafting

Somewhere in an elderly relative's mouse-chewed attic there probably sits a dusty photograph of you – you as a child, smiling and proud one Halloween, wearing a tiny uniform of the thing you were going to be. You had it all planned out; you were going to be a farmer or fireman, cowboy or doctor, or some other role that a child can instantly identify and adore.

For most of us life hasn't worked out that way. A few become firefighters, of course (one in a thousand) or doctors (two in a thousand), but most of us -- for the first time in human history -- do not work at jobs that any child would understand or care about. Telemarketers, Customer Experience Staff, Assistant Diversity Officers – all titles that never existed until yesterday, all to describe where we fit in an ecosystem of office plankton.

It was a shock, then, to hear my elderly neighbours talk of their work life, or to read the memoirs of Ireland's craftsmen. Many started as children, absorbing skills passed through families until they became surnames – smith, mason, miller, thatcher, tailor, baker, carter, cooper, wright. They often worked with other craftsmen, around family or neighbours. They spoke of shaping wood and iron and leather in ways everyone could see and respect. Saddlers and scutchers, farriers and felters, cobblers and cordwainers – even grave-diggers and churchbell-ringers spoke of their jobs with an enthusiasm I rarely see today.

"I jump out of bed on a Sunday morning for my ringing day," said bell-ringer Leslie Taylor. "I am the elected ringing master, chosen by my fellow ringers who are members of the society. This is a happy coincidence of loyalty and pleasure. I'm one of the people who have in one way or another serviced the cathedral in some way since its foundation in 1038. ... I'd like to die in the belfry ... when I'm ringing."[194]

***

It's worth examining why most people in traditional societies spoke so fondly of their jobs and modern people do not, since work would seem to be one area where life has unarguably improved in modern times. My elderly neighbours grew up in what we would consider extreme poverty; Patty Bolger told me the local factory paid ten shillings (about 30 euros or $36 in 2023) *per week*, a fraction of the US minimum wage today. Decades further back were the long hours, unsafe and toxic surroundings, and other horrors we remember from Dickens and Upton Sinclair. Again, many things have improved, and for that we should be grateful.

Victorian factories and coal mines, though, were a historical anomaly, appearing only with the discovery of fossil fuels. Before the mid-1800s in Britain, and the mid-1900s in Ireland, most people were farmers or craftsmen like the elders I interviewed. Also, when people today refer to "modern" jobs, they tend to be those of First-Worlders, not those of the near-slaves that made our clothes and laptops. We compare the worst of their time with the best of ours.

If we compare our eight-hour day in a cubicle to the 15-hour day of a Victorian factory worker, both working corporate jobs for hourly wages, of course we come out far ahead. As Jaques Ellul pointed out, though, we can't compare our office job to the day of a village craftsman, who chooses their own tempo and rhythm, who mentors and is aided by apprentices or children, and who stops to chat with passers-by. We can praise the progress from 1850 to 1950, he said, but "we cannot say with assurance that there has been progress from 1250 to 1950. In so doing, we would be comparing things which are not comparable."[195]

Even then, Ellul was assuming a 15-hour day, but most of our ancestors -- craftsmen and peasants – worked far less. Historian James Thorold Rogers estimated that medieval peasants – whom we think of as the most menial peoples of the most backward age – worked no more than

[194] *Dublin Voices*, 72.
[195] Jaques Ellul, *The Technological Society*, p. 93.

eight hours a day, a figure backed up by several other studies. Labourers rarely worked an entire day for a lord; half a solar day's work was considered a full working day, so peasants who worked sunrise to sunset were credited for two days' work. Medieval Christians, moreover, had so many holidays – in the literal sense of "holy days" – that they only worked half as many days per year as modern Americans.[196]

In Dublin into the 20th century, craftsmen continued to keep such flexible hours, as former master cooper David O'Donnell recalled. "Coopers were well-paid craftsmen," he said. "... you could go in to work whenever you liked provided that you could make your own week's wages for yourself. You made so much for each cask. And you could go home whenever you wanted."[197] Walter Love, who drove a cart around his rural area, said that "the thing I liked best of all was the freedom. You were your own boss ... I was tired at the end of a hard day, but I was usually happy and when I think back the thoughts are usually happy ones."[198]

Of course their work was physically demanding, whether ploughing fields or hammering iron – but most of these men grew up exerting themselves, and could handle the work in ways our bodies could not. My neighbour Jack worked construction jobs in the towns around him, and often had to ride his bicycle 20 miles there and 20 miles back every day just to get to work, something that "younger people wouldn't dream of doing nowadays," he said. "You had to be pretty fit," he added with a smile. Dersie Leonard said few dig turf the old way, for "I doubt present generations would have the muscle and bone of their forefathers."[199]

***

Just as men formed meithals to bring in the hay or build a house, women to turn pigs into sausage and flax into linen, so did they form teams to lay rail tracks or carve stones or unload ships. "There was no need for leaders or bosses back then," John McArt said of the men stringing the

---

[196] Knoop 1961, Ritchie 1962. Also, Bennett H.S., *Life on the English Manor* (Cambridge: Cambridge University Press, 1960), 104-6.
[197] *Dublin Voices*, 204.
[198] *Times of Our Lives,* 24.
[199] *No Shoes in Summer*, 15.

first electric lines across the country. "Every man was a leader and if one man was flagging there was always a colleague at hand to pick up the pieces and not let the side down."[200]

Even ringing church bells required surprising training and precision. "The most complicated are sequences that have long and tricky gamuts of changes requiring a difficult and lengthy pattern to be retained in the brain as a route map and consulted all the time in the mind's eye," Taylor said. "The tolerance of error is a tiny percentage. Mis-timing will have a devastating effect on change-ringing, one person's error running like a cancer through the ringing. It can only take one person to cause bad ringing, the ripple of defect running through the whole thing, a domino effect and a catastrophe..."[201]

Most jobs were not done in isolated offices as they might be today, but in company and often in public, with the work and the results visible to all. Even in Dublin, each neighbourhood was like its own village, and elders remembered passing dozens of shops every day. "I was born in Blackhall Place and this part of Dublin, to me, always had a sort of 'villagey' atmosphere," O'Donnell said. "In this area I remember saddlers, wheelwrights, blacksmiths, bootmakers, tobacconists, and bakers, and they all did a great business."[202] Friends gathered around the barbers' or the smithy to chat and watch the work. "There was something very special about the forge," Ann Gardinier said. "It was a place people were reluctant to leave."[203]

While corporations today might call their employees a team, they are not responsible for them, nor are the workers loyal to each other; everyone just puts in their time and leaves to their far-flung addresses at night, while their children are mostly raised by strangers and neighbourhoods evaporate into mere collections of houses. In today's workplace one can build up many relationships, but they amount to a pile of threads, not a tapestry. Many of these craftsmen, though, had grown up in the same neighbourhood, sat together in church and were destined for the same

---

[200] *Then There Was Light*, 200.
[201] *Dublin Voices*, 68.
[202] *Dubliin Voices*, 203.
[203] *The House Remembers*, 14.

churchyard, and had an interest in seeing each other do well. "There was a great feeling of comradeship," O'Donnell said of the 300-or-so coopers in Dublin, and the same was true for most crafts.[204]

They also celebrated together once the day's work was done. Gerry Rafferty remembered the teams of men that laid rail lines near their town came to the pub in the evening with their violins and banjos, and "were not only skilled workers but were also musicians and storytellers, the last of a dying race."[205]

"Publicans [bar owners] knew all the men," said William Murphy, who worked the docks in the Ringsend neighbourhood of Dublin. "And in Ringsend every publican knew who he was dealing with and if you were short and stuck for a pint he'd give it to you and you'd pay him when you got a job." When a docker took sick, Joe Murphy said, "a loaf of bread was sent in or a bag of sugar or bag of tea. That's the type of people they were."[206]

Tombstone carvers all gathered after work at O'Neill's pub on Pearse Street for a surprising pastime. "Oh, they could all tap-dance," said Stephen Bracken. "You see, tap-dancing came into the trade years ago around the country ... Don't ask me why! But all my uncles could tap-dance and my father was even on the stage here in Dublin."[207]

Craftsmen mingled so much with others in the craft, people told me, that their children often married – the son of a cooper often married the daughter of another cooper, and of course their children took up the trade. This went on for generations until all the men of a certain profession knew each other only by nicknames, as they all had the same few surnames. Glance through this chapter and notice that all the Ringsend dockworkers are named Murphy.

Corporations today work hard to replicate this sense of community, advertising smiling family scenes and hiring greeters to simulate normal human friendliness. Most of us grew up surrounded by similarly fake

---

[204] *Dubliin Voices*, 204.
[205] *And the Band Played On,* 30.
[206] *Dublin Voices*, 136.
[207] *Dublin Voices*, 96.

interactions, from actors on screens to employees reading scripts, until we have forgotten – if we ever knew -- what real cameraderie felt like.

Of course, not everyone was a craftsman, but even factories in Ireland were not Dickensian pits; Chrissie McAdam remembers all the workers at the rosary factory chatting together all day, "and the place would be full of singing. They all sang when they were working."[208]

Many men got a bit of extra money from odd jobs on the side, as carters, porters, dockers, scrap collectors, and construction workers, and women worked as servants, washers, street traders and many other things, or walked to the countryside and picked vegetables for farmers.[209] Anyone who needed workers announced it in the pub, John Gallagher said. "You'd go into a pub and somebody'd say, 'Look, we're starting work and we're looking for a few men,' and you'd give him a drink for that bit of information. Then you'd be out there early the next day waiting for the start."[210]

Rural men who needed extra money hired themselves out at fairs to "get hired on a farm for a place to sleep, to share in the food, and a weekly allowance of tobacco," Gerry Rafferty said.[211] Malachi Horan said each man stuck a pipe in the band of his hat to show that he had yet to be hired, and put it in his pocket to show when he had been hired.[212]

More regular workers, too, spoke of the cameraderie of their neighbourhoods. Dublin was networked by trams – streetcars -- and former drivers described knowing all their regular passengers and getting gifts from them at Christmas.

"The tram men and the passengers in those days seemed to be nearer to one another, more familiar," said former tram operator William Condon. "People were different in those days. Oh, the politeness. And you were respectful. Children then wouldn't give you any impudence or anything like they do now. And if you'd get some old crotchety passenger who'd

---

[208] *Dublin Voices,* 156.
[209] *Dublin Tenement Life*, 30.
[210] *Dublin Tenement Life*, 133.
[211] *And the Band Played On,* 77.
[212] *Malachi Horan Remembers,* 35.

accuse you of doing something wrong you'd always get passengers to speak up for you. They'd stand up for you."[213]

Economic models tend to assume that all humans pursue only their own interests, but we are also social animals, and find meaning in what we do for others. Sociologist Amy Wrzesniewski studied janitors in a hospital and found that what got them out of bed every morning was helping patients – joking with them, calming them down, helping families find them in the hospital – even though that was not their job.[214]

For thousands of generations, virtually all humans were engaged in straightforward, tangible tasks that had immediate and self-evident benefits, for themselves and their community. "If you made a cask you wouldn't think about the money, you always wanted to make a good cask, and have a look at it and get pride out of it," David O'Donnell said.[215]

"We are not famous, most of us like the fact that we are unseen most of the time," said Taylor. "It is, in a way, part of the solidness of the tradition that you get nothing in the way of reward, neither much money nor much recognition. Yet you feel you are doing something special and the doing of it is the reward. … I jump out of bed on a Sunday morning for my ringing day ... I'm part of the bells, absolutely part of them."[216]

"We're always striving toward perfection, if that's possible," he said. "When it's done well there's a feeling of a job well done, an elation and satisfaction. Ringers will aspire to the more difficult ringing for the sense of achievement it gives them. And their pleasure will not be less knowing that it makes no difference at all to the listener that the band had rung a very fine sequence of changes of Double Dublin Surprise Major instead of a very fine but simple sequence of Grandshire Triples. Some of us would aspire to ring the Double Dublin and if we were then struck by lightning we would die proud!"[217]

Even grave-diggers spoke of the pride they took in their work. "I've buried many a famous person," said Jack Mitchell. "I helped to put Dev

---

[213] *Dublin Voices*, 53.
[214] Wrzesniewski 2003.
[215] *Dublin Voices* 206.
[216] *Dublin Voices*, 72.
[217] *Dublin Voices*, 68.

[de Valera, prime minister of Ireland] into it [the ground]. I'll always feel part of that history."[218]

* * *

In an age when children roamed freely and every village had craftsmen, they grew up watching men at useful work. "The forges fascinated us," Paddie Crosbie said. "I thought then that the blacksmith was the greatest man on earth. ... Tom Byrne often allowed us into the forge and on one occasion he let me pump the bellows. I have never forgotten that."[219] John Lyons' local forge "was our rambling house at night, and on wet days when we were not able to work in the farms, we went to the forge, where we were always welcomed. The smith was a highly intelligent man, and listening to him was as an education. His wit was great, and his writing was copperplate."[220]

Boland spent so much time with his neighbourhood smith in Dublin that he was allowed to assist with more and more tasks until he could shoe horses himself. "The smithy was very proud of me too, but then I had served a six-or-seven-year apprenticeship to the trade, on and off," Boland said. "The next time I called in, the smithy had a special present for me: My own made-to-size leather apron."[221]

Other elders described spending time with carpenters or bakers and absorbing their trade, but most learned the craft of their parents. John Vaughan's earliest memories were of his father and grandfather's forge; as a boy his job was to turn on the furnace with a stick, as the wall lever was too high for his tiny body to reach. "From our house I always knew when someone was working in the forge, for the sound of the anvil carried down the street," Vaughan said. "Every anvil must have its own tone, because I remember this anvil, and it's quite different than any other."[222]

[218] *Dublin Voices*, 92.
[219] *Your Dinner's Poured Out*, 43.
[220] *Joy of My Boyhood Years*, 127.
[221] *Tales from a City Farmyard*, 185.
[222] *Door into the Dark*, RTE documentary.

"My family lived above the shop," said John Read Cowle of his family cutlery business. "We started in 1670 …Now when this firm started they were sword cutlers. Now sword cutlers were important people."[223]

Few elders, however, exulted in their family traditions as much as 78-year-old tombstone carver Stephen Bracken. "My sons are seventh generation [masons]," he said. "Oh, we're stone mad. *Stone mad!*"[224]

Still others joined a craftsman as an official apprentice, which required a fee. My neighbour Patty trained as a teenager to be a servant at Howth Castle, learning the precise way to polish buttons, pour sherry or press trousers. "Whatever people that were there, you watched them and you learned it," she said, "And the next thing was you were an improver."

Joe Murphy of Ringsend came from a long line of shipwrights, yet still had to apprentice under another. "in those days you couldn't serve your time under your own father or grandfather," he said. "You had to serve your time elsewhere." He was trained like a soldier, and everything had to be perfect. "You'd sharpen every instrument in your tool box and don't you dare be seen sharpening tools during the week! Everything had to be razor sharp for the following week's work. In those days the chisels were silver steel and it was forged under iron and when you sharpened it, it was like a lance."[225]

Even grave-digging required training. "In them days you were a year in before you'd be made permanent," said Mitchell. "You were known as a 'leveller.' The leveller, he'd be at a plot and if he seen a mound of clay he'd level it down, keeping the plots tidy. You can visualise men opening graves and there's clay here and clay there and it was up to you to level it down … and as you were at your first year of levelling you would always be somewhere near somebody that was opening a grave and you'd watch him."[226]

Every apprenticeship impressed a tradition, the distilled culmination of hundreds of lives of experience. Taylor said his group of bell-ringers uphold traditions dating back centuries, and could name prominent ringers

---

[223] *Dublin Voices.*
[224] *Dublin Voices, 93.*
[225] *Dublin Voices, 132.*
[226] *Dublin Voices, 89.*

of the 1600s. "In effect, we salute their memory every time we ring and we remember, when we are nostalgic, the ringers who were senior when the oldest of us started to learn."[227]

My daughter and I were visiting a local farmer friend when the farrier came by to shoe his stallion. He looked no more than a boy, with a face you'd expect to see in a fast-food window, but as he wrestled the stallion's leg with one arm while clamping a searing horseshoe in the other, he was obviously a man, and one who knew his business.

Four times he propped a horse leg on a pedestal – with difficulty, he told me, as the stallion far outweighed his usual clients in this racehorse country -- and scraped the blackened hoof white. After each such cleaning he stepped over to the van he had backed into the stable; the entire inside folded out like a tackle box into shelves, drawers, and rows of tools ready for use.

Most importantly he had a furnace inside like a barbecue, with a grill for the horseshoe, a bellows for the flames below, and a small anvil for hammering the shoe to fit. He moved swiftly and easily, and when the metal arch still glowed faintly he grabbed the horse's leg and set the shoe to it. I have seen horses shy at distant noises or blowing scraps of paper, but the stallion remained undisturbed, even when the heat burned the hair on his fetlock.

When I asked how long it takes to learn his trade, the young man said he apprenticed for four years, so he must have left school early, yet is one of the few of his age to be employed. If people didn't want to take the full four years, I asked, how long would it take to learn the basics? Without looking up, he said "Four years." No shortcuts.

***

When I write articles or give talks about traditional craftsmen, I sometimes encounter a surprising hostility from "woke" people today. To them, *any* authority must be oppressive, authoritarian, patriarchal, fascist, and so on.

---

[227] *Dublin Voices*, 69.

The impulse to question authority and to side with the underdog runs deep in Western culture; when we see a movie about Spartacus fighting the slave-masters, Robin Hood versus the Sheriff, or rebels rising up against the Galactic Empire, we instantly understand which side to root for. It's a shock to Westerners to hear legends or see films from cultures that lack these core values, and see characters that would be heroes to us treated as villains. An ancient example would be from *The Iliad*; at one point King Menelaus commands his weary troops to keep fighting, and when a lone hunchback talks back to him, the king strikes him down. Everything about the situation -- the futility of the war, the king's arrogance, and the hunchback's disabled status -- signals to us that we should side with the hunchback, but that's probably not how Homer's audience saw it. Their descendants, by the time of Euripides or Sophocles, would think differently.

If the woke hostility to authority took the form of building back democracy, with masses of activists attending utility board meetings and debating community issues, I'd be all in favour of it. Instead, though, most of their activism centers not on the reconstruction of community and civic life, but the destruction of symbols like statues or monuments. They do not focus on making more people authorities, but on eliminating authority.

There are several problems with this. First of all, the woke movement seems to be concentrated mostly among the upper classes; infamous riots take place at the most expensive colleges in the country, rather than small-town plumbing schools, and global corporations have taken up the ideology, but not Mom-and-Pop hardware stores. Their targets -- say, police officers – tend to be the institutions that provide some small measure of safety to lower classes.

For another thing, the desire to live without authority requires the belief that living without authority is possible, which has never happened in any human society. Woke literature often cites tribal cultures – always conveniently far away or extinct – that allegedly lived without conflict or leadership. These claims ignore the fact that many Native American groups made almost constant war on their enemies – in certain Amazonian tribes more than 50 percent of males die violently, compared to 0.3 percent of Americans and 0.09 percent of Irish today --- and more complex empires like the Aztecs held rituals of mass human sacrifice.[228]

Most human societies were not so brutal, but all have some kind of leadership; hunter-gatherer tribes have less formal hierarchies than empires, but some people are always more senior than others. The same is true of our animal relations, from the literal pecking order of chickens to the savage dominance struggles of chimpanzees.

Also, even the most anti-hierarchical of woke activists have hierarchies of their own, with organisers and figureheads. No babies are born espousing French post-modernism; the students learned at the feet of someone they follow, who follows someone else. These are hierarchies of persuasion and peer pressure rather than violence, but so were most relationships in traditional communities.

Of course authority can be unjust and brutal, but it doesn't need to be. All human groups have some measure of seniority and hierarchy for a simple reason: some of us know more than others about certain subjects. If woke activists were hit by a car they would not want to be treated by any random passerby, but an emergency doctor, not because they have been brainwashed by an oppressive conspiracy, but because a doctor would know what he or she is doing. When they have a leaky pipe they would call a plumber, and if violent gangs were to attack your neighbourhood you want to know which of your neighbours is good with weapons.

We can and should treat people as equals, if we mean under the law or in the eyes of God or as fellow human souls making their way through this Earth. We will not, however, all be equally good at the same things, or have the same experiences. Mothers can do some things for children more easily than fathers, and vice versa. Older people will know more on average than younger people. Even if a community is run by democracy – which I encourage – I can say from experience that everything will be decided by the few people who show up to meetings.

Since hierarchies of authority are inevitable, we have a choice between types of authority: visible and invisible, accountable and unaccountable, earned and unearned. Democracy, science, public justice and other

---

[228] Walker 2013. Also, *War Before Civilization: The Myth of the Peaceful Savage.*

Western traditions demand authority be visible and accountable, their status earned through election or expertise. Attack such institutions into oblivion, as the woke movement is trying to do, and we are only left with invisible hierarchies, based on hidden relationships, secret deals and unspoken prejudices.

***

Apprentices learned responsibility at an early age, and did not spend their adolescence in an agonised search for "identity," for by their teen years they already were someone. Eventually the apprentice could produce his own piece worthy of a master – a literal "master-piece" – and take up the trade as an adult, no matter his age.

To a craftsman the physical world around us is intelligible, as Matthew Crawford said in *The World Beyond Your Head,* and can be shaped by his will into objects of utility and beauty imbued with part of his life. The objects – this nail, that chair -- can be as recognisable as a signature, carrying an imprint of the craftsman's thoughts long after their body is dust. Thomas Aquinas defined humans as beings with brains and hands, made in the image of God -- not in the sense that God is a giant human, but in that we, alone among animals, emulate the Creator. As unthinkably vast and incomprehensible as the world can be, craftmanship takes a part of that world and makes it something that our minds can understand, and therefore love.

"The satisfactions of manifesting oneself concretely in the world through manual competence have been known to make a man quiet and easy," Crawford wrote. "They seem to relieve him of the felt need to offer chattering interpretations of himself to vindicate his worth. He can simply point: the building stands, the car now runs, the lights are on. Boasting is what a boy does, because he has no real effect on the world. But the tradesman must reckon with the infallible judgement of reality..."[229]

Craftsmen paid attention to the reality of the situation, not to their own image of how things ought to be. "The man who recognises his own work in the world can take pride in it, is transformed by it," Waters said. "But

---

[229] *The World Beyond Your Head,* 15.

learning to do so requires a lot of failure, which protects one against too much conceit. The experience of failure tempers our sense of mastery."[230]

The ability to create also generally bestows the ability to repair, and for generations almost all humans fixed their own devices, from baskets to roofs to swords. Those skills applied even when hand tools gave way to machines; Dennis Leonard, for example, grew up a farmer and knew how to work a forge, and that knowledge served him well when he became a pilot and electrical expert, and could use his forge to create or repair new machine parts. Repairing one's own belongings was once so normal that cars and appliances came with schematics of the insides, since it was asumed that the owners would want to maintain and repair them. These skills started young as well; boys' magazines had instructions on how to build their own dynamos, windmills, bicycles, and many other machines. Tony Carr and his friends created boxcars to race down hills, and Martin Keaveny created a device that lit the inside of a chicken coop, persuading them to lay more eggs when needed.[231]

Today most of our belongings are made to break and be thrown away – even furniture that appears to be entirely wood might have plastic bits designed to break, so we will be forced to buy replacements. Almost all the products we see in around us have been designed to be unfixable, to remove our ancestral right to shape and repair our world.

Increasingly, people in the modern world can even be sued for trying to fix their devices, as the tractor company John Deere did when farmers repaired their tractors. The company claimed that because their tractors contain software – because of course they must – its owner merely has an "implied license," and must bring it to the company and pay for it to be repaired. "Smart" technology means our possessions can not only spy on us, but were never really ours.

Many elders complained about similar rules in Ireland. "Later in my career ... I would be in charge of four power plants, each one of which could supply a whole village," said Dennis Leonard. "Yet, in my

---

[230] *Give Us Back the Bad Roads*, 203.
[231] *Growing Up With Ireland*, 25.

retirement, I am forbidden by law to do so much as install a light or move a power socket in my own house. And that is progress."[232]

Whether we can legally fix our own cars in theory, we usually cannot in practice. As Crawford pointed out, many new cars no longer even have a dipstick; car owners must rely on what was once called the "idiot light," as we are all now treated like idiots. Modern corporate spaces collude to enforce this kind of helplessness; even when we wash our hands, we must wait for the water, without being able to use a handle, and then for the air to dry it. Technology trains us, in Crawford's words, to "supplicate to invisible powers."

Even if we had something to repair, learning how to do so for a modern person can be surprisingly difficult; learning repair skills often requires long and expensive courses made for specialists. Schools used to teach shop classes, but most have been eliminated, and a 2009 poll showed one-third of teens spend zero time per week doing anything hands-on at all.[233] "Most young people today have no real skills," said elder Steve Manry. "Even the things kids used to do, building and making things with their hands, isn't done anymore, so the hand-eye coordination is gone."[234]

They can leave school and get an office job, but the well-paying ones require college, which for most of us meant spending our most productive years in debt. It's a system that benefits corporations, who get employees desperate to work, and government agencies that get monthly tributes for decades, but hobbles young people trying to find their way in the world.

Until recently, all the tasks we unthinkingly relegate to machines today were done by people, so most people's jobs had obvious value; everyone needed shoes, so everyone needed a cordwainer to make them and a cobbler to fix them. Everyone needed tailors for their clothes, haberdashers or milliners for their hats, butchers to cut their meat and grocers for their flour, masons and carpenters for their homes. Everyone needed publicans to serve the beer on Saturday night and priests to forgive them the next morning. When they died they needed carvers of headstones.

---

[232] *Let There Be Light,* 162.
[233] Why your teenager can't use a hammer," *Maclean's,* 25 May 2011.
[234] "The Many Sides of Steve Manary," RTE documentary, 15 November 2012.

Modern people usually tell me that people back then had fewer choices, and that's true if you, again, compare the richest today to the poorest then. Census records from the late 1800s, though, show not just the basic crafts I've mentioned, but around 1,500 job titles: ale tunners, archil makers, battures, bozzlers, camlets, clouters, arbalesters, brachygraphers, culvers, danters, and many others just in the first few letters of the alphabet. They represent a way of life so alien to most of us that even when we look up the definition we still don't understand what they did. A modern person can read on their screen that a "garthman" was the proprietor of a weir, but they'd need to learn what a weir was, and why people depended on them, especially during Lent.

There was little chance for a carpenter to become a CEO, but there is little chance you will become a CEO either. If you were a carpenter, though, you had a status and an identity no outsourcing or artificial intelligence could take away. Even if you lost your physical ability with age or accident, you could mentor others, for you had the knowledge that apprentices needed and that no book could convey.

"A man who was a carpenter was more than a man," Waters wrote. "A woman qualified as a dressmaker was someone from whom an opinon emanated in a new way, seen to be born of a depth of endeavour and application to reality that made her worth listening to."[235]

Each craftsman represented a distillation of centuries of experience, of lore and secrets. "… a hatter was a very secretive person and a very proud person, very proud of his knowledge which he wouldn't give to anyone else ... in tricks that you learned when you were growing up," said William Coyle, who worked in the days when no one would be seen outside without a hat. "...There are things I can do with a hat that nobody else would know about. And I wouldn't even share it with anybody because that's my trade and it'll die with me."[236]

That came up again and again when talking to craftsmen about their trades – most knew they were the last of their line. "Me father and me grandfather and me great-grandfather were all shipwrights, and I'm the

---

[235] *Give Us Back the Bad Roads,* 182.
[236] *Dublin Voices,* 200.

last of them because neither of the two sons I have are following the trade," said Joe Murphy.[237]

All the crafts disappeared in a generation or two – the coopers, wrights, milliners, cordwainers and other crafts. So did the apprenticeships, lodges, clubs, co-ops and guilds. When I walk around Dublin or Paris or St. Louis, I see breathtaking architecture that spans the ages, church sculptures that shape marble like silk, art that ennobles and inspires, all works that – if they are not demolished, as many have been – are likely to outlast all our fragile modern architecture. These buildings used to house clubs and libraries and schools that taught philosophy, literature and political organising. They survived unimaginable hardship to overthrow empires and create free, healthy and safe societies. I realise that we could not build some of these structures now; the crafts to create them are forgotten, along with the conviction to devote a life to them, and the social organisation, and the families to support the craftsmen, and ... everything. The entire human infrastructure.

And I think: *None of this world could have been built by the people now living in it.*

* * *

Today most of our jobs have no traditions, for we are trained to disdain the past. Yet the more modern the skill is, the more short-lived it is, easily replaceable by Third World labour or artificial intelligence. In such an economy, to "work" merely means to cling to the undersides of corporations like fleas and hope to be transported somewhere in life before being dislodged.

Those who have not yet been replaced by machines are required to emulate machines – say, standardised tests in schools that remove the teacher's judgement, or sentencing laws that take away the discretion of a judge -- all to surgically remove human "error," meaning humanity. Most of us answer to machines, whether to software that tracks our phone calls and keyboard movements, cameras that track us like prison inmates, all designed to prod us down the right path at the right speed. We fantasize

---

[237] *Dublin Voices*, 137.

about hidden conspiracies run by shadowy elites, but it's difficult to imagine them doing better than our we do ourselves.[238]

And while traditional jobs have limits -- at some point the house is built, the pipes are fixed – there is no natural stopping point to the amount of surveillance, or paperwork, or billable hours. Keeping up with these trends make every job, in Tim Wu's phrase, "like a football game where the whistle is never blown."[239]

In addition to all this, most of us must spend many hours every week travelling back and forth to these jobs. I rode a bus for three hours a day, 15 hours a week, for 15 years, and could chat with my elderly neighbours, but for most Americans this means driving a car, usually alone. Those hundreds of hours per year are hours not spent chatting over the fence with neighbours, or playing ball with children, or anything else. Commuting is such a drain on our lives that when the COVID pandemic forced millions of Westerners to work from home, most preferred it; a UK newspaper polled asked readers how many looked forward to the world returning to normal, and only nine percent did.[240]

Finally, most job advertisements -- for marketing managers down to cleaning ladies -- demand employees who will be "enthusiastic" or "passionate" – even McDonald's employees, who may well be sleeping in their cars out back, have been encouraged to "high-five" customers to create the illusion of excitement. In other words, we are asked to lie flamboyantly, all the time, and never, ever stop.

Because there is one thing worse than working in the modern world – not working. In a world where our jobs consume our lives, unemployment leaves us without purpose; a UK study found that 40 percent of jobless young people had experienced symptoms of mental illness, and almost a third have considered taking their own lives.[241]

With all of these pressures, then, it's not surprising when employees rebel in whatever passive-agressive way they can; a (pre-pandemic)

---

[238] Umar Haque, "The Asshole Factory," *Medium*, 21 April 2015.
[239] Tim Wu,"You Really Don't Need To Work So Much," *New Yorker* magazine, August 21, 2015.
[240] "Just 9% want things to 'go back to normal' after coronavirus lockdown, says poll," *Daily Mirror*, 17 April 2020.
[241] Prince's Trust MacQuarie, Youth Index 2014, p. 8.

Gallup survey found that 70 percent of US workers said they were "not engaged" or "actively disengaged" from their jobs. You're not imagining it; most people you pass on the street, see at work or talk to on the phone are mentally checked out, and have been for a long time.[242]

The elders I talked to worked harder jobs for longer hours, and with none of the technological distractions we have, for a tenth of our minimum wage, yet their lives had meaning – and what is anything else for? "Everyone worked so hard and we never heard a word of complaint, yet now you turn a press a button and everyone is stressed," Susan O'Driscoll said. "Everyone is bringing the stress on themselves with expenses they could do without, if they only realised the years pass so quickly and the older you get the faster they go."[243]

***

If you asked almost anyone why we abandoned a world of craftsmen, the answer would probably be: *We have technology now.* Yet humans created ingenious technology in every era, long before we had fossil fuels or electricity: astrolabes and orreys and gear clocks, masonry stoves that use little wood, pedal-and-chain mechanisms, and other inventions that people could make themselves.

We can also adapt a lot of the machinery around us for new purposes, if we become as mechanically inclined as most boys were a few generations ago. When I learned how to forge metal here in rural Ireland, my teacher had made his own bellows by reversing an old vacuum cleaner into a blower. There are millions of used car alternators in the USA, and any of them could easily power a wind turbine, providing a small but vital part of a home's electricity. I know people in America who have similarly fiddled with their diesel engines, and happily run their car on old fast-food grease.

Many of these technologies are being rediscovered by the "steam-punk" subculture, which has ballooned from a marginal literary genre to a network of enthusiast web sites, conventions and clubs. Its writers mix the vintage – usually Victorian Europe – with science fiction, like sepia Goths.

---

[242] https://www.gallup.com/394373/indicator-employee-engagement.aspx
[243] *No Shoes in Summer*, 47.

Its musicians mix folk and antique styles into a junkyard-retro sound. And some fans tinker with old machinery and make it work again, or turn it into something else elegant and functional.

Subcultures appear to fill voids in the culture, it's easy to see why the genre has achieved such a devoted following. Science fiction offers us fantastical space adventures that seem farther away now than they did decades ago, or doomer porn that ramps the despair ever-further downwards. Steampunk reboots science fiction entirely, giving the 20th century a do-over, and reviving everything that we liked about the genre in the first place.

It's also easy to see why fans go back to steam-punk, rather than oxen-punk or flint-punk; they are returning to that historical moment of balance between craftsmanship and technology. For thousands of years before then, smiths and coopers made tools that were useful and graceful, and those men must have regarded the first railways and canals with an awe we will never feel. The Victorian era was the last heyday of that artisanal tradition, but on the grand scale that fossil fuels allowed. Even the most mundane bridges or prisons or sewage plants from that era are breathtaking to look at as well as functional, while our glass skyscrapers are neither. We have torn most of that world down, but the few buildings that remain could stand a thousand years from now, long after many generations of glass and plastic buildings have collapsed.

It was the last time that machines could be repaired continuously for decades or centuries, in a way that our iGadgets cannot. It was the last time household items were made of steel and wood and suede, pleasing our eyes and skin in a way that plastic never will. It was the last time battles took place between men rather than machines. It was the last time that machines looked like works of art, and art looked like something recognisable. It was a pre-Google world when old libraries held secrets.

Whatever you might think of steam-punk culture, they are on to something. They realise that they can revive the craftsmanship and artistry that our world had recently abandoned, or tinker in their sheds as their grandparents did, all without replicating the less pleasing aspects of those eras. And once they are no longer dependent on the latest computer to create, and no longer bound by the culture of the present moment, a whole new world opens up before them.

Chapter Six

Schooling

Tens of thousands of children walked across hills and fields each morning, often for miles in rain and chilly weather, often barefoot and wearing sewn-together flour bags, to go to school. Their tiny hands often carried bricks of hand-hewn turf, or sticks that they picked up along the way, to keep their single rooms warm – or less bitterly cold – as they studied. School budgets effectively did not exist; children often carried a few coins here and there for the teacher when the parents could afford it, or paid in fireplace turf. Nor did children go to school all year; they left whenever the parents needed an extra pair of hands on the farm, or to baby-sit their brothers and sisters, or to bring in the turf for winter, or to make some extra money at a job. Some described going to school until they were 16, or 14, or 11, and then never again.

Now: Tell me what kind of education they got.

Every modern person assures me the results would be pathetic – just the "three Rs," so named because we assume that backwoods hillbillies would have spelled the subjects "reading, 'riting and 'rithmatic." We assume that the poorer you are, the worse your education, and these days that's often true in my native USA, where two-thirds of all adults cannot read at a proficient level, and a third cannot handle a basic level.[244]

Also, some of these children lived a century ago, and we assume knowledge only becomes vaster and more refined over time. This is why we spent 15,000 hours of our youth in giant cement warehouses – our parents wanted us to keep up with the competition in a race forward. It's

---

[244] U.S. Department of Education, "Literacy, Numeracy, and Problem Solving in Technology-Rich Environments Among U.S. Adults," 2012.

is why so many of us spent years in college, and decades paying off college, to join the future and not be left behind.

This belief, held by almost every man, woman and child today, crumbles the instant one reads descriptions of schools from a century ago, or actual school-papers of children then, or newspapers and magazines of the time, or reading the books normal children once read. Children used to read sophisticated literature that few college students – or professors – attempt anymore. So did mechanics and farm-hands, house-wives and fishermen.

They discussed these works at the lodge and the shop and the pub. They wrote about them in their diaries. All this, you'll recall, in addition to their practical skills, their knowledge of local lore, of the natural world and the people around them – all of which are also rare today.

Ann Gardinier remembered learning John Bunyan's *Pilgrim's Progress*, Dante's *Inferno*, and Milton's *Paradise Lost*, as well as Latin, poetry and Shakespeare, all at the age of 11.[245] Alice Taylor remembered translating Virgil from Latin to English and back again.[246] My neighbour Sean described performing Gilbert and Sullivan operettas in school, translating them into the native Irish language.

Nor was their schooling limited to literature; Liam Bradley remembered having to prove geometry theorems in grade school. "Mental arithmetic was a daily feature in our school life. My old school companions would be horrified at the hesitancy of modern schoolchildren in mental computations ... there was really no need for pocket calculators."

Country schoolhouses might have been only one room with children of many ages, but that was a great advantage to which modern students have been denied, Bradley said. "Students of many ages had to be taught together, and younger children, instead of being isolated, overheard some of the things that their older peers were learning." They also learned facts through mnemonic chants, which few schools use today but which any memory expert will tell you is the best way to learn. Bradley learned the names of the towns around our area, like Athy (pronounced a-TIE) and

---

[245] *The House Remembers*, 136.
[246] *Quench the Lamp*, 104.

Naas (rhymes with face) with a couplet: "Kildare, Athy, Naas, Maynooth: My hair, my eye, my face, my tooth."[247]

Of course, free-range urchins required a firm hand, and some teachers – especially the Christian Brothers – gained a reputation for strict rules and corporal punishment. At the same time, Christy – who was taught by the Brothers, and became a teacher himself --said they were dedicated to their students. "They gave 24/7 in their teaching," he said. "They were there after school, and they were there in the morning. The principal would have done the secretary work, the accountancy, the timetable, everything" without much of a salary. In contrast to pale and pious movie monks, they were "men with ruddy, weather-beaten faces who might have been .... uncles or neighbouring farmers, men who could turn from teaching honours maths to fixing the tractor," according to one former student.[248]

In the countryside where there were no monasteries or convents, Taylor remembered that teachers rented their own schoolhouses and rode bicycles for miles every morning to school. "Those young educational entrepreneurs could have found jobs in well-established convents or colleges, or emigrated to exciting new places, but chose instead to face an uncertain future and invest their time and money in renting premises to set up these small schools," she said. "These teachers are the unsung educators and enlighteners of many young minds around Ireland. We owe them a debt of gratitude."[249]

Just as smiths or hatters taught children craft traditions, so teachers taught them national traditions. Monks were especially patriotic, Christy said, having suffered under centuries of British rule; they taught Irish history as far back as ancient legends, he said, and only allowed Irish sports in the schoolyard.

For many children, book-learning was not limited to school, but was a part of daily life, in-between farm chores. In the countryside of the early 1900s, Mary Fogarty estimated she read five hundred books a year, waking with her mother and sisters at 5 am to read for two hours, and then again before bed. "We read *Lorna Doone* – I was in love with John Ridd for

---

[247] *No Shoes in Summer,* 68.
[248] "Ballyfin – A Boarding School Memory," RTE documentary.
[249] *Books in the Attic,* 15.

weeks – *The Vicar of Wakefield*, more Dickens, Thackeray, Kingsley, and the Brontes, returning now and then, for little Annie's benefit, to the loved books of our first days – *Little Women, Masterman Ready, Scottish Chiefs, Gulliver's Travels*, and Mayne Reid," she wrote in her memoir. "Mother enjoyed Maria Edgeworth more than we did, also Jane Austen; we much preferred George Eliot."[250]

Ann Gardinier remembered reading *Robinson Crusoe* and Charles Dickens around the fire with his family.[251] Alice Taylor devoured Dickens as well before moving on to the Brontes.[252] Crosbie began reading with crime novels, as well as *Treasure Island* and *Kidnapped,* but soon was reading any kind of book.[253] "Reading had always been our great escape," he said. "We devoured anything we could get our hands on, suitable or not, though my mother kept a close eye."[254]

Of course, everyone was poor by our standards, and schooling varied wildly from one person to another; a survey around the time of Irish independence in the 1920s found that 14 percent of the population were illiterate – but that is no lower than the USA now.[255] And even the unschooled valued the written word; some elders remembered illiterate neighbours dropping by to listen to the newspaper read to them.

Most said that everyone they knew read whenever they weren't working. Sometimes they did both at the same time; one elder described farmers holding books in front of them – usually something we would consider a classic – as they ploughed, or craftsmen employing a boy to read to them from such a book as they made barrels or shaped leather. Taylor said that her father loved poetry and recited it for his children. "His favourite poet was Goldsmith and *The Deserted Village* rolled off his tongue with such relish that you knew he approved of all the poet's sentiments."[256]

---

[250] *The Farm by Lough Gur*, 172.
[251] *The House Remembers,* 129.
[252] *Quench the Lamp*, 127.
[253] *Your Dinner's Poured Out*, 131.
[254] *The House Remembers*, 10.
[255] The National Literacy Institute, www.thenationalliteracyinstitute.com
[256] *To School Through the Fields*, 61.

Farmer Stephen Rynne, who chronicled his life in the early 1900s, described passing the winter nights reading Burton's *Anatomy of Melancholy*, Cobbett's *Rural Rides* and *Advice to Young Men*, Darwin's *Voyage of the Beagle*, and Joseph Joubert's *Thoughts*; without them, he said, "the long winter nights would be too long by streets."[257] Nor were any of these people wealthy; Rynne remembered one of his farm-hands spending his leisure hours reading the *Confessions of St. Augustine*,[258] and the local greasy mechanic in Rafferty's village had read Gibbons' *Rise and Fall of the Roman Empire*, Chaucer's *Canterbury Tales*, Dickens, Gerard Manley Hopkins, WB Yeats, and Paine's *Rights of Man*.[259]

"That generation .... seemed on average to have greater facility with words – better handwriting, even – than we do and to use language more precisely," Gene Kerrigan said.[260] If you want first-had evidence of this, read from Rynne's private journal from almost a century ago. Read it aloud to yourself, slowly, letting the words roll around like music:

"One pauses to look at the bronze and golden trees: every beech a Titian, every lime a Norse goddess, elms like sunsets, and oaks like Vandyke's old men. Boastfully a Spanish chestnut holds up her unlocked seed-vessels. The berry clusters of the hollies bite out like rubies from the rich velvet of foliage. The brownish-green masses of the sycamores seem like tapestry in which one could imagine pictures: horses and huntsmen, or medieval battles. In the wood, this year's leaves lie with the skeletons of their ancestors.

... Yet give me gleaming autumn with its fast hours, its replete grandeur, its pacific beauty languishing on earth and bending from the sky. Just now the world is like a Dutch kitchen: all bronzes, lustre and pewter. There are calm, gold days making up weeks together, each day as rich as the woven costume of a mandarin. Leave me autumn with its threat of winter, and let romantic-minded urban dwellers enjoy the summer to their hearts' content."[261]

---

[257] *Green Fields*, 69.
[258] *Green Fields*, 76.
[259] *And the Band Played On,* 85.
[260] *Another Country,* 67.
[261] *Green Fields*, 19.

When I describe this to people today, they are sceptical: these must have been the few rich farmers, people tell me, the oppressors rather than the oppressed. Or they must lie to justify how miserable their life was. And if we use simpler language, they tell me, it must be an improvement – back then, people were too ignorant to use small words. And why, they ask, would anyone want to read works from long ago, before anyone knew anything?

They never ask the more obvious question: If so many people were so literate, what happened to us?

***

If you've watched or read any science fiction, there's one scene you know well; maybe you've seen it in *Star Trek*, or *Doctor Who*, or *Mad Max*, or any number of imitators. It goes like this: Amid the ruins of a post-apocalyptic landscape, barbarians – perhaps wearing pelts or holding spears, or using some kind of patched-together junk technology – find a lost book or see engravings on the crumbled monuments, and read slowly, "We ... the... people" or some other familiar phrase, words whose meaning is lost on them.

As grim as they seem, post-apocalyptic stories remain popular for a reason – in their own way, they flatter us. They tell us that even when our buildings and books are ruins, the survivors will look back on us with awe and fascination, and that we – the pinnacle of civilisation --- will inspire them.

In the real world, though, apocalypses almost never happen, and when they do, as in Ireland during the Famine, the results are not what you see in movies -- more on that later. In real life, civilisations rise and fall, but slowly – the "fall" of Rome unfolded gradually over four centuries. News of the time – and histories since – might have focused on maps and emperors, Huns and Vandals, but these came and went, and life went on. They did not think they were living through a decline and fall any more than we do, as trends spanning centuries were too gradual for anyone to truly notice. By the time Rome was a ruin, no one alive remembered when it had been otherwise, and no one mourns what they do not remember.

Remembering is what makes a people who they are, and for thousands of generations every tribe and people had their own oral traditions. In the last few hundred generations, though, humanity created one of the most astonishing inventions ever – the ability to freeze their thoughts on a surface in writing. At first it was used by only a few elites, but once a critical mass of free people learned to read and write -- in the Athens of 25 centuries ago -- it resulted in a new and radical kind of human society.

Reading the thoughts of strangers forces us to see them as individuals, challenges our views, and erodes the gulf between rulers and ruled. And in fits and starts that the Greeks documented for us in detail, it created the first free Western civilisation, whose values are so fundamental to our lives that we strain to recognise them – but would instantly recognise their absence.

Before the Ancient Greeks – and in many places today – leaders had absolute power; openly criticising the ruler would get you killed very quickly, and even today criticising the government in China, or Islam in a Muslim country, would not get you pleasant results. In Athens and some other city-states, however, leaders were elected – not just political leaders but military ones as well – and were to step aside peacefully when voted out. Every free man could criticise and question officials; soldiers could even question their commanders, as Creon's guards did in Sophocles' *Antigone*, and Aristophanes could perform anti-war comedies in the middle of a horrific war.

The common man was valued as important, and playwrights of the time endowed their menial workers – shepherds, farmers, guards and messengers -- with a common sense the rulers needed. As Victor Davis Hanson and John Heath put it, in Greek plays the hero is often the underdog, the trouble-maker, who criticises what everyone else blindly accepts. Ajax, Philocretes, Lysistrata, Electra, Prometheus, Antigone, he or she – often a she – harshly condemned the leaders, and did so publicly.[262]

They created the first society where people debated on and voted for laws that applied equally to everyone. They had a free economy, and not just tribute to the overlord. They worshipped a different religion, but they

---

[262] *Who Killed Homer?* 33.

had a separation of church and state; there was no Great Pyramid of Solon, no mummies of Socrates. When this spirit started to slip, and generals like Alexander and Caesar deified themselves, Alexander's men mutinied and Caesar was murdered.

They had schools, elections, libraries, comedy, tragedy, history, philosophy, a justice system, human rights, public debates, markets, public speakers, news and opinion pamphlets, protests, and "Athens' Got Talent"-style music competitions. Their lives are comprehensible to us because we still enjoy the free Western culture that they invented.

The Romans, despite their many faults, kept Greek writings alive, and added their own to a growing canon of what became known as the classics. As Rome declined, though, and barbarians burned cities and libraries across Europe, it seemed like all memory of free Western culture would go with it, a brief and singular moment in human history.

Since you're reading this today, of course, that didn't happen. You know of science, democracy and human rights today because they developed from people reading the Greek and Roman classics, after they had been preserved and kept alive for a thousand years by Christian monks, especially here in Ireland.

Ireland converted to Christianity just as Rome was falling, fusing its classical learning with existing Celtic traditions to create its own brand of Catholicism, which remained standing when mainland Europe and Britain collapsed. Monks not only kept and re-copied the classics but taught people – commoners as well as nobility, girls as well as boys -- to read them, and understand why they were important.[263] As writer Seb Falk notes in *The Light Ages*, medieval people were not as illiterate as we imagine; perhaps half of the population in England could read and write, and sometimes hired monks to teach them, creating the first universities.[264]

A classical education meant more than enjoying the stories; for more than a thousand years classical education meant teaching children how to think, beginning with the Trivium of grammar, dialectic and rhetoric. Grammar – reading – was an act so transformative and spiritual it became

---

[263] *The Hedge Schools of Ireland*, 96.
[264] *The Light Ages*, 30.

the word "glamour," a magical spell; it's also why the word "spell" means both writing and sorcery.

Dialectic meant learning how to argue about what they had just read. Later generations mocked medieval scholars for arguing over issues like how many angels could dance on the head of a pin – a straw-man example, by the way, that never happened in real life – but they missed the context of those arguments; they were academic exercises to teach students to follow premises to their logical conclusion. Finally, rhetoric taught students how to speak and write about these ideas to others.

Our entire legal, political and scientific infrastructure is based on these now-endangered skills. Juries and voting assume everyone can hear logical arguments and pick them apart, and our legal system remains full of Latin phrases that now only lawyers understand. Science assumes the ability to test assumptions and argue them before peers, and its names for animals and plants, subatomic particles and asteroids are all from Greek and Latin. When doctors operate on patients, they still use Greek and Latin terminology, whether in Japan or in Brazil. This is not imperialism, for these languages belong to no living people and no country, but to everyone.

Western Civilisation isn't just the cultural preferences – foods, decorations, festivals -- of Victorian Britons or 1950s Americans or any other Western country. I'm talking about a specific toolkit of social technologies, of intellectual "hacks" that transform society for everyone -- democracy, monogamy, literacy, the scientific method, and freedom of speech. Many appeared in Ancient Greece first and were developed in Italy or England or Germany, but printing was first developed in China, and our numerals in India. Wherever they were from, however, they caught on because they *work*.

You can see the distinction easily in music. All cultures have had their own music, and we all have our preferences. When Westerners created musical notation, equal temperament, harmony and chords, however, they opened up whole new possibilities which can now be used by musicians in all styles around the world.

Nor was the Western Canon an unchanging set of texts, but an ongoing conversation that lasted thousands of years – from Homer to Socrates to

Aristotle to Aquinas to Dante to Milton to Shelley, each generation building on what came before. It became a growing canon that enabled people of every country and every era to reference a "Trojan Horse" or "Horatius on the Bridge" without having to re-invent the cultural wheel. Only modern people think they can create a culture superior to the past while refusing to learn the lessons of the past.

Many of their students brought these classics back to mainland Europe, spreading both the classics and a re-invigorated Christianity as far as Russia. Without this injection and re-invigoration of faith and learning, Europe would probably have fallen long before to the Muslim invasions. None of the great churches of Europe would stand, the great works of painting and sculpture of the Renaissance would never have existed, the Enlightenment would never have happened, and the England or Paris of 1900 might have looked like Afghanistan today.[265]

Because of these generations of monks, Europe already had many readers, and a culture that valued reading, when printing was invented in the 1400s. The first books to be printed after the Bible were Greek and Roman classics, and soon schools appeared everywhere to teach them. According to Neil Postman, when printing was invented were 34 schools in England; by 1660, there were 444, a school for every 4,400 people, one school approximately every 12 miles.[266] Nor were they all for wealthy boys; many were free or inexpensive, and some admitted girls as well.[267]

The British Isles were transformed into lands of readers, all able to reference the same cultural standards. Most of the writers we remember for their original works – Alexander Pope or John Dryden, for example – actually put most of their time and energy into magnificent translations of Greek and Roman classics. It was for this reason that by 1600 Shakespeare could write about Coriolanus or Titus Andronicus, confident that the audience would understand who these people were and would care.

To get an idea of how widespread this was, take the introduction to *Lorna Doone*, the novel Mary Fogarty loved. The narrator describes

---

[265] With mass Muslim immigration to Europe, large and growing sections of them already do.
[266] *The Disappearance of Childhood*, 40.
[267] *The Hedge Schools of Ireland*, 15.

himself as a "nothing but a plain, unlettered man" and an "ignoramus" --
a redneck, we would say. Yet two paragraphs later he describes what that
meant in the 1600s – "...by the time I was twelve years old ... I could
make bold with Eutropius and with Caesar -- by aid of an English version
– and as much as six lines of Ovid," meaning reading it in Latin.[268]

Lorna Doone was fiction, but personal journals of the time tell a
similar story. In 1788 the future novelist William Hazlitt wrote to his
brother how he was reading Ovid and Eutropius – he was ten. A writer in
1715 predicted that "every country milkmaid may understand the *Iliad* as
well as you or I."[269] In 1787 poet Robert Burns wrote of a gardener's wife
who "can repeat by heart almost everything she has ever read, particularly
Pope's 'Homer' from end to end."[270] This might have been exaggeration
– my copy of Pope's *Iliad* clocks in at 428 pages – and these were probably
unusual individuals, but even a populace with a tenth of their knowledge
would be far beyond most professors now.

Having cultural references rooted in Greek and Roman classics wasn't
limited to England either; when Italians created the first operas, they were
consciously trying to emulate the (presumably) sung verses of Greek
plays, and assumed the audiences were already familiar with the stories.
Claudio Monteverdi's last opera, for example -- *The Coronation of Poppea*
-- ends with a love scene between the Roman emperor Nero and his
mistress Poppea, in what seems a happy ending for them. Venetian
audiences of the time, though, would have understood the meta-level of
irony, for they – unlike most of us – knew their Tacitus and how tragically
Nero and Poppea's story would end. They would have seen the opera the
way Monteverdi intended – as an attack on the decadence of Venice's rival
city-state Rome. The subtext would have been obvious to them -- but only
because they already knew the classics in a way that modern audiences do
not.

This is not to say that most farmers or craftsmen in those centuries
knew the actual Greek or Latin languages – those were still mostly for
elites wealthy enough to afford both the books, tutors and time to learn

---

[268] *Lorna Doone*, 1.
[269] *Homerides*, p. 8.
[270] Journal of Robert Burns, 9 May 1787.

them. Puritans in the 1600s described people who could only read English as "illiterate," according to historian David D. Hall; "literate" meant able to read Latin. The Earl of Chesterfield wrote something similar in 1748, that "classical knowledge, that is, Greek and Latin, is absolutely necessary for everybody ... the word illiterate, in its common acceptance, means a man who is ignorant of these two languages."[271] Understanding these languages became a mark of status, which is why Richard Hogarth, father of the painter William, set up a coffee house in London in 1704 where only Latin was allowed to be spoken – a venture that failed, but it says a great deal about the age that it was attempted at all.[272]

***

When I describe how educated people were then, almost everyone today has the same reaction: *those were just the rich elites. Everyone else was illiterate, filthy and starving.* While the wealthy classes had more formal education, though, everyday farmers and factory workers – no matter how poor – valued a classical education and went to astonishing lengths to acquire it.

Next door to Ireland, British workers taught themselves and each other not just to read but to read the Greek and Roman classics, and to use them the way medieval monks did – to think logically, debate publicly, and use those skills to organise people politically. These "mutual improvement societies" started in Scotland in the 1700s and spread rapidly; by the early 1800s, perhaps a quarter of all male workers in Britain belonged to such a club. By the late 1800s, *up to 80 percent* did.[273]

They met in homes or halls or churches, sometimes every night – rag-men and sweatshop workers, dock-men and coal miners, even homeless – to practice reading from Plato or Juvenal or Marcus Aurelius. They engaged in practice debates. They organised their own classrooms, subscription libraries, theatre clubs and musical groups. They paid each others' medical bills, provided unemployment benefits, savings banks, job referral services and burial plans.

---

[271] Letter to his son, 27 May, 1748.
[272] "Hogarth's Progress," *New Yorker*, 16 December 1971.
[273] *The Intellectual Life of the British Working Class*, 58.

Welsh miners – men, women and children -- who worked up to 12 hours a day doing dangerous work for low pay, put what few coins they had to fund vast networks of libraries, as well as theatres, lectures, opera, choir practices, dances, and political meetings. They stocked the libraries with Greek and Roman classics, and used them constantly -- at a typical library at Ygysir, *each reader* borrowed an average of 86 books a year.[274]

Club members started their own publications; *Chambers' Edinburgh Journal*, which began in 1832, focused on the classics, and featured discussions of Livy, Homer, Tacitus, Petrarch and many others. Others, like the *Popular Educator*, also taught mathematics and science. Keep in mind these were not just for working people, but *by* working people; the *Educator* was founded by a carpenter's apprentice, and their pages were filled with articles and letters from coal miners, farmers, shepherds and weavers.[275]

Their evening schools taught ten-year-old factory worker David Livingstone to become a medical doctor and explorer. "With a part of my first week's wages I purchased Ruddiman's 'Rudiments of Latin,' and pursued the study of that language for many years afterward, with unabated ardour, at an evening school, which met between the hours of eight and ten," he wrote. He then studied until midnight and was up again at the factory, propping his Latin book in front of his face as his hands worked the machine. "I read in this way many of the classical authors, and knew Virgil and Horace better at sixteen than I do now."[276]

Britons – widely literate since the 1500s, as mentioned – became some of the most highly educated people in the world, despite their poverty. Fred Kitchen said of villagers in Yorkshire that "The most remarkable thing was the number of books each family possessed ... held in great reverence by the parents, and no one was allowed to open one with unwashed hands."[277] A 1932-33 survey of a poor area of London during the Great Depression found that everyone surveyed owned books, and a quarter

---

[274] *The Intellectual Life of the British Working Class, 251.*
[275] *The Intellectual Life of the British Working Class, 188.*
[276] *Life and Explorations of David Livingstone, 18.*
[277] *The Intellectual Life of the British Working Class, 98.*

owned more than 100 – all people who might have to save up for weeks or months to afford a book.[278]

Some taught even poor Britons how to perform their own scientific experiments. Shoemaker Thomas Edward, born in 1814, had a tiny income, no education, and was self-taught, but discovered many new species, contributed to scientific journals, and was elected to the prestigious Linnean Society. Railway porter John Robertson made observations of sunspots, and slate-loader and dock-worker John Jones constructed a telescope – himself – powerful enough to observe the icecaps of Mars.[279]

Today we think of art galleries, poetry, opera, symphonies, choirs and other creations of Western culture to be exclusively for the elite and pretentious, but a century or two ago their main patrons were the working class. A 1918 survey of Sheffield found that many, if not most, working people to be patrons of museums, art galleries, theatres and operas.[280] A 1940 survey of students in working-class areas – again, people who made less money than the poorest inner-city families today, and who couldn't afford private schools --- found that 62 percent of boys and 84 percent of girls read poetry outside of school.[281]

The clubs inspired generations of Victorian workingmen to organise unions, understand the news, lobby for political causes, and even run for office. William Johnson left formal school at 12 but continued to educate himself through working-men's clubs and night courses, learning geology, physiology, French, German, chemistry, literature and many other subjects, working his way up to becoming a member of the British Parliament. J. Ramsay MacDonald was the illegitimate son of a farmhand and housemaid who joined a member of a mutual society in the 1800s and rose to become Prime Minster of the UK.[282]

When we picture, say, Victorian Britain, we inevitably take images from Sherlock Holmes adaptations and other film and television stories, or perhaps from history books. Almost no one has ever heard of the mutual

---

[278] *The Intellectual Life of the British Working Class,* 231.
[279] *The Intellectual Life of the British Working Class,* 70.
[280] *The Intellectual Life of the British Working Class,* 192.
[281] *The Intellectual Life of the British Working Class,* 232.
[282] *The Intellectual Life of the British Working Class,* 61.

improvement societies, though, as no movie or novel mentions them. Few movements in history have transformed the lives of so many people so successfully, and few have been so quickly forgotten.

***

Europeans took their love of education with them when they colonised the United States, and brought as many books with them as they could -- sometimes too many, as when one shipload of colonists hit a storm in 1586 and were so weighed down by books they had to throw them overboard. Even in the middle of a dangerous wilderness, colonists quickly built printing presses, libraries and colleges; just 16 years after the first Puritans stepped off the Mayflower and 15 years after they almost died of starvation, they founded Harvard University.

Booksellers and printers did a brisk business in every city and town, coffee-shops hosted vibrant debates on all manner of subjects, and wandering preachers paid their way through the countryside by selling books to rural homesteaders. They often read multiple languages as well, many books sold were in Ancient Greek and Latin, and newspapers were shipped in from various European countries – months late, of course, but still prized – in their native languages.

Thomas Paine's book *Common Sense* sold half a million copies in its first year, reaching 20 percent of the population – only the Harry Potter books come close today. And despite its homespun title, its long and complex sentences, subtle philosophical distinctions and references to John Milton and classical literature flummox many a college student today. Take this sample paragraph:

"It is repugnant to reason, to the universal order of things to all examples from former ages, to suppose, that this continent can longer remain subject to any external power. The most sanguine in Britain does not think so. The utmost stretch of human wisdom cannot, at this time, compass a plan short of separation, which can promise the continent even a year's security. Reconciliation is now a fallacious dream. Nature hath deserted the connexion, and Art cannot supply her place. For, as Milton wisely expresses, 'never can true reconcilement grow where wounds of deadly hate have pierced so deep.'"[283]

By 1831, French author Alexis de Toqueville wrote that "there is hardly a pioneer's hut which does not contain a few odd volumes of Shakespeare. I remember that I read the feudal play of Henry V for the first time in a loghouse."[284] English politician Richard Cobden, who toured the USA in 1835, estimated that there was six times more newspaper reading in the young America than in his own country – more than 1,200 newspapers publishing 90 million copies, in a country that had only 17 million inhabitants, implying that every adult read perhaps eight newspapers a day.[285]

Most striking about this level of education is that almost all of it happened without mass schooling; schools were small and few, and many children only went for a few years. People had a literate culture not because they went to school for more years than we do, but because they read almost constantly, at home and at work, to themselves and each other. They had a democracy not because a document said so, but because they debated what they had read in coffee shops and town halls and churches.

When I point this out to people today, most retort, "If they were so much better than we are, how could they oppress Native Americans? How could they keep slaves?" One could answer in a number of different ways; for example, that very few Americans in the 1700s or 1800s killed Native Americans or owned slaves; such things were done by a miniscule percentage of the population. Or that we don't need slaves, as we use fossil fuels, and leave the burden to our grandchildren. Or that we contribute to atrocities as well, but through corporations and governments that commit them far away on our behalf, leaving us with the illusion of moral superiority. The best answer, though, might be: *Why do you think those things ended?*

Paine's writings, and many less famous texts, galvanised a population of fence-sitters to join the Revolution; nothing like this would have happened if Americans were not a people who would buy and read such a

---

[283] *Common Sense.*
[284] *Democracy in America*, Alexis de Tocqueville, Chapter XIII.
[285] *The Political Writings of Richard Cobden* Volume 1, Volume 2 p. 90.

book enthusiastically and follow its sophisticated arguments. Lincoln spoke against slavery in masterful speeches, with extended sentences, expansive vocabulary and logical constructions. They were also, obviously, spoken, so his audience had to follow them by ear in real time – sometimes a long time, as the Lincoln-Douglas debates lasted for three hours, with each speaker lasting up to 90 minutes at a stretch. And the listeners were mostly frontier farmers.

The great social movements of the past few hundred years – the exaltation of universal human rights, the extension of voting to all people, the end of slavery and discrimination – succeeded only because people could, and did, read, write and debate these ideas. If slavery existed in the West today, it might not ever end.

When modern people list the benefits of the modern world, they often mention democracy and equality, literacy and education, human rights and individual freedom. All these things, however, were conceived and reached fruition long before the world modernised with fossil-fuel technology in the 1900s. Most of our great art, music, literature, philosophy and architecture appeared before then. They came from Western Civilisation -- and in the last century, as Western Civilisation declined and modern consumer culture took over, *all these things declined.*

***

As poor as the London ragmen and Western pioneers were, though, there was one thing they did not have to contend with – police or soldiers finding their meetings and imprisoning or murdering the teachers. That was the case in Ireland, however, where for three centuries children who wanted to learn the classics had to do so in hiding, in secret meeting-places in the woods or concealed by hedges – an underground network called the "hedge schools."

As mentioned, Ireland might have been the greatest centre of learning in the Middle Ages, and its monks kept Christianity and the classics alive when mainland Europe fell to wave after wave of barbarian invaders. For a thousand years the monasteries and convents taught Irish children – boys and girls, noble and common – as well as students from across Europe. Ireland also had another, parallel school system as well: the bardic schools, which "represented a highly developed system providing ... a university education."[286] The main subjects were music, poetry and storytelling – ancient epics that might date back to prehistoric times.

The first English colonists in Ireland seemed little different than native lords, but as England became more powerful and split away from the Catholic Church, all that changed. They looted the monasteries, expelled religious leaders, and instituted laws to persecute Catholics. Then, when the Irish tried to rebel in 1641, Oliver Cromwell's government massacred up to *one-tenth of the population* and transferred more than two-thirds of the country into English hands, evicting most landowners. They closed the Bardic schools and forced its teachers into hiding – they became the sennachai (SHEN-a-kee), the storytellers that we'll hear more about later.

The native Irish – specifically Catholics, but generally the same thing -- were banned from owning land, holding office, from educating themselves, and from attending religious services – in short, from doing anything but working for the English overlords. For a while Irish Catholics were forbidden from living in towns. Food and wealth were shipped to Britain, leaving little for the people even in the non-famine years. Ireland was the original plantation, the template for slave-owners in the American South. Anyone who fought back, or was caught teaching children, could be hanged, shot, or burned – more than one elder wrote about old trees that still had shackles of hanged prisoners in the branches.

Astonishingly, that didn't stop children across Ireland from going to school. Teachers held classes in woods or in the corners of fields, surrounded by hedges that hid them from passers-by, with one student on lookout. By winter schoolmasters stayed with local families and did farm work or – when they dared – teaching the children of their host.[287]

Mary Fogarty said her grandmother sent her sons to a hedge school, "for no self-respecting parent ... would let her children go to the charter-school provided by the government for Catholic children, where all the scholars were compulsorily educated to be Protestants. The hedge-school was held in isolated houses or out of doors in lonely and well-screened places where the risk of discovery and interruption was small and the

---

[286] *The Hedge Schools of Ireland*, 7.
[287] *Hedge Schools*, 35.

meeting place could if necessary be changed from day to day. The teachers were outlaws, nominally under the authority of the priest who was sometimes himself an outlaw ...The education they gave was good; they carried many of the scholars from the alphabet to Latin, Greek, mathematics and English literature. Some scholars took orders direct from the hedge-schools, and were known as hedge-priests."[288]

Latin and Greek were not merely their keys to education, but allowed them to communicate with others; in the 1600s Sir William Petty conversed in Latin with peasants living in Kerry, saying Latin fluency was "very frequent among the poorest Irish."[289] Also, as we saw, the classics are full of rebellion, and telling classical stories allowed Irish storytellers to embed coded messages of resistance, as black slaves in the American South used stories of the Israelites in Egypt.

Students would walk for hours barefoot to get to "school" while trying not to be seen. Paper was scarce, so they wrote on slates and even sand.[290] One person described a shelter literally made of mud, yet it held a hundred students, "a good number of them females."[291] Yet they produced playwrights like Oliver Goldsmith and political leaders like Daniel O'Donnell, who rose to prominence despite all the laws and prejudices they faced.

The teachers themselves were often master poets; when they arrived they often circulated a letter describing what they would teach, written in verse as proof of their skill. When two hedge schoolmasters both settled in the same village in County Armagh and the town wasn't big enough for the both of them, they circulated satirical verses about one another, like a modern trash-talking rap battle, until one conceded and moved on.[292]

Sometimes the English tried to set up Protestant schools as a way of "converting and civilising the natives," in the words of a petition to George II. Yet most of these schools were attached to factories and farms, and became sweatshops using child labour, teaching them nothing. In 1773 John Wesley visited the English school and found "nastiness and

---

[288] *The Farm by Lough Gur*, 8 - 9.
[289] *The Political Anatomy of Ireland*, 191.
[290] *Hedge Schools*, 48.
[291] *Hedge Schools*, 36.
[292] *Hedge Schools*, 79.

desolation" with not a single child well-clothed or educated. By contrast, he said, the children from hedge schools were "clean and wholesome" and better educated.[293]

The result of all this was that "generations of visitors to Ireland described ostlers, cowherds, post boys, barefoot servants and other low people displaying classical erudition."[294] A writer in 1776 said that he encountered a poor ragged boy was "well acquainted with the best Latin poets," while another in 1797 said that in the wild backwoods regions of Kerry, "many may be met with who are all good Latin Scholars ... Greek is also taught in the more mountainous parts by some itinerant teachers."[295][296] Another wrote in 1824 that "amongst the peasantry, classical learning is not uncommon; and a tattered Ovid; or Virgil may be found even in the hands of common labourers."[297] When William Makepeace Thackeray visited Cork in the 1840s he heard two barefoot boys discussing the Ptolemys.[298]

Rev. Alexander Ross, writing from Dungiven in 1814, said that "Even in the wildest districts it is not unusual to meet with good classical scholars, and there are several young mountaineers of the writer's acquaintance, whose knowledge and taste in the Latin poets might put to the blush many who have all the advantages of established schools and regular instruction."[299] Another observer wrote in 1808 that most men he knew "in the humblest occupations; [like] broom-sellers, [and] coachmen" who knew Latin and even Greek.[300] The poet Eoghan Rua O Suilleabhain was a farm labourer to a wealthy family, and when he offered to write down a message from a woman to the master of the house, the woman was sceptical that a common Irish farmhand could write. He responded by writing her four copies of the letter -- in English, Latin, Ancient Greek and Irish.[301]

---

[293] *Hedge Schools*, 29.
[294] Higgins, 2007.
[295] *A Description of Killarney*, 8.
[296] *Sketches of the Southern Counties of Ireland*, 151.
[297] *Researches in the South of Ireland*, p. 326.
[298] *Hedge Schools*, 56, 77.
[299] *A Statistical Account, or Parochial Survey of Ireland* Vol. I p. 314.
[300] Hedge Schools, 40.
[301] *Hedge Schools*, 104.

A German traveler visiting Ireland in the 1840s, just before the Famine, wrote about the men of rural and very poor County Kerry. "'Even the cow-boys and the poor farmers' sons know Latin there,' is a common saying." He shared a boat with a Kerryman who was reading an aged book written in the Irish language, stitched together of smaller and larger pages and gradually added to over the years. Some pages, he said, had been passed down from his father and grandfather, and some might have been older still, containing old Irish poems and a treatise by Aristotle, among other things. Such books were probably precious heirlooms, passed down through families at great risk through years of persecution.[302]

Nor did they just learn the classics. A Dr. Smith reported one man in poverty who knew "calculating the epacts, golden number, dominical number, the moon's phases, and even eclipses..."[303] Richard Lovell Edgeworth said that between the barefoot children of poor families and the sons of wealthy English families, it was usually the former who knew advanced mathematics.[304]

***

Once I began to read the classics as an adult, I suddenly understood many of the paintings in art galleries, as most of them reference scenes from Greek and Roman works. When I re-read the writings of Jefferson or Lincoln, I realise how much of their writings drew from the Greek and Romans of their education. I used to think the famous sculpture of George Washington in a Roman toga was a bit of pretentious glorification; now I understand, as Americans at the time surely did, that it was the opposite. It portrayed Washington as Cincinnatus, who peacefully stepped away from power – or as my daughter put it after reading Tolkien, "he put down the Ring."

The same was true until the mid-20th century; black-and-white films, newspaper articles, novels, popular songs and even children's rhymes referenced Horatius or Croesus, assuming everyone would understand the reference. Even when I casually read books or magazine articles written a

---

[302] Quane, 1951.
[303] Dr. Smith, *History of Kerry*, p. 67, 418.
[304] *Hedge Schools,* 60.

mere few generations ago, written not for professors but for regular mailmen, farmhands or construction workers, I'm struck by how liberally they are peppered with references to the classics, lost on anyone reading today.

Children across the Western world once began their Latin lessons by reading Julius Caesar's account of the wars in Gaul, beginning with the line "Gallia est omnis divisa in partes tres," or "All Gaul is divided into three parts." This was so well-known that the 1948 memoir *Cheaper by the Dozen* could begin, "Father, like Gaul, was divided into three parts," confident readers understood. Similar jokes appeared in short stories, Broadway musicals, even cartoons. Classics scholar Wes Callihan described a cartoon in *The New Yorker* magazine from decades ago: a pig teaching a classroom, writing on the chalkboard "Alligay estay nis-omay ivisaday in artespay restay." The cartoonist could safely assume everyone got the joke – it was a pig teaching Latin in Pig Latin. And in those days everyone would have understood, just as their ancestors might have for centuries. Today, just decades later, not one person in ten thousand would understand.[305]

Even if you only watched football, you were expected to know classical references; the Yale football cheer for decades was "Brek-ek-ex Ko-ax," which is nonsense unless you've read Aristophanes' *The Frogs*. The people chanting might well have been in college fraternities, which still use Ancient Greek letters, although they no longer remember why.

Even journals of Irish farmers have passages that are difficult to understand without having some knowledge of Greek and Roman works. Rynne whimsically describes his village as "scourged and whipped by every wind from west to east, by every fat-cheeked rogue that cares to puff: It is the blow-ball of Boreas, the fluff of Notus, the dead leaf of Eurus. And feather of Favonus, Argestes fag, the butt of Corus, and the tea-cup of the proverbial storm."[306]

In the mid-20th century, though, as modern Hollywood culture slashed through our real culture like a Mongol horde, references to the classics bled out with astonishing swiftness – all the more because so few have

---

[305] Wes Callihan, *Roman Roads Media*, Youtube.
[306] *Green Fields*, 79.

ever remarked on it. Not only do we no longer know any of the things for centuries we knew as a people, but *we no longer know that we once knew them.*

Not only are we no longer learning the classics, but when I bring up the subject I'm told that "Western culture" is code for "white supremacy." Yet ancient Greeks and Romans weren't necessarily "white;" Romans could be from anywhere in an empire that stretched from Scotland to Sudan. Some, like St. Augustine, were natives of Africa, and no doubt some had darker complexions, but unlike woke activists today, no Roman thought skin colour important enough to mention.

Of course the Ancient Greeks kept slaves, as did all cultures then and most since; concepts like freedom or democracy had to begin somewhere, and weren't going to emerge from an already-perfect society. But Greek "slaves" weren't like those of the American South in the early 1800s; a pamphleteer in fourth-century Athens wrote that it was difficult to tell slaves and freemen apart, for slaves could speak freely, own their own property and become wealthy. Even if you take that with a grain of salt, it is true that there were laws governing treatment of slaves – a step in the right direction found in few other places. As Hanson and Heath put it, all cultures had slavery, but only the Greeks had a word for "freedom."

Ancient Greek and Roman women might not have had all the privileges women enjoy in our culture, but they were the first cultures to tell stories from a female perspective, as in Euripides' *The Trojan Women,* or to write women's histories, like Plutarch's *On the Bravery of Women.* They had female poets like Sappho, scholars like Hypatia, and later historians like Anna Komnena.

Again, *how do you think these injustices were changed?* Reformers and rebels in all eras were inspired by the Greeks, whose very creation myth involves Zeus rebelling against Cronos and Prometheus rebelling against the gods to aid humans. Toussaint L'Overture read Plutarch's gripping account of Spartacus' slave uprising before he led the first successful slave rebellion in Haiti in 1791, while suffragettes demanding the right to vote in Britain recited Medea's speech. Martin Luther King quoted Ovid, Plato and St. Augustine. This is why Thomas Hobbes, when planning a totalitarian dictatorship, recommended that rulers ban Greek and Roman authors. This is why a British official complained in 1808 about the Irish secretly learning the classics, saying they "inculcate democracy, and a foolish hankering after undefined liberty."[307]

Occasionally I hear some activists pull out Gandhi's quip that Western civilisation "would be a good idea." Of course, Gandhi was commenting ruefully on actual oppression that our armchair activists can't fathom, and of course he was just joking – he read and cited Homer, Socrates, Aesop, Plato, and many others, and actually circulated a Gujarati translation of Plato's *Apology* to inspire his countrymen to rise against their oppressors.

Perhaps this hostility comes from our current reverence for "diversity," and it's true that the Western canon by definition didn't include Indian, Chinese or African writings. Yet woke activists today are not volunteering to learn the Guru Grunth Sahib or the Annalects; rather, they have abandoned any memory of their own culture without embracing any other, save that of Hollywood franchises.

A people whose culture is of the moment, who honour no traditions, are worse than the Visigoths who sacked Rome, and we have few people to preserve these ideas as the Irish monks did. Our society today is coasting on the fumes of the intellectual inquiry of centuries past, severed from the culture that made such inquiry possible and desirable. Culturally, we are already a post-apocalyptic society; our physical infrastructure is still running on inertia, like a cartoon character running off a cliff and not yet looking down.

If you want proof, go to any university, any courthouse, any building or statue from a previous century, and look at the inscriptions over the doors or the writing on the plaques; they will typically have been engraved in Latin, not as a pretentious affectation to keep people out, but a way of letting everyone in, by using the universal language of learning.

Today we are in the position we falsely ascribe to medieval peasants, of seeing these languages as obscure and magical, used to create the quasi-Latin spells of Harry Potter wizards. A century or two ago our scientific and legal language, civic mottos and inscriptions, were not arcane

---

[307] *Letter to the Board of Education, in Reports from the Commissioners to the Board of Education of Ireland, Reports on Free Schools of Royal Foundation,1813, p.109; Stanford, Classical Tradition, 1986, c.215.*

incantations but direct messages to a public that, at the time, could read them, and cared what they said.

We are the science-fiction survivors trying to read engravings that no longer make any sense to us – only our monuments have not yet crumbled, and we are unaware that the barbarians are us.

Chapter Seven

Visiting

Sitting alone in our cars, our cubicles and in front of our screens, it's almost impossible for us in the modern world to imagine how communal and intimate virtually all human life used to be until historically yesterday. Tribal cultures live in small groups in a world with few strangers, and so did all our ancestors, even in villages and cities, for thousands of generations.

In Dublin's poorest areas "You had this great community ... you weren't isolated and you weren't afraid because there was somebody beside you," John Gallagher said. "[Families] slept together; it was this great feeling of unity."[308]

Living uprooted as most of us do, spending our lives adrift on a sea of strangers and rarely seeing loved ones, was in most cultures the worst punishment. Ancient Greeks chose death over exile, and the Israelites grieved to be strangers in a strange land. International law today condemns solitary confinement as literal torture, but that is how many of us spend our lives, alone even in a crowd.

In every society, of course, there were young people who left to seek work or adventure, but even that was often seen as a kind of death. When a son or daughter left for America seeking work, everyone held an "American wake," a funereal celebration, as though the departing were already departed.

Men who went to sea or to war or to a monastery found a new family, a "brotherhood" like the real brothers they might have left. Even today, when people look back at the best times of their lives, it's usually things

---

[308] *Dublin Tenement Life,* 133.

like camp or college, when they were thrown together into the same kind of closeness, and briefly felt as humans should.

Consider for a moment what it means to be social – and as someone on the autism spectrum, I have had to pay conscious attention to a process that most find intuitive. When someone speaks to us, we are forced out of the hall of mirrors in our own mind by the alarming presence of another, demanding something of us. As people rarely state flatly their thought processes and intentions, their words force us to winkle out their true motivations, to imagine ourselves through alien eyes. We have to stretch beyond ourselves, and create a new living thing – a relationship – in the space between us.

Relationships are more than the ratio of the people involved, but create something unlike any of the ingredients, as the green gas chlorine and soft metal sodium combine to become salt. We all know couples who were magical together but not apart, songwriters who worked best as a team, or elderly people who lost the will to live after their spouse – and their relationship – died. Different people bring out different things in us, our identities subtly reshape to fit them, and even when they are gone their imprints remain. As the number of people in a group increases, the number of relationships increases more, and a community is born, with its own personality different than the people who comprise it.[309]

Those relationships can also demand much of us, which is why we find it so easy to flee from them into screens. They force us to be kind when we don't feel like it and to put ourselves in the place of others; that is, to practice the qualities that separate humans from other animals, and thus become full human beings. They make us endure the quirky habits of others long enough to build an immunity to them, and perhaps even appreciate them. We have all known people who hated each other at first and then became friends or romantic partners, and when loved ones pass out of this life, we have all fondly remembered the eccentricities that might have once annoyed us. Our modern world of earbuds and phones, of social

---

[309] If the number of people in a group is N, the number of relationships is $[N \times (N-1)] / 2$, so three people mean three relationships, but four people mean six relationships, five people mean 10 relationships, 10 people mean 45 relationships and 150 people – Dunbar's number – mean 11,175 relationships.

media and online chats, by contrast, lets us unfriend and shut out anyone as easily as changing a channel, filtering out any encounter that would force us to grow up.

In traditional villages, the "close-knit rural community ... was an extension of our home," Taylor said. "... The old were never alone as the neighbours joined hands around them and the young, too, were included in the circle. As in every group of individuals, all had their own idiosyncrasies, and we as children were educated in human awareness by the close association with many people." Some elders said that when they visited cousins in a different village, it felt bizarre it was not to know the people you pass on the road.

"People dropped in every night of the week, there would be someone sitting around the fire, drinking tea, telling stories," Kevin Kealy said. "You have to remember in those days there was no telephone, no radios, no telly. No nothing, as they used to say. But we were happy as Larry."[310]

When everyone knew and needed each other, your well-being became everyone's business. "There were only about thirty people living in our village so there were no secrets, everyone knew everything about each other," Aine Aherne said. "often out for a walk we would see one or two people in the distance ... [and] when they came near, and after the first greeting, the next question was 'Where are you going?'"[311]

If this lack of privacy bothers you, though, consider what people today show of themselves to the world on social media, displaying their fetishes and outbursts in ways that degrade both the exhibitionist and the audience. When people knew that you worked hard, paid back favours, or told a good story, they knew what they should know about you, and didn't know what they shouldn't.

Since they all grew up together, they were literally familiar with each other; they were family, and lived without the invisible walls and calluses we need surrounded by strangers. "Neighbours came to our house and we went to theirs as freely as the birds flew across the sky; invitations were unheard of and welcomes unquestioned," Alice Taylor said.[312] My

---

[310] *Growing Up with Ireland*, 61.
[311] *No Shoes in Summer*, 23.
[312] *To School Through the Fields*, 17.

neighbour Peter remembered that "people would just leave their key in the door. Neighbours would just come in ... it was a much more relaxed society then, with more neighbourliness and people looking out for each other and so on. And we've lost that."

A world without strangers is a difficult world to deceive, as Nazis found trying to infiltrate neutral Ireland in World War II. According to one of my neighbours, one parachuted in and went to the nearest town with a train station, not realising the rail line had closed down. The garda came out right away and -- before locking him up -- brought him to the local pub and asked, "do you have a pint for Heinz, who's just dropped in to see us?"

As poor as people were, "the inner city was great," said former garda Paddy Casey. "You just went along – one man walking the beat then – and at that time people spoke to you. And there were street traders and paper sellers and buskers on the street playing banjos and singing songs and selling knick-knacks. And we had balladeers, fellas writing ballads and getting them printed in a sort of cheap printing house and selling them for a penny or two pence each ..."[313]

On weekends or holidays, my neighbour Christy said, families from the neighbourhood took the bus to the seaside or park together. Incredible as it sounds, Gene Kerrigan said some of these were "mystery buses" that refused to say where they were going; the destination was somewhere relaxing for the day, and other than that it was kept a surprise. Wherever they ended up, he said, they usually had a great day, and "on the way home in the dark everyone sang ... and someone took off their cap and went up and down the aisles, collecting tips for the driver."[314]

City streets were packed with neighbours, as people lived so much of their lives outdoors. "Before television became the mental disease it is today, imprisoning people in their homes and softening their brains, people visited each other more often, to chat, play cards, tell stories and have a sing-song," Boland said. "Groups of friends going walking would sometimes link arms and sing songs as they walked along. .... sometimes

---

[313] *Dublin Tenement Life,* 156.
[314] *Another Country,* 79.

the boys would try to get on chatting terms with passing groups of girls, out for an evening's walk."[315]

When Susan O'Driscoll's family got the neighbourhood's first radio "the family two doors down would send us in to tell my mother to turn the horn out the door so they could hear it – all doors were open at that time, and one thing I know, we never had a key to our front door. You could go in anytime, so could breadmen, milkmen and friends. I wonder will we ever see those times again. It's so sad we have to lock our doors now, even if we go across the road."[316]

"Fitzwilliam Street and Merrion Square were always lovely places and full of life when I was a kid," Deirdre Kelly said. "There were families in all the houses. I often remember going down Fitzwilliam Street on a Christmas and all the Christmas trees in the windows and just full of life and people going in and out of all the doors. And now ... there's no lights in the windows because it's all offices. It's like a tunnel of darkness. It's dead as can be."[317]

***

When I describe this world to modern audiences, they often say I am romanticising a time of desperate poverty, especially in Ireland – and it is absolutely true that people then lived on a fraction as much money as people do now. Dubliners, especially, lived in a world many of us would find hellish – whole families living in one room, sleeping on beds of straw, taking turns eating off a single plate, wearing someone else's cast-off clothes or sewing their own from flour bags, using an outhouse behind the building.

Yet elder after elder, in my interviews and their memoirs, all told the same story; whatever the injustices of the world, they got by because they "shared everything with one another," Elizabeth Murphy said. "Same with births, deaths and marriages, they all came. Everybody helped." Neighbours cared for each other when sick, helped each other on jobs, and gave each other food and clothing. When they died, as we will see, local

---

[315] *Tales from a City Farmyard*, 112.
[316] *No Shoes in Summer*, 47.
[317] *Dublin Voices*, 109.

women prepared the body and local men carried it to the grave. Local pubs often helped pay for the funerals of their longtime patrons. "See, the way it was, if one was in sorrow, we were all in sorrow," she said. "Everybody knew everybody else. It was a *community*."[318]

Patrick Boland remembered that his parents made extra food to distribute around the neighbourhood. "But my parents were not alone in their concern for others," he said. "Other people on the street, even those in poor circumstances themselves, made sure no one was forgotten or neglected. Gosh, how times have changed."[319]

Surprisingly, most of the former slum urchins missed their old neighbourhoods ---not the poverty itself, but the camaraderie and support. "It was a hard life," Murphy said, "but I wish I was back in it again, in the tenement again," she said. "When they started tearing the old tenements down it was like tearing us apart. It tore me apart. We were all one family, all close. We all helped one another. If I had a tenement house now I'd go back and live in it ... yes, I would."[320]

Father Michael Reidy, who worked among the Dublin poor, remembered ... and remembers their "tremendous resilience and spirit ... they *helped* one another, they were great neighbours."[321] Paddy Casey, a policeman in Dublin's roughest neighbourhoods in the 1940s, said they were "extraordinarily happy for people who were so savagely poor. They had a great community spirit and code of honour among themselves... That was the extraordinary thing, they were *fulfilled*."[322]

A number of elders thought the poverty of the time gave people a sense of solidarity, and that once the country became wealthy, that spirit disappeared. "It's a thing that happens when people are together in privation," my neighbour Mary told me. "A community spirit grows, as grew in England during the war. People really pulled together; the traditional English reserve disappeared, and people talked to each other buses, perfect strangers helping each other. It digs into some deep human

---

[318] *Dublin Tenement Life*, 90.
[319] *Tales from a City Farmyard*, 15.
[320] *Dublin Tenement Life*, 91.
[321] *Dublin Tenement Life*, 25.
[322] *Dublin Tenement Life*, 26.

thing. Whereas once there is wealth, there is automatically separation and gradation."

"...The funny thing is people were happier, in a way because the human connection was so heartfelt and so strong," she said. "This is a secret thing of the human psyche; we need real relationships, with other people."

According to many of my modern friends, all our ancestors lived in oppressive conformity, filled with hatred for anyone different than themselves. Actual elders who remember the past, moreover, say the opposite; people then were allowed to be themselves in a way they no longer are. "We live in an age of conformity, compared to when I was growing up, strange as that might seem," Patrick Boland said. "To step out of line these days, whether by expressing a controversial viewpoint, or doing something silly at the Christmas Party, you get tagged and pigeon-holed, in a way that can affect your promotion prospects or even your job."[323]

Many elders fondly remembered the eccentrics in their community; old Dublin shops still display photos of "Bang-Bang," a character who jokingly pointed a house key at people and pretended to shoot them; adults usually ignored him and the children joyously shot back. Maire Walsh remembered three elderly sisters who lived in a cottage by themselves and made all their own clothes, wearing heather for earrings, and looked like time travellers from a different era.

Singer Maura O'Connell, speaking on RTE radio, remembered newspaper delivery man Michael Tierney in County Clare, who dressed in women's clothes. Since he was otherwise a respectable neighbour, the locals regarded him with bemused affection as the local eccentric – probably the right response then and now.

Because all human societies have differences, they all have conflicts, and at the time my elder friends were growing up Ireland seemed like it should have more than most; it had just been through a revolution that overthrew centuries of British rule, and when that was done a civil war broke out among the revolutionary factions. Occasionally these tensions showed up in everyday life; Boland remembers one neighbour who

---

[323] *Tales From a City Farmyard*, 160.

continued to fly the British flag, to the distaste of most local families. He remembered giving her one of his hen's eggs, not telling her that it was one the hen had laid in the toilet. She thanked him and in exchange gave him a few chocolate pieces, not telling him they were laxatives. [324]

The same neighbours who bickered, however, also "told stories, played cards, drank endless cups of tea, and discussed and argued over nearly every subject under the sun. But when the arguments were over, the slates were wiped clean, and there were no hard feelings."

***

Unbelievable as it sounds today, most areas had a house "where all travellers were welcomed with open arms," all year long, John Lyon said. These "rambling houses," they were simply local homes known to everyone as the place for travellers to ask for a place to sleep. Anyone who opened the door would get room and board – not for money, but in exchange for singing songs or telling stories to entertain everyone else staying there.

My neighbour Tony Carr remembered his neighbour's rambling house, which welcomed distinguished visitors from the city and wandering homeless alike. "You could meet a tramp, a millionaire and a professor all together and Eileen had the same time for them all. There was no class distinction ...." [325]

Some were itinerant workers or evicted families wandered the roads, and "it always amazed me how the farmers' wives were able to give alms to up to three travellers a day in very bad times; if it was the last bite in the house, they would share it with them," John Lyon said. "The people were poor but honest and God-fearing, and the travellers made many a bad winter's night enjoyable for them with their stories and songs." [326]

My native USA, a vast and mobile nation of the uprooted, might never have had that degree of faith in complete strangers, but Americans used to be much more trusting as well. Some of my countrymen are old enough to remember when hitch-hiking and picking up hitch-hikers was familiar to

---

[324] *Tales from a City Farmyard*, 137.
[325] *Some Time to Kill*, 123.
[326] *Joy of my Boyhood Years*, 26.

everyone. Today both would be regarded as extremely hazardous, and perhaps rightly so; as hitch-hiking stopped being normal, the normal stopped hitch-hiking.

An episode of *The Twilight Zone* made in the early 1960s showed a married couple waking up in a strange house, remembering only that they were driving home from a party the night before. They conclude that they must have fallen asleep at the wheel, and someone must have found them and put them to bed in his own house. The inevitable twist – alien abduction –doesn't sound strange to us, as we've had decades of that. What is remarkable to us is the assumption that some stranger would do that.

Some Americans might remember when it was common for neighbours to visit each other and trade things – to "borrow a cup of sugar" in a common saying. There is a lost civilisation buried in such phrases. They reveal that people cooked for themselves using simple ingredients, walked around neighbourhoods without fear, and knew their neighbours well enough to feel comfortable asking for such things.

We can see some of this lost world through old black-and-white movies like *Our Town* or *Marty* or *An Apartment for Peggy*, which – while they were works of fiction – were set in the kinds of close communities audiences would have recognised as their own. Or, again, we can see it in American comic strips: In *Blondie* Dagwood stumbles out sleepily to meet his carpooling co-workers just as many Americans did decades ago. He chats to the local diner cook like an old friend, something few of us could do today with the teenagers at a McDonalds.

If you only had old movies and comics to go on, you might dismiss these as fantastical conceits, like the way people burst into song in musicals. Yet in his excellent book *Bowling Alone*, sociologist Robert Putnam used dozens of polls, surveys, diaries and other statistics to back up their depiction of what American life used to be, a culture rich with neighbourhood gatherings, card games, fraternal lodges, dinner parties, bowling leagues, PTA meetings, political caucuses, town bands, Boy Scouts and many other groups. This, by the way, was true for *both genders and all races;* even where ethnic groups were legally separated into different neighbourhoods, each group created their own social network and trusting society.

A world where people knew and trusted their neighbours, whether in Ireland or the USA, is a world where everyone could relax their guard a little. As Putnam put it, life expectancy itself is greater in more trusting and trustworthy communities, perhaps because background stress of everyday interactions is reduced. None of us notices all the times that we *don't* fear the person walking behind us at night, or don't have to count our change, or don't tense up when neighbourhood kids walk by, but millions of such moments add up to an immeasurably better life.

People who trust those around them, in turn, are more likely to volunteer in the community, participate in politics and local organisations, give blood more frequently, and are less likely to cheat – even in private – on tax and employment forms.[327] They are also more likely to come to the aid of people in need, as George Bailey's neighbours did in *It's a Wonderful Life*.

Or take board games from a century ago. If you've played Monopoly, you might remember the "Community Chest" square that gives you money when you land on it. At the time the game was invented, however, those were real funds for neighbours who had fallen on hard times; an estimated 1,318 communities had them in 1950, covering 57 percent of the US population.[328]

* * *

Just as people gathered in "mutual-improvement societies" for education and debate, so too did they gather in fraternal orders – to some extent in Ireland and Britain, but nowhere more than in the USA. Most people have heard of the Freemasons as the inexplicable target of conspiracy theorists, or parodied as the Stonecutters on *The Simpsons*, but there were dozens of similar organisations, each with hundreds or thousands of chapters in almost every town and neighbourhood.

They included the Elk, the Odd Fellows, the Knights of Pythias, the Knights of Columbus, and such sadly extinct and magnificent-sounding

---

[327] Putnam, 137.
[328] "Philanthropic Giving," *Social Work,* 1951.

organisations like the Prudent Patricians of Pompeii, the Modern Aztecs, and the League of Friendship of the Supreme Mechanical Order of the Sun. They took many forms -- quasi-religious orders, paramilitary groups, social clubs, health funds, college funds, unions, co-operatives, and grass-roots political organisations, many of these at the same time.

Each lodge member contributed a small amount of money each week to a fund, and when any member took sick, the lodge typically gave them sick pay to cover the loss of employment. According to John Michael Greer, lodges often hired a doctor or nurse to check up on all its members; called "lodge trade," it offered work for thousands of medical professionals, and unlike our modern medical system, it was affordable and gave patients a say in their own care. When a member died, the organisation often paid for the funeral and perhaps a pension for the widow(er) and children. Many did more than that; a lodge called the Knights of Labour evolved into the first labour union.

As recently as the mid-20th-century a large minority, if not a majority of Americans, were members of these organisations – again, *of both genders and all races*. And while they are called "fraternal," many existed solely for women and were run by women, some independent of any men's organisation.

This doesn't even include the PTA, Lyceums, Chataquas, Temperance Societies, Agricultural Societies, Philosophical societies, educational institutes, book circles and church clubs. These organisations were deeply woven into community life for generations, and their sudden and astonishing decline after the 1960s has been rarely commented on or even noticed.

* * *

Almost everything else declined in my native country around the same time. Putnam cited numerous surveys demonstrating that between the 1960s and 1990s – the exact years varied by survey – the time Americans spent socialising fell by a third. The number of Americans working in a community organisation fell by half. Union membership fell by two-thirds. Entertaining neighbours at home fell by 50 percent. Picnics declined 60 percent.[329]

Pastimes disappeared as well. In the 1940s more Americans owned decks of cards than radios or telephones, and as recently as the 1970s 40 percent played with friends at least once a month. Now card games are mainly played by the elderly; in 1999 the average age of players was 64.[330] Membership in bowling leagues fell by 75 percent.[331] Playing a musical instrument fell by half.[332]

In short, take almost any normal thing your great-grandparents used to do outside of work – go on, pick one. Whatever it is has almost disappeared. *All forms of human interaction*, the thing our species needs to stay sane and human, had plummeted when Putnam wrote his book in 2000; since then, they have continued their freefall toward zero.

In the USA, at least, we are working longer hours, often alone in cubicles. Americans are also spending more of their day commuting – usually alone, unlike Dagwood – and every 10 minutes on the road cuts your involvement in the community by ten percent, according to Putnam.[333] We have also become used to driving everywhere, often living in areas that require a car, so neighbours see each other only as dim shadows inside a chassis.

If Putnam, a left-wing sociologist, supplies the statistics, conservative Christian Anthony Esolen vividly describes the effects in his 2017 book *Out of the Ashes*. Walking through an American town, Esolen wrote, "here is a state park that used to be thronged with people on a sunny weekend.... You don't want to go there now. The nervous man in the parking lot is waiting for an assignation that has to do with either of two things. One of them is drugs. The other one isn't."

"... here is a room in a Catholic High school. Its closet is filled with books on German and French. They have not been opened in 40 years.... here is a church sold off to people who have turned it into a mattress warehouse. Here is a sandlot where boys used to play baseball without

---

[329] *Bowling Alone*, 100.
[330] *Bowling Alone*, 104.
[331] *Bowling Alone*, 108.
[332] *Bowling Alone*, 115.
[333] *Bowling Alone*, 213.

adult supervision. You would never know that now.... here is what used to be the city's vocational high school, for boys who wanted to learn a trade. Here is the American Legion hall, the terminus for the town's grand Memorial Day parade. There has not been a parade in 50 years. This is a bandstand, for what used to be the town band. There is no town band. This is what used to be a parish hall, built by a priest with his own family money... this is a ball-field, where the town's baseball team – men, not boys – used to play against teams from other towns. There is no team. There aren't really any towns, either, if a town implies a community life."[334]

Ireland has not transformed as completely, but is moving in the same direction; where each house once had a large family, my neighbour Jack said, "now we are the only old family left here ...We don't know any of those people; everyone gets up in the morning, gets into a car and is away, and that's the way it works now. There's no communication whatsoever."

If we know little about each other as neighbours, we know too much about each other on social media. The elders I talked to said Ireland certainly had gossip; in Dublin "the Mammies and Grannies were also watching, but from behind their lace curtains, sometimes taking their meals there for fear of missing out on some street activity," Boland said.[335] In traditional communities, though, gossip has a function; it allowed women to let each other know who was having problems or not pulling their weight. And when everyone had to get along, gossipers themselves had to be judicious and discreet.

None of our forebears had to deal with the situation today, where online we can over-share, steal, lie, abuse and make hyperbolic statements in ways that few people did when they had to look each other in the eye and possibly get punched. None ever faced the turbocharged gossip machine of social media, where anyone can take a photo or record you and spread it to millions of people in an instant, in a world where everyone can pile on with no consequences.

People will still crave human contact, of course, but these days we are more likely to hire pretend friends. In the 1940s, as Ronald Dworkin

---

[334] *Out of the Ashes*, 9.
[335] *Tales from a City Farmyard*, 113.

pointed out, the USA had 2,500 clinical psychologists, 30,000 social workers, and fewer than 500 marriage and family therapists. By 2000, the country had 94,000 psychologists and psychotherapists, 592,000 social workers, 50,000 marriage and family therapists, 325,000 mental-health and substance-abuse counsellors, and 30,000 life coaches. Put together it's a more than 33,000 percent increase, a mass outsourcing of decency, alongside a similar surge in the proportion of police, security guards, judges and lawyers for all the times decency fails us.[336]

* * *

We are told that poverty causes crime, and looking around American cities that seems to be true. Yet Irish decades ago made only a fraction of the income of inner-city Americans today, so you'd think the crime would be unimaginably high.

In fact, murder was rare – often single-digit numbers for the whole country, as opposed to 80 murders in 2022 -- one-fourth the rate of Ireland today, one-fortieth that of the USA, and one-540th that of the inner-city neighbourhood near where I grew up in Missouri.

In rural areas, crime of any kind was rare, both according to official statistics and the memories of people who lived there. "In Ireland you left the doors open," said my neighbour Mary, in a sentence echoed by many others. "We couldn't imagine locking the door, or being afraid – you just couldn't imagine it. Even in Dublin."

Many doors didn't even have locks, as no one ever needed them; one apparently hardy soul named James McPat, interviewed for Irish radio, left his front door wide open in all weathers for thirty years.[337] "There was just an ethos; people just weren't that way," my neighbour Mary said. "Ireland was virtually crime-free ... It would be absolutely astonishing to people today."

Occasionally rural families made their own poitin (pa-CHEEN), or moonshine; a number of local families made it and hid it when the garda came by. When they transported jugs from house to house, Walter Love said, they inserted coded messages about their schedule in the songs they

---

[336] Dworkin, 2010.
[337] "The Curious Ear: Blue Door," RTE documsntary (2010).

sang at the pub.[338] Police often had a "need to know" attitude about local naughtiness; at dances the police were required to make an appearance and ask if admission was being charged, the organisers duly said no, and everyone could happily go their separate ways.[339]

Even in the poorest areas of Dublin crime was unthinkably low; Kevin Kearney, in his generally grim anthology *Dublin Tenement Life*, noted that "robberies, vandalism, muggings and sexual crimes were virtually unknown. Tenement doors were left unlocked, even open, and people walked the streets at all hours without fear of violation."[340]

"The roadside was cluttered with bicycles and your bike could have been left there for a week [unlocked] and it'd still be there when you went back," Gerry Rafferty said.[341][342] Delaney's Bike Shop in Dublin even let prospective buyers take their bicycles for test drives, assuming – correctly – that no one would ever steal one. In an interview with Irish radio, the owner said that one girl was gone for five hours, as she had to ride home and get permission from her mother to buy the bicycle, and then rode back and bought it.

Even the poorest of Dubliners "had a code of honour among themselves and were extremely religious," said former gardai Paddy Casey, adding that rape was "non-existent," and that most fights were simply between drunken men outside a pub, giving everyone in the neighbourhood a free show.[343] "Everyone was out walking on every corner, and no one ever felt afraid," people told me again and again.

All this might sound strange if you read Irish newspapers from the era, which played up the violent activities of the so-called "Animal Gangs." The drama around these gangs clearly sold a lot of papers and are still fondly remembered – and fictionalised in television series like *Peaky Blinders*. But the real groups were nowhere as violent as their small-screen counterparts, and nothing like the heavily armed and drug-dealing gangsters of today. Across 20 years or so only one person died in their

---

[338] *Times of Our Lives.*
[339] *Irish Country Childhood*, 67.
[340] *Dublin Tenement Life*, 43.
[341] *And the Band Played On*, 105.
[342] *Dublin Voices*, 61.
[343] *Dublin Tenement Life*, 43.

brawls; in my city of St. Louis, the same size as Dublin, 4,000 people were murdered in the last 20 years.

According to everyone who remembered them, the animal gangs rarely used anything other than their fists, and only members of other gangs. They mostly sold newspapers by day and went to dance halls and pubs at night, or – implausible as it sounds -- sang in choirs on streetcorners. "They were great harmonisers," said former gang member Timmy Kirwan. "People'd be looking out their windows all night looking at them and listening to them."

Their more organised actions, though, made them local heroes. When the boys weren't making enough money selling Irish Republican Army newspapers, they marched into IRA meetings demanding better terms, like employees lobbying for a union. When the battle-hardened IRA men tried to physically throw them out, the boys – teenagers and schoolchildren – stood their ground and brawled, were accused of "behaving like animals," and the name stuck.

"They were Robin Hoods in the neighbourhood!" Kirwan said. "...we'd no food or nothing. So they went in and robbed a butcher's shop and took two cows off the hook and cut the cow up in pieces and delivered it to all the people at night-time..."

When poor families couldn't pay their rent and the sheriff came to evict them into the street, "all of the sudden people got together. And when the sheriff used to come then the animal gang used to come in with them ... So you had hand-to-hand fighting up and down the streets and people'd stand beside the animal gang and throw water and all (from windows). And then the sheriffs wouldn't go back to that area for a while! And that gave them time to collect money for that woman or family ..."[344]

When no poor tenants were being evicted, though, most police walked a regular beat in a community and had a good relationship with residents. Former gang members like Johnny Campbell spoke glowlingly of certain officers, even ones that had arrested them. Officer Christy Byrne walked the Dublin tenements every day, Campbell said, and understood that young men needed to test their limits; when he saw young men roughhousing, he offered to box them himself, saying he would arrest them

---

[344] *Dublin Tenement Life*, 57.

only if he won. Byrne always won the fights, according to Campbell – and while he arrested some of the gang members, they had immense respect for him.[345]

All of these, however, were extraordinary situations, far removed from the everyday lives of most Irish, who – according to every elder I talked to – lived with a sense of safety that everyone has lost, and that few people remember once existed.

Only when Ireland's traditional culture has been supplanted by modern pop culture, and its economy plugged into a global network of money and debt, did the crime rate rise and people feel in danger. Modernising increased the amount of wealth, something our culture talks about exclusively as a benefit while ignoring the cost; more wealth means more possessions, making crime profitable. Second, it means more money for people to engage in their worst impulses; when consumerism took over the West in the late 20th century, drugs and other addictions followed. Third, going modern meant becoming more mobile and uprooted, spending more time commuting and staring at screens, until few neighbours knew or cared about each other.

In *The Cow Book*, his memoir of returning to his family farm in Longford, John Connelly wrote that "...in recent weeks I have heard news of several cattle raids in the area. It is the worst crime we farmers can imagine ... People no longer feel safe in their homes, for gangs of thieves roam the once-quiet countryside. I do not know a farmer without a gun, for the police are fewer and we are all alone. In the last three years, over 10,000 cattle have been stolen."

"In these lawless days, we are perhaps closer to the Wild West; we too have frontiers, there are cowboys here, and rogues and villains. We know a local man who shot two thieves that broke into his property. He is not ashamed of it, for they were armed too. The police are mostly absent, so men have taken things into their own hands, and each family is now an outpost. These times have made the country people harder."[346]

* * *

---

[345] *Dublin Tenement Life*, 77.
[346] *The Cow Book*, 114.

When young Harry Mullery minded his parents' Dublin bakery in the 1950s, he often gazed out the front window at the young nurses waiting for the bus. When one particularly caught his longing eye, he sent his friend Patrick Boland to deliver them a fresh-baked roll with a message, "Tell her Harry loves her." Once, Patrick wrote decades later, one sent back a love message of her own. Sometimes courtship was just that simple.

Sometimes there were complications, of course – as he continued to slip notes between them, Boland once gave it to the wrong person, an old woman with a moustache, and when she looked around for the sender Harry had to hide behind the bakery counter. Another time he carried a love note from Harry and a racing tip from a bookie, and got the two notes confused.

Courtship was easier then, elders tell me, because it grew out of the socialising that people did every day. "Groups of friends going walking would sometimes link arms and sing songs as they walked along. .... sometimes the boys would try to get on chatting terms with passing groups of girls, out for an evening's walk."[347] Or young priests – back when there were young priests – organised neighbourhood dances, which Christy said allowed young people to mingle without getting into trouble they would later regret.

"At that time the girls and boys growing up was really innocent," May Hanaphy said. "... All we ever done to a fella when we were young was rob their caps. If you fancied a fella you robbed his cap and you ran and he ran after you. There was an awful lot of chasing done."[348]

In the 1940s, Rafferty said, "if you had a date with a girl you agreed on a place along the road to meet, or being bolder, ventured to within whistling distance of the house."[349] Parents kept a watchful eye on their conduct, and everyone in town knew who had been courting and whispered when people had been dragging it on and should just get married.

Sometimes, of course, people needed a little help; when teams of workmen strung Ireland's first electric cables through a village they found

---

[347] *Tales from a City Farmyard*, 112.
[348] *Dublin Tenement Life*, 218.
[349] *And The Band Played On*, 95.

that the barman at the pub – handsome but shy -- secretly adored a local lady. The workmen sought out the lady, and through mutual friends found that she, too, loved the barman. In a plot out of a romantic comedy, all the workers conspired to bring them together on a date; they were married soon after, and the barman "was the proudest man in the world the day they tied the knot."[350]

Neighbours often conspired to get unmarried people together, Ann Gardinier said. One woman from the area, Bridie, had moved away for work years ago, but had returned to look after her aging mother, and was "on the wrong side of forty." Her brother Tom went to Gardinier's father, handed him a pack of cigarettes and asked, "Would you have any fellow over your way that would suit our Bridie?"

Ann's father brought the word to local bachelor Mossie Maloney, and arranged for the two to meet. When they hit it off, "the dowry fixed and a date set," and Bridie was "well-pleased with her new man." Mossie's cottage definitely looked like a single man lived there, and when she saw the state of the place, Bridie said "'There's work to be done here, Mossie' ... taking off her wedding finery and knuckling down to business." The two were "close as two peas in a pod and lived and worked happily side by side" for thirty-odd years.[351]

Modern people recoil at the thought of arranged marriages, and of course no man or woman should be forced to marry against their will. Yet arranging could simply be match-making, as we would use dating apps. Surprisingly, studies have found that such marriages do better in the long run than marriages based on romantic love. In one Indian study of 50 couples, half from "love marriages" and half from arranged marriages, psychologists Usha Gupta and Pushpa Singh found that love – as far as survey responses can measure – continued to increase over time in arranged marriages and decrease in love marriages.[352]

Paul Yelsma and Kuriakose Athappilly found the same result in a comparison of Indian and American couples; the Indians in arranged marriages reported being happier than either Indians or Americans in love

---

[350] *Then There Was Light*, 28.
[351] *The House Remembers*, 151 - 154.
[352] Gupta 1982.

marriages.[353] In a January 2013 study, "How Love Emerges in Arranged Marriages," psychologist Robert Epstein found that when parents and other interested parties are involved in a relationship from the beginning, they can do "background checks" on the prospective mate, looking at them more objectively than two young and hormonal people can.[354]

In our modern culture, when elderly couples are still together after fifty years, we assume it's because fifty years ago, they fell in love. We don't consider that perhaps they are in love because they've been together for fifty years.

***

No aspect of traditional cultures draws more attention or generates more rage than the relationship between men and women. According to most modern people I talk to, all women were slaves until recently, beaten and sexually harassed constantly. Anyone who defends any part of traditional life is accused of trying to "turn back the clock" to a time when that was all most women knew.

Yet almost everything I heard or read from my neighbours was the opposite. Everyone insisted that courtships were innocent, sexual crime was rare, and couples not only stayed together, but were happy. In volumes of private letters between Irish women of all classes, writing to each other privately over centuries, I read barely a mention of violence or abuse or catcalling.

Of course, those things surely happened, and of course these are the memories of elderly people, who might have a rosy view of their youth. You could argue that such things were kept private, only to be revealed later, like the Church's sexual scandals. You could argue that the elders remembering had been brainwashed by their culture into accepting these things as normal, and so not mentioning them. Yet it's worth asking how we think we can know their lives better than they did. It's also worth asking why it's always other people who are brainwashed, and never us.

In fact, when I look around today, I do not see anything closer to a sexual utopia, but further away. Half of marriages do not last. Half of

---

[353] Yelsma 1988.
[354] Epstein 2013.

young people have never had a partner.[355] Women's self-reported happiness has plummeted.[356] In one survey, more than a quarter of all young women had reported symptoms of mental illness *that week*, and self-harm had trebled in the 2000s.[357] All recent developments, all unprecedented.

Let me be clear: women were treated horrifically in many times and places, and are in many cultures today. Let me also be clear that people in most traditional societies, even those of my neighbours, had attitudes that I would disagree with.

Yet we should not picture human history as a single choice between modern feminism vs. slavery. Modern feminism is a complex thing with many moving parts, some unique to our strange modern culture; people in other times and places might have had equivalents to feminism that suited their indigenous culture. Our society, for example, treats men and women not just as *equal*, but as *interchangeable* pieces of a corporate economy, with few jobs or roles or spaces just for one sex or the other. Whether you consider this a good thing or not, it didn't happen because of a cosmic transformation in human consciousness; it happened because we began burning fossil fuels. They power the factories that make birth control pills, the laptop jobs that men and women can perform identically, and devices like washing machines that save household work. When the fossil fuels are gone, we will struggle to maintain this technology, and will have to reverse-engineer some older set of social rules.

Also, technology doesn't automatically create gender equality. Women are more oppressed than ever in Muslim countries today, parts of the world we see as "stuck in the past." Yet countries where women are forced to wear burkas today were not always so; as recently as the 1970s women in Iran and Afghanistan looked similar to women in Illinois or Denmark. Islamic fundamentalism is a new movement, one that Westerners underestimate by seeing it as their past, rather than their future.

---

[355] *Survey Centre on American Life* 2023.
[356] *National Bureau of Economic Research* 2009.
[357] NHS Survey 2016. Also "Young women at 'highest mental health risk,'" BBC News, 29 Sept 2016.

Nor are gender-neutral societies necessarily benevolent ones; genocidal dictatorships like the Soviet Union and Mao's China also tried to make men and women into replaceable cogs in a state machine, to weaken the family bonds around which people could resist authority.

Nor did all traditional societies forbid women from having power. Celtic mythology teems with powerful women, like the goddess Morrigan or Queen Maeve from the *Tain*. Irish history is filled with female leaders of all kinds. St. Brigid challenged Dark Age warlords. "Pirate Queen" Grace O'Malley was received as a foreign dignitary by Elizabeth I. Constance Gore-Booth Marckievicz helped lead the Irish Revolution, was spared a firing squad on account of her sex, and then – astonishingly – became the first woman elected to the British Parliament.

Of course, most women had little formal authority, but in an agrarian world there was little formal authority to be had. Until recently people did not live as consumers in an economy, but as participants in a network of relationships, an area where women can have immense power. Many men will risk death to protect their families, and since a woman with a baby can't outrun a lion, we are descended from thousands of generations of men who did just that. Boys will fight for the honour of their mother, brothers their sister.

In rural Ireland, if a husband smacked his wife, he could often count on a beating from her family. Aine Aherne remembered a neighbour knocking on their door one night, his face bloody. He said he fell off his bicycle, but Aherne later heard that his brothers-in-law had beaten him up.[358] In the 1700s and 1800s, if word got around that a man was beating his wife, neighbours dragged him out of his house and gave him "rough music," beating him through town in ritual humiliation. Just like the boy racer from the introduction, people in traditional communities took care of things themselves. It wasn't always fair, but neither is our court system today.

Men and women in every era were adults with their own minds and agendas, and negotiated the fact that they had gendered bodies with their own social rules. We can disagree with some of those rules, but we can understand why they were created.

---

[358] *No Shoes in Summer*, 22.

Take, for example, Christianity's rules about sex. In the rape culture of the late Roman Empire, Christianity would have been a godsend to many women, as it gave them permission to turn down sex for virtue. It dictated that men and women were equal in the eyes of God. It imposed monogamy on men, who had to promise long-term commitment to one woman.

By creating celibate orders it took a certain percentage of potential partners out of the mating game, reducing conflict among those still playing. It gave monks and nuns a chance to find life-long family and support among others of their sex. It gave women safe spaces which no man could enter. And it gave them immense social power – in Catholic Ireland, no man would disrespect a nun.

In the 1970s Irish radio interviewed a group of nuns --- even then a remnant of once-powerful orders – and asked one of them about feminism. The sister responded, gently, that they were part of an ancient, self-sufficient, female-run society; what did feminism propose to do for them?

Even when women dd not take holy orders, they often inhabited a world of other women, just as men spent most of their days with other men. Men formed a meithal to bring in the harvest, women formed a meithal to turn the pig into sausage. When men gathered for fraternal orders, women gathered for parallel organisations. Some elders reported men and women sitting on different sides of the church. Even when the family went to the pub they might go in separate entrances; most Irish pubs still have two doors, one to the men's "bar" and the other to the more comfortable women's "lounge" or "snug."

Women's roles were different than men's in every traditional society, but for pragmatic reasons: Farm life requires a lot of skills, and it makes practical sense for different groups to specialise in different duties. As a 21st-century man, I want everyone to be free to pursue their own interests, but women and men will, on average, often be interested in different things.

Nor are traditional gender roles necessarily better for men, as any man knows who's had to clean sewers or work on an oil rig or fight in battle. In the 1950s Irishman Desmond Doyle came home to find that his wife had abandoned their children, and had to sue the Irish government to get them back from an orphanage. As told in the book and film *Evelyn*, authorities were sceptical that a man could raise children without a woman.

Women also organised and even became violent when their families were at stake, as when landlords tried to evict the Blasket Islanders with three boatloads of police. To their surprise, Tomas O'Croghan wrote, the police found a crowd of women waiting for them on the shore, holding rocks. The police pointed guns at them but did not fire, as no one wanted to shoot a woman, and the women lobbed so many rocks at them that the police fled.[359]

Women built communities, in Ireland and everywhere else, and when women started to leave in the 1970s to find work in cities, many communities collapsed. John Healy's *Death of an Irish Town* and Hugh Brody's *Inishkillane* describe an epidemic of alcoholism and mental breakdowns among bachelor farmers who could find no wife, and so had no children and nothing to live for, like so-called "incels" today.

"Few persons realise how much the stagnation of the country villages is a woman's question," wrote Lord Ernle in his survey of Ireland, *The Land and its People*. "Without their help every remedy is foredoomed to failure."[360]

Throughout history it has been largely men who have ploughed fields, constructed cities and fought battles – but not because they were part of an evil global conspiracy to keep women from doing these things. It was because they were trying to feed a wife and children, or defend them, or build up enough money to afford a wife, or impress a woman. It is true that most things we record in history were done *by* men, but they were done *for* women. Once a man has no chance of children, however, there is often nothing to live for, or to lose.

Never think that women lack power. Women are the only reason that anything that has ever happened in history has ever happened.

---

[359] *The Islander*, 48.

[360] R. E. Prothero, 'Women on the land, 1917-19,' *The land and its people* (London, 1925), p. 169.

Chapter Eight

Storytelling

As naturally and compulsively as bees build hives or beavers build dams, you tell stories. When you unload your troubles at the end of the day, when you declare your love or pitch a product or argue a point, you tell a story. You are the hero of your own story, and your life has whatever meaning the story gives you. Suicides are people whose stories failed them.

Author Neil Gaiman once retold a story from Ancient Egypt, found in hieroglyphics and only recently rediscovered, of two brothers who were split apart by a treacherous woman. After one died, the other travelled the Earth to find a way to bring him back, until finally – after many adventures – the two were reconciled.

That we could read a story thousands of years old, and find it funny and moving, is remarkable enough – but it gets better. Years after reading the story, he said, Gaiman chatted with an archaeologist recently returned from excavating ruins in Egypt. Around the campfire at night, she said, the local Egyptians took turns telling stories, and one offered a tale he heard from his grandfather. It was the same story of two brothers, passed down through four thousand years.

A good story outlives any other man-made thing, Gaiman said, so if we want to pass on something important, we'd be wise to wrap it in a story that everyone will want to retell. People who live in the shadow of a dormant volcano could simply warn their children that it occasionally erupts – but the more generations pass without another eruption, the more likely no one will believe the story enough to retell it.

If, however, they tell the heartbreaking tale of a maiden who fell into a forbidden love affair and was sacrificed to the fire in the mountain, everyone will want to pass it on. And in the tale is the knowledge that the land itself is not as solid as it appears, that every so often the ground could shudder and mountains can breathe fire and ash.[361]

Nor are Egyptians even close to holding the record for the oldest stories; as mentioned, Australian Aborigines tell stories of the rising seas that seem to date from the last Ice Age. Just as with children's games, oral histories can be preserved so long as people care about them, and for thousands of years we did.

When Seosamh O'Dalaigh sat down with Peig Sayers of the Blasket Islands, she told him 375 stories, including some of epic length.[362] In rural Ireland, my neighbour Mary remembered, almost all communities had their own Peigs. "there was an institution called cortorach, Irish for visiting, and the people would visit each other's houses," my neighbour Mary said. "It was huge in the country ... they would have a sennachai – a storyteller – and he'd be spinning great yarns and tales, some of them the old, old stories. Some of them might be two thousand years old, really stories from prehistory -- stories of Cu Chucullen and Meave, stories from long long ago. Senna is the Irish word for old, so a sennachai was telling the old stories."

"[It happened] at least once a week at least, and nearly every night at times," Mary said. "You can imagine it, the kitchen and ... a turf fire, and very warm, and the people gathered around listening to the sennachai telling his story ... And the children were supposed to go to bed but were allowed to stay up, and would listen to the sennachai, their eyes wide like saucers."

While every family and village had their own born sennachais, "storytelling was a natural art that most people had," Edward McNerney said.[363] At family gatherings they recited poems, they recounted histories, they told jokes and ghost stories, and "all formed part of the family's unwritten heritage."[364] Stories were passed down around the dinner table, in front of the hearth, ensconced in the local pub, with crowds gathered around listening attentively. "There was always great craic [merriment,

---

[361] Speech to the Long Now Foundation, 9 June 2015.
[362] *An Old Woman's Reflections*, ix.
[363] *No Shoes in Summer*, 227.
[364] *Jaysus Wept!* 55.

pronounced "crack"] round the fireside," Bridie Matthews said. "Seven or eight neighbours might drop in of a night. Often it was just for a bit of conversation or to tell a yarn or two."[365]

The slums of Dublin, Sidney Davies wrote in the early 20th century, were "made bearable, at times even delightful, by their own vivid imagination. They are loquacious, fiercely interested in their neighbours, in the things they see in the street .... The poor classes dramatise every minute event of their daily lives in such a way as to lend a natural excitement and glamour to even the hardest and most squalid forms of existence."[366]

It was a world saturated with stories, in which every bend in the road, every mound, every branch of the family came with a melodrama. It was a world where stories were universal currency; remember that rambling houses let anyone stay in exchange for a tale. Stephen Mooney said that he and his friends couldn't all afford the cinema, they would pool their money for a local storyteller to go in, knowing he would describe it to them all later as an epic tale that was often better than the actual movie.[367]

"There was a great sense of community, of warmth, of laughter, of fun," one old neighbour told me. "There still is, I think, if you strip back the layers ... One thing I love about Ireland is the craic; you say something absurd, and other people see if they can say something more absurd to top you. If you do that in, say, Germany, people would be worried for your mental health."

Such stories were more to convey truth than fact, to teach lessons deeper than words. When Alice Taylor's neighbour told stories, "some he made up as he went along and others were old myths and legends. It made no difference to us because there were no boundaries between reality and fantasy in our world."[368]

"I often tell foreigners that Article 37 of the Irish constitution says that you shouldn't spoil a good story for the sake of the truth," my neighbour said. "There's a lot of that in Irish storytelling."

---

[365] *Times of Our Lives,* 29.
[366] *Dublin Types,* 1918.
[367] *Dublin Tenement Life,* 150.
[368] *Books from the Attic,* 118.

***

Just as Homer could recite the *Iliad* and *Odyssey*– each perhaps 500 pages written down – from memory, so did storytellers in most traditional cultures. My neighbour Jack said his local sennachai "could spin those stories so well that no one would go home until it was daylight."

Declan Gowran remembers his uncle Ned telling them stories of "black Bran," Bran Dubh MacEchach, an ancient warrior from West Wicklow whose exploits are recorded in the annals of Ulster.[369] Alice Taylor's neighbour recounted the ancient story of the Goban Saor as they worked the fields. "Storytelling was a natural art that most people had," Edward McNerney said.[370]

Such men and women had kept those stories alive in secret through centuries of persecution. "The literature, which has been preserved entirely by oral tradition, includes ancient legends, some of them older than *Beowulf* ... and a wealth of folklore, still only partly collected," wrote Moya Llwellyn Davies.[371]

Mary Fogarty described the stories of the enchanted lake of Lough Gur, where locals said an ancient city once stood before an earthquake flooded the valley and submerged it. "Even now, the peasants say, when the surface of the lake is smooth one may see from a boat, far down and down again, the drowned city, its walls and castle, houses and church, perfect and intact, waiting for the Day of Resurrection. And on Christmas Eve, on a dark night without moon or stars, if one looks down and down again, one may see lights in the windows, and listening with the ears of the mind, hear the muffled chiming of church bells."

The older people said a race of giants lived in Ireland before the coming of the Celts, and "On Baile-na-Cailleach hill one of these giants lies buried in a stone coffin with a long gold sword beside him ... No wonder that they who travelled the roads, the wandering beggars, pipers and harpers, story-tellers, Poor Scholars, drovers and tinkers, all feared to

---

[369] *Then There was Light*, 150.
[370] *No Shoes in Summer,* 227.
[371] *Peig,* introduction.

be benighted within a mile of Gur's enchanted waters, feared even to sleep in broad daylight, so great was the magic in the air."[372]

In Ireland, uniquely, Christianity did not conquer nor convert an existing empire, but merged with the folk spirituality of the ancient Celts. As Thomas Cahill put it, it replaced the human sacrifice of the Celts with the living sacrifice of the monastic traditions, and the pagan sites with churches, but kept many of the traditions and holidays: May Day, Lughnasa, Halloween. Even now some of the older Irish churches have Sheila-na-gig -- very explicit fertility carvings -- on their walls, a puzzlement to many tourists. Each tradition filled in the cracks of the other; one dealt with the universal, eternal and literate, the other with the local, capricious and primeval.[373]

Many stories dealt with the fairies --- but not what you're thinking of, the tiny winged girls of cartoons and costumes. The fairies of real legend were the primaeval spirits of the land, the *sidh* (pronounced "shee") -- the anguished ghost of a woman ("ban" in Irish) was a literal "banshee." They could replace babies in the crib with changelings -- impostors that withered and died -- or curse anyone who offended them. Phrases like "the Good People" or "the Little People" were euphemisms, as the Ancient Greeks called the Furies "the Kindly Ones" or the characters in *Harry Potter* are reluctant to say the name of Voldemort.

As William Butler Yeats put it in *Irish Fairy and Folk Stories*, "... behind the visible are chains on chains of conscious beings, who are not of heaven but of the earth, who have no inherent form but change according to their whim, or the mind that sees them. You cannot lift your hand without influencing and being influenced by hordes. The visible world is merely their skin."[374]

Such beliefs were common to all people, until our generations. A life hewing wood for warmth or wresting an animal for meat is one in which everyday acts have meaning, and a life by candlelight is one where ghost stories have power. "Growing up in an Ireland where fairyland was part of the landscape added an extra dimension to life, especially for us children

---

[372] *The Farm By Lough Gur*, 14.
[373] *How the Irish Saved Civilization.*
[374] *Irish Fairy and Folk Tales*, 2.

for whom nothing was outside the realm of possibility," Alice Taylor said. "To us these unseen people were as real as the farm animals and our constant dream was to take one of them by surprise and have a chat with them."[375]

They were said to live underground, and wells and springs that reached into their realm were often sacred. Sites said to conceal passageways to their realm, like the ancient ring-forts used by Celts in the Bronze Age, were left alone even when poor farmers could have used the space for more crops, or could have cut their trees for firewood. "[British] plantations they frequently rob," said a German visitor in the 1840s, "but the wood growing wild on these fairy mounts they never touch."[376] In the 1960s electricity cables had to go far around such places, Joe Keane said, as they were "considered no-go zones by many of the older people."

Whether most people believed they were literally true is the wrong question; these stories predate literacy, and were not to be factual but *meaningful*. They passed on the distilled wisdom of generations, and warned against ingratitude, discourtesy, dishonesty and other vices. Leaving the ring-forts alone meant keeping some trees alive while the rest of the forests were being felled.

Just a few years ago, a member of the Irish Parliament blamed the fairies for a local road that crumbled no matter how many times it was repaired. The international press laughed at him, quoting county officials that it was merely an "underlying subsoil/geotechnical problem." Be that as it may, road planners who believed in fairies might not have kept making the same expensive mistakes.

Most of all, though, these beliefs ensured the Irish would treat their past with respect, at least until recently. To this day Ireland is unusual in that so many archaeological sites remain undisturbed – 45,000 in a country the size of South Carolina. "Many farmers who had old forts on their land followed this practice and thus preserved these historic places which are part of our heritage," Alice Taylor said.[377]

---

[375] *Books from the Attic*, 26.
[376] *Travels in Ireland*, 33.
[377] *Books From the Attic*, 30.

***

Just talking to the elderly about the neighbourhoods they grew up in, or reading their memoirs, reveals a connection to the land and its people that any other traditional society on Earth would have had until yesterday. Martin could tell me about the spat between two landowners in the 1800s that defined our postal area, and Jim could walk me around ruined Carbury Castle, pointing out the now-caved in kitchens and dungeons. They are rooted in a way that everyone used to be, and people have trouble imagining now. At one farm, the wife told me about the area, and said her husband was local. "Are you not?" I asked. "Oh, no," she said. "I'm from several miles away."

If that seems like people were more stranded in space than today, they were less stranded in time, for they lived alongside all the spirits of their ancestors. Francie Murray described that a family of ill repute stole a calf from St. Patrick, who cursed the town so that no man from it would become a priest. Sure enough, no priests come from there, although there are plenty from the neighbouring villages. Whether the legend is true, it refers to events from the 600s AD.[378]

My neighbour Tony Carr noted that the nearby town of Naas dates back to about 400 AD, and that Brian Boru stopped there on his way across Ireland to wage war against the Vikings, finally defeating them in 1014. The town's full name, Nas Na Riogh (NACE-na-REE-a), means "meeting place of kings."[379] People continued customs over centuries as well; the monastery on Scattery Island washed their flagstone floors every Friday, and told radio interviewers why – it was to honour the memory of the 42 monks murdered by pirates in 1188.[380]

Talking to other older people across Ireland I heard about almost any small church, any woods, any mountain, any ruin, and they could tell you all about it – and most of the stories I verified later through history books, so few if any were telling me tall tales. This is not, in and of itself, because they are old – remember the children from chapter 1, who wore oak leaves

---

[378] *Them Golden Fields I Trod,* 1.
[379] *Some Time to Kill,* 92.
[380] "Scattery of Senan." RTE documentary.

in their lapels -- but because they were among the last people to truly live *in* a place, and not *on* it.

"There's a very strange thing – I can't explain this – when I grew up in that area, there was this very interesting sense of the presence of the past," my neighbour Peter told me. "And almost the benign presence of the people who had lived there before ... the sense of the kind presence of the past."

Even within a few blocks around my old neighbourhood in Dublin, I can see the place where George Bernard Shaw lived, where Bram Stoker was born, where Brendan Behan drank, and the pub where Sheridan Le Fanu set his novels. Here is buried Jonathan Swift, author of *Gulliver's Travels*. Here is the old Parliament building, where the largely British aristocrats voted to dissolve Ireland's home rule; the statue of nationalist Henry Grattan forever faces away in disgust.

When I walked through Dublin I wondered at all the delightful place names – Tolka, Stoneybatter, Grangegorman, Smock Alley, Fishamble Street, Thundercut Alley. Conversations and memoirs of elders explained them to me: Grangegorman after Gormo, the Viking warlord in the 900s, named when Dublin was still a Viking slave market. Thundercut Alley because men cut through the alley to get to the long-destroyed Thunder pub. And these are passed-down memories that go back a long way: St. Michan's church dates to 1095, Oxmantown from 1192, the Brazen Head pub from 1198, Stoneybatter Road supposedly from the 300s AD.

A tour of the Irish countryside reveals the scope of history, and puts our present troubles into perspective. The pub down the road from me is almost as old as the Mayan temples we have uncovered from the jungle, which we consider ancient and mystical. A number of hills in the West Country still have small dolmens, slabs of rock assembled into tombs, which are so old that we can't tell how old they are. The best guess of archaeologists is that they are as old as the monument of Newgrange, making them far older than Stonehenge, older than pyramids. When they were built woolly mammoths still walked the Earth.

***

Just as we rarely tell stories anymore, we rarely sing, except perhaps meekly in church, and laugh at those who do. When my elder neighbours were young, through, postmen whistled on the streets, men sang as they worked in fields, factory workers sang on the assembly line, and women sang together in kitchens.[381] Girls sang as they milked the cows, street vendors sang their wares to passers-by, and in the evenings everyone sang with gusto in the pub.[382]

When workmen were hired to string the first electric lines across Ireland, they remembered singing most of the way -- sometimes cowboy songs, sometimes operatic arias.[383] Women had songs just for certain tasks, like cutting seaweed for fertiliser, and on the day when all the women gathered on the shore they all knew the right song to sing. People sang in church choirs and company choirs, and as mentioned, even teenaged gangs harmonised on the street.[384]

"People used to sing on the bus," Christy told me. "Say you went to the seaside, and you came home, and the whole bus would be singing. The whole bus -- just amazing. And one thing after another, and someone would bring up one of the Irish songs – they'd be more or less ballads. But everybody would know them. And nobody would complain, that you shouldn't be making noise – it was just a happy thing. Everybody just sang."

Most of our ancestors, of any culture, probably did the same. At the Last Supper, Jesus and his apostles sang a hymn; they did not have hymnals at hand, but knew it by heart. The Greeks sang of Troy, and we still have the lyrics three thousand years later. Most American schools had singing clubs, and many had a school song, meant to be sung by students together; as Anthony Esolen pointed out, Princeton in 1873 had a songbook a hundred pages thick. Small towns had their own singing clubs, and people waiting for a haircut could sing along with barbershop quartets.

People were expected to sing, and to know the songs of their people. My American cousins once visited a rural Irish pub where everyone took

---

[381] *Around the Farm Gate,* 135.
[382] *The Farm by Lough Gur,* 23.
[383] "Rural electrification," RTE documentary, 2016.
[384] "The Lewis Folk," RTE documentary, 1976.

turns singing local songs, and when the locals invited the foreign guests to take a turn, my cousins sat frozen for a moment. Finally, they dredged up kindergarten memories of "She'll Be Coming 'Round the Mountain," and everyone joined in obligingly.

When neighbours came to each others' homes in the evenings, or went to the pub, they brought their instruments. "There was one pub in Werburgh Street and here was musicians and you were merry in the morning till the last thing at night," said Dublin dockworker William Murphy. "Singing and melodeons and fiddles and everything. They were very good, lovely singers and musicians. And if you went in you were leaving the musicians a pint. Oh, great sport. And dancing and all on the floor, waltzing around on the floor ... In the summer you'd be sitting outside and the house'd be full and you'd be listening to the songs."[385]

Few today realise how common it once was, a century or two ago, for regular people to play musical instruments. Some musicians played classical or operas, which even poor people knew. Some played American country music or the "showband" style that was popular here in the 1960s. Many neighbourhoods and even companies like Guinness had their own brass bands, said Christy, and competed with one another. Most of all, though, they played the traditional Irish music, whose distinctive pipes and harps sound like nothing else, and which had been handed down secretly through the centuries.

Music holds immense power over us; babies who can't yet speak will giggle and bounce to a familiar tune, and elders who can no longer remember their names will revive at the sound of an old standard. We form our musical tastes in youth and never abandon them; the teen anthems that played during your first kiss or last fist-fight remain with you forever, the intensity of feeling gone but the tastes frozen in amber. Such inborn switches served us well for thousands of years, allowing children in Tipperary and Turkmenistan alike to hear songs over and over and pass them on as adults, letting musical traditions accumulate through the generations.

We are just as imprinted today with the music of our childhoods, but for most of us those are television commercials, video-game sounds, or

---

[385] *Dublin Voices*, 118.

electronic pop hits. A playlist of this music follows you through your day – gym, coffee-shop, doctor's office, train and the earphones of the kid sitting next to you, cranked up so loudly you can recognize the song.

After generations of this, we have lost touch with what music is *for*. For thousands of years, in every part of the world that I know of, songs were made to be sung by ordinary voices in communion, and they told the basic stories of the human condition. In workers' fields and prison yards, from birthing beds and deathbeds, men and women swelled taut with grief or joy or rage, gave their bodies over to the song and were lifted into a better world.

The songs sung in a rambling house or farmhouse could be from the Middle Ages ("Greensleeves, Scarborough Fair"), the 1600s ("Whiskey in the Jar"), 1800s ("She Moved Through the Fair") or 1900s ("John O'Dreams"), but they were never museum pieces. When each family and community had their own versions, songs could evolve and cross-pollinate, and over time the most viable experiments remained. Sometimes the music changed in a new land – becoming, say, country music in the USA – and were re-imported so that now there are Irish-language American-style country music singers.

This unwritten songbook, however, would have something to alienate almost every culture warrior in my native country today. Many liberals I know would be put off by the lack of utopian idealism in the songs, or that the lyrics do not treat men and women as interchangeable. Many conservatives I know would be shocked to hear labour songs that in the modern USA are confined to marginal leftist countercultures.

The songs told them who their people were, and why this day was different. They kept the rhythms of churns and scythes, of tanneries and looms, and grew and changed as they were passed on. They were sung secretly about the days when earthly kings would be overthrown, by farmers who feared a rapping at the winter door.

When Britain conquered this land, they "cut the hands off the pipers and hanged all the harpists during the 18th century," my neighbour Mary said, and Irish music was nearly exterminated. When families gathered to sing and play, they were not merely visiting; they were committing treason. Irish dancing – which Americans might know through shows like

"Riverdance" -- was also an act of rebellion, and some of the famous dancing masters were genuine underground militia leaders. One man in the 1800s wrote that his instructor had been in the rebellion of 1798, and that his back was covered in whip marks.[386]

The music "nearly died out here," my neighbour Mary told me, but millions of Irish secretly kept it alive over the centuries, just as they secretly held Mass or sent children to school. Instruments were expensive, yet even in starving times families saved up to buy them. When Ireland finally gained its independence, its coins and passports were stamped with a harp, and still are.

* * *

You can imagine that a world of storytellers and musicians embraced theatre; my neighbour Sean remembered his school class performing Gilbert and Sullivan operas – which they had translated into the native Irish tongue – at the city theatres every spring. The theatres were required to have at least half their shows be live local talent and not movies -- a move by the Irish government to boost local art and employment -- so for theatre owners the school shows were a guaranteed income.

Travelling theatres went from village to village, especially during Lent when dancing was forbidden. "They always started with a vaudeville act – singing, violin, and a comedy act," Kevin Duffy remembered.[387] Larger cities had opera houses, which even the poor people appreciated.[388] "People would sing on stage to crowds; can you imagine people today doing that without sound effects."[389]

Movies were just coming in, nowhere near ubiquitous enough to replace traditional culture, but could be enjoyed alongside it. When people in the larger towns went to the cinema, "it was more of a special occasion then to go to the pictures," said Herbie Donnelly. "They would treat it as a special thing, much as people now would going to the theatre at night. An usher in those days, you were more like the guardsmen outside

---

[386] "Hayfoot Strawfoot Dancing Masters," RTE documentary, 1976.

[387] *50 Years Behind the Counter*, 21.

[388] *The Way We Were*, 24.

[389] *No Shoes in Summer,* 167.

Buckingham Palace. You were impressive, very impressive."[390] When television came in, families initially treated it like movies; they would dress up in their Sunday best to sit in front of it, "like they were in the presence of a great man."[391]

When elders talk about the movies they loved, they are always surprised when I know the films; I was raised in a family with a love of black-and-white movies, and grew up knowing Groucho Marx and Cary Grant the way other children might know rappers or wrestlers. I sometimes made the mistake of thinking that everyone else had the same cultural touchstones. Invited to a Halloween party a few years ago and at a loss for a last-minute costume, I put on my most raggedy suit, bought a cigar, applied three strips of greasepaint, and walked in the door as Groucho Marx. I thought Groucho would be as iconic and recognisable as Elvis or Dracula, and not one of my educated, middle-aged neighbours had heard of him.

Most people these days are unfamiliar with the classic movies of the 1930s and 40s, and seem perplexed, even repulsed, that I would recognise my grandparents' cultural references, even though that's how everyone used to be. They find the conventions of black-and-white movies as alien as opera, familiar only from decades of countercultural spoofing. When a film like *Metropolis* or *Dark Victory* plays in cinemas and we get to the dramatic scenes, the audience around me erupts in horse laughter. When a young friend of mine said he liked the awful monster movies of the 1960s – the only black-and-white films he knew – I recommended *The Maltese Falcon,* but he later reported back that it wasn't as funny. He didn't realise he wasn't supposed to mock it.

Once in a while, though, someone I know discovers that *12 Angry Men* -- nothing more than actors in a single room talking in real time – absorbs them more than two hours of computer effects. Or they sit down to really watch *It's a Wonderful Life*, rather than just have it playing in the background, and notice what a dark masterpiece it is. And then I tell them that, while those were great movies, they weren't that unusual – for a few

---

[390] *Dublin Voices*, 75.
[391] "Dan Joe's TV station," RTE documentary.

decades there were hundreds of good movies, and at least a dozen or so great ones, *every year*.

I grew up with these movies, and my family passed every supper with trivia contests, with games our parents and grandparents had created. In one game we were given two actors – say, Charlie Chaplin and John Wayne – and had to link them with the shortest possible number of co-stars. Yes, it's the Kevin Bacon game; years later a bunch of college students patented it, marketed the idea and gained fame and fortune. No, I'm not bitter.

This love of movies stayed with me over the years; I worked as a film critic for a newspaper chain in my twenties, which sounds like a dream job until you realise how many bad movies you need to sit through. The more I saw, the more I realised that no recent decade had as many great movies as a single year of the 1940s. Nor, for all their films' spectacle, did any of the writers or directors do as much as John Huston or Woody Van Dyke did with a plywood set.

While these movies were a mass corporate product, their stories drew on hundreds of years of Western tradition. The writers and directors of these films had often grown up familiar with Livy and Shakespeare and the Bible, and these references showed up in their movies. They often grew up knowing physical labour and hardship, had fled persecution abroad or had seen the horrors of the battlefield, and knew well the value of freedom. Film scores – even cartoon music – built on operas, symphonies, hymns and folk music from across Western history.

Classic films also treated courtship and violence with a discretion that seems alien today, now that our mass media have spent six decades celebrating every new broken taboo as a victory against The Man. What people today miss, though, is that films from that era were democratic and populist, meant for everyone. Anyone too young to get innuendo could still watch the films without seeing anything inappropriate, while those old enough to understand the more mature elements of the story would do so. This required subtlety made stories better and more layered.

They often depicted normal problems far more realistically than our media today. The ensemble casts of *Destry Rides Again* or *Boys' Town* were from many ethnic groups and cultures, all with their own personalities and flaws, forced to work together and bring out the best in each other. They were genuinely diverse, without the fake "diversity" of films today, in which characters are cast as heroes or villains based on their sex or skin colour.

The heroes of movies back then were menial labourers, homeless (*Meet John Doe, Our Daily Bread, My Man Godfrey, Beggars in Ermine*), the falsely accused (*Captain Blood, Saboteur*) and imprisoned (*I Am a Fugitive from a Chain Gang, Sullivan's Travels*), and refugees from tyranny (*Three Faces West, Casablanca*). However lowly their circumstances, though, they rose to become heroes, giving audiences an example to follow. Frank Capra's movies have become synonymous with Norman Rockwell Americana, but their bright moments were powerful because they were surrounded by darkness, their decent characters – John Doe, George Bailey — framed, harassed and pushed to the edge of suicide and madness.

Many working people struggle to keep health care these days, but if I want to see that depicted I have to go back to 1938's *The Citadel*. More people must care for elderly parents, but I don't see many films dealing with that part of life, outside of 1937's *Make Way for Tomorrow*. For people trying to keep up with the rent, take King Vidor's 1934 film *Our Daily Bread*, in which a young couple about to be evicted find they inherited a farm, and don't know how to farm. They find dozens of homeless families willing to work, and the problems solve each other.

Such ideals drew accusations of Communism even then, and some of those writers and directors did become entangled in the more misguided intellectual causes of the 1930s. "A surprising number," though, write authors Paul Buhle and Dave Wagner in their book *Radical Hollywood*, "came straight out of Middle America and made their choice on old-fashioned moral grounds."[392]

When the Great Depression hit, movies shifted away from the big-budget fantasy spectacles of the 1920s into more modest and realistic fare. In part they were responding to the demands of newly invented talkies, but also to the desires of an increasingly desperate America. Hollywood saw an intellectual movement – imagine! – of writers and directors determined

---

[392] *Radical Hollywood*, xiii.

to tell useful stories by and for ordinary people. American films have never been more well-written or resonant than in the 1930s and 40s, because they have never been more gently and consciously populist.

And they are one of the last things we do in community. I took my daughter to see a rare public screening of Buster Keaton's *The General*, and while she chuckled when I showed her clips on YouTube, we had tears in our eyes laughing with an auditorium of people. It felt like a good football game or a revival tent, with waves of emotion rippling over a crowd, and for a brief moment in the darkness you are reminded that we're all in this life together.

***

Going to the cinema didn't discourage them from telling stories at home, or singing songs together, or playing music at the pub. For a few cents they could dress up, see some of the great storytelling of cinema's golden age in a hushed and darkened space, and return to the world. Television, though, is piped into homes all day long, and as it swelled to fill our time, all the other human activities declined.

"People got more out of life then," said Mary Bolton. "But when television came in the whole body seemed to go out of it. It changed the whole atmosphere. Television was the ruination of the world."[393]

Today the average American watches 24 hours of television a week – 10 years of an average life, more time than we spend in school or with family or doing anything else outside sleep and work. It has become such a basic part of any home that furniture is now made with a place for the remote control. Family vans are now made with televisions in the back seat for children. Restaurants, pubs, gyms and offices increasingly have televisions all over the walls, and when I ask staff to turn off the pimple-popping show while I'm eating, or the rape rap while I'm talking to my daughter, I get baffled stares.

It destroyed the neighbourly bonding at the local Irish pub, Joe Cox said. "Today it's 'Come in, sit down, and shut up,'" he said. "Conversation is gone … they shouldn't have it in the pub at all."[394] For a long time they

---

[393] *Dublin Voices*, 8.
[394] *Dublin Voices*, 8.

didn't, and a few still don't; recall the publican that allegedly threw out the Rolling Stones. Tomsie, Tony Carr's publican in nearby Naas, finally gave in to demand and brought a television into the pub, but then refused to turn it on.[395]

Television simulates the feeling of having friends – that's its job – until we no longer seek the real thing. The characters on television are better to look at and listen to than any ordinary person around us. Most of us grew up more familiar with the living room on *Friends* or the deck of the Starship *Enterprise* than the interior of our neighbours' homes – although I'm pretty sure all their seats face the television.

Neil Postman noted that television flickers between jarring images every few seconds to pull emotions out of us. It is good at visceral images like the death of George Floyd, but it is not good at complex thought, logical debate or focused attention, and after a lifetime of watching neither are we. As far as we can tell, attention-deficit disorder did not exist before television, and we struggle to imagine the farmers who listened to Lincoln and Douglas debate for hours.[396]

By the time Postman was writing in the 1980s, television had not only taken over entertainment, but all of culture, so that politics, news education, religion, sports and sex became subdivisions of the celebrity industry. Newscasters were chosen for their charisma and attractiveness, teachers judged on how well they entertained their classes, and politics became a matter of five-minute "debates" that were chains of slogans.

Every moment we spend watching is one we are no longer telling our own stories, or even thinking our own thoughts. No one voted for it, but television has become our mythmaker. Activists protest chemicals in our food or water because we rightly care what we put into our bodies, yet regulating what we put into our minds would be seen as comically backward or intolerant.

It separated generations for the first time, so that one's stories and songs were no longer those passed down through the ages, but whatever you absorbed as a teenager. It retroactively changes our memories, so when we think of, say, "the 1990s," we think not of our real memories but

---

[395] *Some Time to Kill,* 150.
[396] *Amusing Ourselves to Death,* 86.

of the exaggerated pop-culture version we saw more repeatedly and recently. It changes how we perceive the present, as we compare dramatic events to "something out of a movie."

Its version of the world becomes the one we know. Most Americans I know, for example, think they have failed in achieving a "normal" life, meaning normal on television. Unlike the popular films of the 1930s and 40s, though, in which heroes were often working-class, poor or homeless, "normal" characters on American television would be considered wealthy in real life. Even "working-class" characters on *Roseanne* or *Shameless* live in palatial houses, and characters in post-apocalyptic dystopias -- *Elysium, The Matrix Reloaded* or *Dredd* – have more spacious apartments than most of us can afford.

Fewer young people are getting married or even having sex, finding everyone unattractive compared to the imaginary people on the screen to whom we feel a stronger connection. Television used to at least give us models of behaviour to which we could aspire – yet the happy families of 1950s shows have been mocked for so many decades that most of us reflexively see such relationships as ridiculous.

It changes our conversations, as we litter them with pop-culture references and pattern them after the snarky scripts we grew up seeing. When we look back at people's speech and actions before the age of television, it's shocking how people talked like actual grown-ups; no one is making an attempt to be a goofball, how no one is cracking cheap jokes or throwing zingers to shock and titillate. These days, Irish journalist John Waters said, the epic storytelling "has largely vanished from the public realm, banished by what is called political correctness, pseudo-sophistication and the self-referentialism of what is laughably called 'popular culture' as well as by the mimicry of imported witticisms and the escalating contempt for what is native."[397]

Hollywood has been shocking us for so many decades that it can find little left to skewer. As people today are discovering, a counterculture doesn't have much purpose without a culture to counter, and irreverence has no power if nothing is revered.

---

[397] *Give Us Back the Bad Roads*, 37.

Television, though, is rapidly becoming a subdivision of the Internet, along with our politics, our religion, social life, games, reading, romance, and time in general. The appearance of smart phones – adopted by consumers faster than any technology in history – allowed us to carry the internet with us everywhere. We check our phones an average of 221 times a day, according to a UK study —an average of every 4.3 minutes.[398] This number actually may be too low, since people tend to underestimate their own mobile usage. In one study, female students at Baylor University reported using their cell phones an average of ten hours a day.[399]

Social media tempts us away from human contact; in a 2015 Pew Research Centre study, 89 percent of mobile phone owners said they had used their phones during the last social gathering they attended, even though 82 percent of them felt they were hurting the conversation by doing so.[400]

When everyone is addicted, no one realises it until they must go without. Tim Wilson of the University of Virginia asked people to sit in a chair and think without a device or book for up to 15 minutes; in one experiment, many subjects opted to give themselves electric shocks rather than sit alone with their own thoughts.[401] In one 2015 study a group of people who signed up to quit Facebook for 99 days, and many couldn't even make it to the first few days, while others had other social media to follow and so displaced their addiction. The ones who truly stayed away, though, reported themselves happier at the end.[402]

Just as flowers evolve to dole out just as much nectar as is necessary to keep the pollinators hungry for more, social media gives us just as much neural stimulation as we need to get addicted but not enough to make us not need social media. It makes it easy to fall into a trance of scrolling, swiping, liking and moving on, the world flitting past like the view from a car window.

---

[398] "Smartphone users are busy 221 times a day," *The Times*, 8 Oct 2014.
[399] Roberts, 2014.
[400] "Americans' Views on Mobile Etiquette," Pew Research Center, 26 Aug 2015.
[401] "Doing Something is Better Than Doing Nothing for Most People, Study Shows," *UVA Today*, 3 July 2014.
[402] Baumer 2015.

As my neighbour Christy said, young people exposed only to the social media of the moment never gain the ability to compare the fads of the moment against the wisdom of all the people who came before them. "They only know what's now," he said. "They're told they're free, and that we were all oppressed. It's so sad because they're the ones that have been enslaved and imprisoned ... If there's no morality, no right and wrong, then the biggest and the wealthiest are the ones who will survive."

If television undermined our culture, social media shattered it, launching millions of "creators" all creating their own mythology, their own version of the past, their own tribes. We get our news from sources with no values or canon in common. It has been our Tower of Babel, removing any common understanding of the world around us. We live uprooted in time, knowing no stories older than our bodies. We die strangers to each other.

Chapter Nine

Trading

Whatever you do today -- buy groceries, fill up the car, get that lump looked at – you'll probably accomplish it by swiping a bank card. Same thing tomorrow and every day until your time on this Earth runs out and you swipe that card for the last time. Even if you use cash, you got it swiping the card. Those ones and zeroes in the bank computer are your life; you've given up most of your breathing years to accumulate them, and without them your lights go out, your payments lapse, and people step over you on the sidewalk.

No wonder that bank crises these days – and we've had a lot of them in Europe – come with a now-familiar montage of reporters, riots and emergency backroom deals to avert Doomsday. Here in Ireland the government forced the entire nation into bankruptcy, bailouts and decades of debt, all to keep a small number of irresponsible banks from closing even for a day.

Imagine, then, a modern country – cars, televisions, everything -- where not just one bank closed, but all of them, and not just for a day or two, but for weeks, months, a year. Imagine a country where suddenly you can't withdraw money, or put it somewhere safe, or even verify legal documents in vaults. Any economics student could tell you what happens next: everything stops. Economic brain death. Your basic Zombie Apocalypse.

Yet when this happened in Ireland in 1966 -- and again in 1970, and again in 1976 -- none of those things happened. There was no mass panic, no riots, no starvation, no increase in violent crime, and few bankruptcies. And every time the banks shut down, gross domestic product grew.

If this sounds insane, it's because most of us live so far from normal that we can no longer see it in the distance; we only know it by reputation.

Most humans in history, whether Vikings or Africans or Irish villagers, didn't rely on daily infusions of money to function; rather, they grew and raised and made most of what they needed, and traded for what they couldn't provide themselves. They owned few goods, bought them to last, and fixed them when they broke. Shops traded with their customers. Even as recently as the 1970s, wrote Hugh Brody in *Inishkillane*, each family "maintained its own independence and self-reliance," creating an "invulnerability of each peasant community to the distant centres of change."[403]

Other things made a loss of banks an inconvenience rather than a cataclysm. Most people were paid weekly in cash, including 90 percent of manufacturing and construction workers. A few foreign banks kept offices in Ireland and continued to function, albeit mostly in Dublin, and credit unions remained open. The Irish post office allows people to keep and withdraw money in accounts like a bank, and some money from the UK next door circulated and was accepted.

Still, when Ireland's national banks went on strike they closed off around 85 percent of the country's money, according to economist Antoin Murphy – and while the longest strike lasted six months, bankers worked reduced hours for months before and after, so the Irish were without normal banking for a year. Bank employees were flown en masse to the UK for work; Murphy said that whole planes were chartered to fly them out of the country like refugees from Afghanistan.

Once the banks closed, how did people buy things they couldn't get from the garden – stationary, motor fuel, a beer after work? When they ran out of cash they paid with cheques that would clear when the banks opened someday. Murphy estimated that five million Irish pounds were in circulation when the longest strike began in 1970; by the end of it five *billion* pounds of cheques – almost $100 billion today or $50,000 for everyone in the country – had changed hands.

Some businesses were paid in cash and had nowhere to deposit it, remembered then-bank employee Niall Murphy, while others ran out of cash to give customers in change. In both cases, the business owners put the word out on the street to find a business with the opposite problem to

---

[403] *Inishkillane,* 132.

theirs and traded cash for cheques, bringing thousands of pound-notes in bags and walking away with what was effectively an IOU.

Cheques were written against other cheques. They were traded for other cheques. They "acted like certificates of deposit in that they changed ownership often during the closure," Antoin Murphy wrote.[404] In effect, cheques became the new currency; the country became, as one wag put it, the Cheque Republic. The cheques were worth something because everyone believed they were worth something – which is all money is these days.

When they ran out, they simply went to the local bank manager – on strike, of course, but still living in town and with a personal stash of chequebooks – to replenish their supply. When those supplies ran dry people made their own cheques –former bank official Ernie McElroy recalled them written on cigarette boxes and toilet paper,[405] and as long as everyone treated them as money, they were. "An Irish solution to an Irish problem," Niall Murphy said.

While the Irish Stock Market did go down, only a few businesses went bankrupt, ones that were in trouble anyway. Twenty percent of manufacturing companies had to cut back operations and many construction projects were postponed, although this was also due to a cement strike at the same time. Property deals halted as most legal documents were sealed in now-closed banks. Still, retail sales – largely at neighbourhood pubs and corner shops -- went down only slightly.

When the longest strike ended, Niall Murphy said, the bank employees had literally millions of cheques to go through, and worked from 9 am to 10 pm for months to get them cleared. "The overtime was astronomical," he said.

You'd assume that fraud would be rampant, and while some cheques inevitably bounced, an investigation afterwards revealed only 750 cases in a country of three million, or one bounced cheque for every 4,000 people. "I'm sure that there was some fraudulence – there always is -- but by and large no," my neighbour Peter told me.

---

[404] Murphy 1978.
[405] "How a Six-Month Bank Strike Rocked the Nation," *Irish Independent*, 28 Dec 1999.

All this was made possible by Ireland's intensely local culture of pubs and corner shops in every village and neighbourhood. Pubs were not just bars, but town halls, dance floors, restaurants, hotels, even mortuaries. Corner shops could also be post offices and thus mini-banks. Both allowed people they knew well to run up tabs, in what Antoin Murphy called "a highly personalized credit system without any definite time horizon," so cheques to be paid in an indefinite future were no different. Many business owners were accustomed to customers paying intermittently; Alice Taylor notes everyone got their clothes from the local tailor, Jack, and paid him whenever someone bought their milk or pigs or crops. "When the farmers did well, Jack did well."[406]

Business owners decided which customers were allowed to run tabs, and "their information was likely to be much better than a bank manager or his staff," wrote journalist Patrick Cockburn. "The accuracy of their judgement was demonstrated when the strike came to an end with most pieces of paper turning out to be worth what was written on them."[407]

"If you're the son of Mick who's at the bar every night," your cheque could be trusted, said my neighbour Christy. "If the son defaulted, the family would pay up ...There was huge pride in a family, and a thing like that would be a huge scandal."

The country had 12,000 shops and 11,000 pubs in a country of fewer than three million people – one of either for every 129 people in the country. That's just below Dunbar's number, the theoretical upper limit on natural human social groups; below that number, the theory goes, we can personally know everyone in a group, but above it we need formal hierarchies and legal codes to maintain order. Almost all humans in history lived in such close-knit communities; they are what our human natures evolved for, the default for our species. Combined with Ireland's long history of Christianity, poverty, and solidarity under oppression, and the result was a deep culture of reflexive mutual aid.

"The same families had been in most of the shops for several generations and had built up and passed on a deep understanding and

---

[406] *Quench the Lamp,* 20.
[407] "We can all get by quite well without banks - Ireland managed to survive without them," Patrick Cockburn, *Independent*, Sunday 12 July 2015.

knowledge of their customers," Alice Taylor said. "It was a relationship that worked both ways, and when money was scarce we gave each other mutual support."[408] The same was true in the USA, as noted in Robert Putnam's *Bowling Alone*, as seen earlier.

Even when the strikes ended and the returning bank workers slowly made their way through literal mountains of cheques, Niall Murphy said, they made decisions based on community trust, asking friends to top up accounts before they went into overdraft. Most people had only a few hundred pounds in the bank, but a year's worth of cheques could mean thousands of pounds into someone's account and thousands out, until the account was almost exactly what it had been.

Cockburn said his father "spoke of the strike as an enjoyably stress-free period when he was able to get on with writing books and articles... He was not alone in enjoying the crisis which turned out to be no such thing. Almost half a century later, many Irish people remember with relish how they successfully replaced the banks with other ways of dealing with payment and credit."

Even in Ireland, most people my age and younger have never heard of the strikes, and the few articles about these remarkable periods typically describe Ireland's community networks as an unexpected substitute for banks. They have it backwards. Our daily feedings from the global financial system are themselves a substitute for a healthy society, as we now need to pay babysitters, therapists, lawyers, teachers, nursing homes and charities to do what everyone once did as a normal part of being human, without authorization from governments or corporations. To paraphrase Putnam, what we have now is economic Astroturf, only necessary where the real thing will no longer grow.

***

"While all the shopkeepers were our neighbours, my mother always bore in mind that we were related to some of them, for she was a great believer in looking after the needs of the extended family," Taylor said. "Allegiances of all kinds were important to her, and if somebody's

---

[408] *Quench the Lamp*, 21.

grandmother had been good to my mother's grandmother then my mother was not going to forget that, and so ... [they] were not just shopkeepers to us; they were our friends, and shopping was as much as social outing as the acquiring of goods."[409]

The women who came daily to Duffy's shop were more interested in chatting than buying, for "they bought only the bare necessities," he said. "Tea and sugar were vital. They could produce most other edibles themselves. They all had hens, vegetables, milk, butter and did all their own baking, daily."[410]

As mentioned, even the shopping didn't need to involve exchanging money, for wives traded home-made butter and eggs for what they needed. At the same time, this meant that some shopkeepers took other jobs on the side purely to get hard currency, no matter how wealthy they were in butter and eggs.[411]

When they think of the shops of their childhood, elderly here remember the smells most, whether the "loose tea, a wheel of cheese, candles, snuff, [and] dried meat" smells of Taylor's shop, or the "cathedral" to the "odour of fresh bread" that was Christy Kinnealy local bakery. One man interviewed on Irish radio navigated his entire street by smell memory – "the raspberry smell of Jacob's biscuits... The stale beer smell from the pub. The clean clothes smell of Tommy O'Keefe's."[412]

Butchers, bakers, tailors and others had their own establishments, but most shops simply sold whatever else locals needed: boots and bicycle parts, tyres and tubes, flour and sugar, tea and raisins. No packages were thrown away; mothers across Ireland sewed their children clothes made out of cloth flour sacks, and "the empty tea chest was always promised to some customer, who wanted it for the clocking hen at hatching time."[413]

Store clerks or tellers today have been trained to act as machines, and we in turn to treat them as such. Shopkeepers then had to rely on their own judgement, as when to extend a tab, or how much to estimate the value of

---

[409] *Quench the Lamp*, 21.
[410] *50 Years Behind the Counter*, 15.
[411] *Then There Was Light*, 222.
[412] *Quench the Lamp*, 20; *Maura's Boy*, 17; "The Smells of Life," RTE documentary, 2010.
[413] *50 Years Behind the Counter*, 14.

a trade. They had to calculate prices on the spot, as when people brought in their own containers for boot polish; Duffy said he weighed the jar, looked up the price per volume, calculated the volume of the jar, and came to a price, all on the spot with a pencil and paper.

Nor was business confined to shops and markets, much less to global corporations as it is today; every man, woman and child had several enterprises going. "Everyone earned a little money on the side – fattening pigs, rearing turkeys," Francie Murray said. "My grandfather had many strings in his bow, not only growing his own food but fishing the river, owned a boat and hired it out, and carried provisions to [his] neighbours."[414]

"Now when I was a kid I was always earning money, always," Paddy Mooney said. "I was even out singing in the streets."[415] Teddy Delaney and his friends fished wood out of the river and ripped apart pallets and sold them for firewood. "In time we became something of scrap merchants ourselves."[416]

Francie Murray remembers armies of children hunting the local fields for mushrooms and the shores for periwinkles, selling them to the hotel in the nearby village. Boys snared rabbits, John Curran said, and "hawked [them] from door to door in the village ... for two shillings."[417][418] Boland's father started a pig business in Dublin, which struggled until he realised he could pay the staff of the Clarence Hotel for all the guests' uneaten food, and his pigs quickly fattened.[419]

Some of that commerce took place under the table, as when certain shopkeepers quietly kept a bit of poteen [pa-CHEEN], or Irish moonshine, on special request. Moonshiners took barrels around the countryside, "some of the local ballad singers passed on information at the ceilidhs [dances, pronounced "KAY-lees"] by including references to local places in the words of the songs they sang."[420]

---

[414] *Them Golden Fields I Trod,* 12.
[415] *Dublin Tenement Life,* 99.
[416] *Where We Sported and Played,* 79.
[417] *Them Golden Fields I Trod,* 144.
[418] *Tides of Change,* 77.
[419] *Tales of a City Farmyard,* 73.
[420] *Times of our Lives.*

Those who grew up in World War II, with battles taking place in the oceans around neutral Ireland, remember wreckage and cargo washing up on the beach, and locals selling it. Dockworkers at Ringsend didn't ask too many questions, and "when the rest of Ireland was on its knees during the war years from 1940 up to 1945 Ringsend had a very good time of it" with all kinds of otherwise rationed supplies, David Murphy said. "It just made its way to Ringsend, let's put it that way."[421]

Pubs, as mentioned, were also meeting-places, community centres, funeral homes, supply stores and banks, and like the shopkeepers, publicans were lords of their kingdom. They decided whether to trust someone enough to cash their cheque or extend them credit. Many pubs allowed trusted customers to stay on after legal hours for a "lock-in," when the pub would shutter its windows and appear dark and empty from the outside, but continue celebrating inside. Tony Carr remembered his publican, Tomsie Broughhall, allowing "people he'd taken a liking to on the night" to stay after for a sing-a-long into the wee hours of the morning, and they all turned out the lights and hid when the garda came by to check the place.[422]

Most Irish villages still have a pub and butcher, but most of the old shops have given way to chain stores and supermarkets. Ireland's small towns, like the USA's, are seeing more and more rows of shops boarded-up and covered in graffiti.[423] The new businesses don't have time for socialising, Gerry Rafferty said. "Time was when you were a customer of a grocer's shop you were treated as something of a VIP, but now you are just one of the throng."[424]

Generations raised with this now expect nothing else. "You still have older people coming in -- but the younger people, they don't want to have the one pair of shoes for ten or fifteen years now," said cobbler Lauri Grennell. "The old customers, they love a yap. But some people have no time for talking now."[425]

---

[421] *Dublin Voices - An Oral Folk History*, 224.
[422] *Some Time to Kill*, 148.
[423] "Con Carey and the 12 Apostles," RTE, 2014.
[424] *And the Band Played On*, 41.
[425] *Dublin Voices*, 226.

***

Outside of Ireland, we've lived with supermarkets for so many generations that we've forgotten what strange creations they are. The whole idea of a supermarket is to make you do work – finding an item, carrying it to the till, and often checking it out --- that used to be the shopkeeper's job. If they can get you to also clean up the mess in aisle three, you will have completed your journey to become an unpaid employee. When supermarkets first appeared in Ireland, people called them "huckster shops."[426]

Many supermarkets now hire elderly employees to greet people at the door, trying to replicate the feeling of neighbourliness that people once got from shopkeepers. The most basic items – vegetables, eggs -- are placed at far corners of the cathedral, making you walk past all the other things you could buy, and the shelves at eye level have the most expensive items. They make you stand in line next to magazines and trinkets that you also weren't planning to buy. Of course, most shops then offered only a small range of items and brands, but they were the necessities that everyone needed and wanted; shopping was not a pastime for them.

All the same, modern people tell me, more choices are always better. It's an understandable response, for every major political faction in every country, left or right, claims to love freedom, and defines freedom as more consumer choices. When Americans wanted to show how much better they were than the Soviets, they pointed to the 30,000 products on the shelves of the average US supermarket. More choice is the one thing we all say we want.

Of course we are fortunate to live in a time of such plenty, when we are literally spoiled for choice. Yet how meaningful are most of these choices? Do more consumer goods always mean more freedom? And if more choices are better, why do we have higher rates of depression, addiction and suicide than almost any previous society?

Let's look at what happens when we choose to buy something – for example, the last thing I bought, laundry soap. There were several brands on the shelf – which one gets the clothes cleaner? (All of them equally, as

---

[426] "Markets Without Middlemen," RTE documentary, 1975.

far as I can tell.) Which brand is made more or less locally, and which one treats its employees best? What chemicals will each of them wash into the sewage system? I try to be a discriminating consumer, but I don't know the answers to most of these questions, and neither do you. The hours I could spend researching all would cost more than the soap.

Most of our choices are meaningless to us, worse than useless. Spotify offers 40 million songs, or around 380 years of choices, and Youtube as I write this offers (I estimate) two million years of videos. Yet I'm not going to listen to more than one song at a time, so if I only listen to only new music until I die, less than a millionth of those choices are meaningful to me.

The act of choosing itself creates a momentary uptick in stress, which can paralyse people into putting off the decision; a study of company pension plans found that the more choices employees were offered, the less likely they were to choose any pension plans at all. When we do choose, we are often left with a residual dissatisfaction and lingering thoughts of the roads not taken.[427] As Ann Gardinier said about shopping today, "unlimited choice can be confusing and ultimately is no choice at all."[428]

Of course to a man with one choice, two is far better. Three is better still. But beyond a point each additional choice becomes noise, so fewer choices often leave us happier. In one series of studies some shoppers were given a few items to sample, and others a large number of items, and the shoppers were *ten times* more likely to buy from the small sample. Fewer choices made choosing easier and more satisfying.

This is why couch potatoes can endlessly flip across stations without ever finding something to watch – something that never happened when people had two or three channels. This is why our grandparents in an Irish village or small American town found someone to love forever, while Tinder addicts never will.

How do we avoid the problem of overwhelming choice? The solutions, I'm sorry to say, are three of the most unfairly maligned words in our modern culture: restrictions, routines and rules.

---

[427] Redden 2017; Iyengar 2000; Read, 1995; Redden 1990.
[428] *The House Remembers*, 97.

Restricting your choices actually makes them more satisfying, as we saw earlier, and everyone from medieval monks to modern motivational gurus realised that self-restraint in the short run makes us happier in the long run. When we know we absolutely won't gamble or commit adultery, for example, we remove dangerous variables from our decisions.[429]

Routines, likewise, are something every advertisement and movie presents as something to escape; movies often start with characters stuck in a routine and their character arc is to learn to live spontaneously. Among real humans, though, routines take (hopefully already good) choices and set them on automatic pilot, lifting some of the daily decision-making burden.

Rules are similarly misrepresented. Philosopher Garret Hardin wrote a famous essay called "The Tragedy of the Commons," in which local farmers all graze their cattle in a common pasture, but each cow is privately owned, and its meat and milk profits the owner. The pasture is a collective resource from which each individual can draw a private profit. The pasture can only support so many cows at a time, though, and beyond a certain point – what ecologists call the "carrying capacity" – too many degrade the pasture for everyone.

Each farmer, though, profits when they increase their herd, and if only one farmer does so, all the others are pressured to increase their herds to stay competitive. If each farmer acts rationally in their own self-interest, though, as modern economic theory says they should, everyone loses. The cows overgraze, the soil erodes and everyone's cows die.

Hardin's essay has been cited in more than 100,000 papers since then, debating its meaning and its applications. What few point out, though, is that Hardin's scenario is purely hypothetical. He wasn't a real farmer using a real commons, like my sheep-herding neighbours on the Curragh have done for hundreds or thousands of years. Real humans in those situations act like neighbours, not economic models, and they work out rules and compromises.

Rules became a curse word in modern commerce because our governments and corporations grew so vast and complex that rules to regulate them grew equally Byzantine, removed from our influence and

---

[429] *The Paradox of Choice*, 228.

understanding. In pop culture we idolise the action-movie hero or business guru who "doesn't play by the rules."

Yet you live in a society with rules, spoken or unspoken, that guide us through human situations. As Joseph Heath and Andrew Potter point out, no one likes to wait in line, but a line speeds everyone up safely; in a fire or other panic, the resulting crush slows everyone down. Most behaviours would be terrible if everyone did them, so no one should do them. Following the rules doesn't mean you're a conformist or brainwashed, but just a good citizen.[430]

* * *

While village shops were more personal than today's supermarkets, even they were not necessary for commerce, for farmers and craftsmen often sold directly to buyers. "When fairs were frequent, shops were not needed," William Cobbett wrote in the 1830s. "A manufacturer of shoes, of stockings, of hats; of almost anything that man wants, could manufacture at home in an obscure hamlet, with cheap house-rent, good air, and plenty of room. He need pay no heavy rent for shop; and no disadvantages from confined situation; and then, by attending three or four or five or six fairs in a year, he sold the work of his hands ...."[431]

That's exactly what they did in town squares and Dublin alleys; "all the farmers brought their produce to the street markets ... and would amiably chat and haggle prices with everyone who passed by."[432] The older neighbourhoods still have a few market vendors, loudly singing their wares.

It was in country towns, though, that markets and fairs were absolutely vital, Markets and fairs were "an important part of the farming and social life of Ireland fifty years ago. ... Fairs were held in every town in Ireland, three or four times a year."[433] "In many market towns there were, in fact, two markets each month, the first of these usually being the more important and attracting large numbers of farmers and their families from

---

[430] *Nation of Rebels,* 79.
[431] *Rural Rides,* p 474.
[432] *Your Dinner's Poured Out,* 66.
[433] *The House Remembers,* 122.

outlying districts."[434] Families came from all around; Gardinier remembered a special "market bus" that drove around picking up all the families. "It would stop anywhere; outside houses, shops, boreens or gateways."[435]

Market days were holidays, Martin Keaveney remembered. "The schools were closed on fair days, not so much so the children could enjoy the fair, but because so many stray animals would be wandering around the village – and remember the school and everything else in the village might only be huddled around a single junction or stretch of road."[436]

Farmers started walking their herds and flocks to town the day before, and by market day, Duffy said, "thousands of sheep lined the footpath," and "the square and, indeed, much of the rest of the town, was choc-a-block with every type of animal form sheep to cattle to horses to donkeys," Ann Gardinier said.[437] Horses were bought and sold at the fairs, and horse-racing was one of the main attractions. The markets themselves "had a carnival atmosphere about them"[438] and brought "travelling showmen, amazing and amusing characters, some with performing bears, monkeys and parrots," Maurice McAleese said. "There were jugglers, too, acrobats and ballad singers..."[439]

Itinerant craftsmen wandered the countryside – "tinkers," they were called, as they fixed tin pots – while others repaired shoes or simply sold trinkets. "The cobblers were not just useful, but they also brought all the gossip and news from the surrounding countryside, and that was a cause for celebration – often a dance."[440] Farmers, too, carried all the local news from their village, sometimes transporting messages back and forth for friends, from their own community to the people they'd meet at the market.

When market day ended, the bus came back again, and families boarded carrying anything and everything, from wheels of cheese to ducks

---

[434] *Back Through the Fields*, 91.
[435] *The House Remembers*, 90.
[436] *Growing Up With Ireland*, 20.
[437] *The House Remembers*, 123.
[438] *Back Through the Fields*, 91.
[439] *Back Through the Fields*, 93.
[440] *Back Through the Fields*, 105.

and geese – plants, chicks, ducks, geese – and one woman, who brought a large cloth bag to market, came home with a calf in the bag. Gardinier remembers all the families singing together on the bus, all the way home.[441]

* * *

If those markets worked better, you might ask, why did anyone change? The shift took decades, and required people to be convinced that everything is moving in a better direction and they need to get on board. They needed to be sold on the idea of progress.

You might think that progress is an easily provable thing: we have mobile phones, our ancestors didn't. For most of us, though, progress is far more than that. It is an idea that caught on quite recently, yet dominates how we view the world.

As John Michael Greer pointed out,[442] progress is how we describe the story of our past, from stone tools to farming to chariots to engines to laptops, always "forward" in a straight line. It's how we describe social ideas, from "backward" sexists and racists to modern "progressives." It's how we describe the evolution of life on Earth, an ascent from primordial slime to fish to apes to humans to the stars. It's how we describe our future of flying cars and mile-high skyscrapers. It's how we describe geopolitics, calling First World countries "developed" by more progress, while Saudi Arabia and China are "developing" – supposedly on the road to becoming us.

What progress means, then, is an invisible force that makes everything better – in Martin Luther King's words, "the arc of the universe is long, but it bends toward justice." When we are prosperous we thank progress, when we are not we wonder why progress abandoned us. Someday, we are told, humanity will ascend to the heavens, and if we choose to side with progress we will not be left behind.

---

[441] *The House Remembers*, 90.

[442] See, for example, *The Long Descent: A User's Guide to the End of the Industrial Age, After Progress: Reason and Religion at the End of the Industrial Age,* and *Not the Future we Ordered: Peak Oil, Psychology and the Myth of Progress.*

Replace the word "progress" with "God," and you see why we're not just talking about a set of mechanical devices, but a religion -- evangelical Christianity with one word changed. As modern Hollywood culture spread over the last century or so, smothering local folk culture in country after country, progress has quietly replaced every other religion. Even most atheists, so proud of rejecting every other belief, are fanatics in this faith.

Take, for example, how evolution is portrayed in pop culture, as an invisible force that makes all life better until it becomes us. Fundamentalist Christians denounce this as a rejection of God, and fundamentalist atheists embrace it for the same reasons. Neither group, though, is actually talking about evolution in the biological sense. They're talking about progress, a dark god that rewards the superior and kills the rest.

In biology, evolution simply means change over time. Plants and animals that are best at surviving survive, and whatever genetic traits help them survive get passed down to their offspring, but they do not become "superior" in a moral sense. Biologists observe this process but they do not "believe" in it any more than chemists worship catalytic combustion.

So if life did not follow a path of progress, what about the arc of history that took us from caves to the moon? Surely that's progress?

Our human story, though. did not follow that arc, or any arc. For our first 95 percent of time on this Earth modern humans hunted and foraged. Even when they bred crops and domesticated animals they lived within the hard limits of Nature. They could keep warm in winter by burning wood in the fire, but cut down too many trees and they don't have enough for next winter. Killing more pigs this year left fewer to use next year. Humans were subject to the same natural laws as all other living things, and all our cultural attitudes and religious teachings were based around this.

What changed was the discovery that fossil fuels could be burned in a metal engine to do the work of many horses – "horsepower." Coal, oil and gas allowed us to humans to move faster than anyone had imagined, from trains to cars to planes. They power turbines to create electricity, surrounding us with brilliant light at all hours. They power machines that construct buildings far higher than ever imagined, with electric elevators to reach the top. They allow us to broadcast images and sounds on screens, to converse across a planet in real time. Innovations were so frequent and world-changing that we became used to the idea that it would continue forever.

However you frame it, though, progress – in the sense of the runaway growth of those decades -- was always going to be temporary. Its founding principle was growth, and not linear growth (2,3,4,5,6) but exponential growth (2,4,8,16,32,64,128). Take anything our modern world depends on – interest rates, GDP, inflation, production – and it all grows by a percentage each year, meaning it doubles in a number of years, then doubles again and again. Nothing in Nature grows that way, with one exception – cancer, and then not for long.

Take the amount of rubbish in the world, which rose tenfold between 1900 and 2000 and almost doubled since then, to around two billion tonnes a year. That's more or less exponential growth, which means that in 800 years – and for reference, the pub down the road from me is 800 years old --- we will have 268 million times more rubbish, or enough to cover the Earth a few miles thick. I'm not predicting that will happen – it will never happen, because it's ridiculous. Since our economy relies on throwaway goods, however, that means that our economy, as we know it, will be replaced by something else one way or another. And we know that something else is possible, because a world of throwaway goods never existed until historically five minutes ago.

Or imagine that our oil consumption continues to double about every twenty years; in a century we will have to burn 32 times what we do now. Yes, I know that some "peak oil" writers in the early 2000s predicted an imminent apocalypse that never happened, but I'm not. I'm saying there's nowhere near enough oil to continue as we have been -- and since oil powers all our cars, planes, ships, trains and tractors, we'll have to do some things differently.

When activists point out the problems with fossil-fuel use or climate change, they make the same mistake every time; they yell that we only have a few years left until Doomsday unless we repent and change our evil ways. A few years later, when we're all still here, many naturally conclude these issues were imaginary, and dismiss their prophecies as we do those of street-corner preachers. My point is the opposite. These doomsday scenarios are impossible – but because they are impossible, our culture will not continue forever exactly as it has in the last few generations. One way or another, we will have to rediscover some more traditional ways of doing things.

When people today picture the future, they usually fall back on familiar tropes of flying cars and mile-high skyscrapers, but those tropes have remained much the same for a century, always ten years away. Most of the inventions people cite as proof of progress– electricity, cars, planes, phones, computers, televisions – appeared in the 70 years between the 1870s and 1940s. Look at a 1950s movie and the characters have dishwashers, cars and televisions just as we do, 70 years further on, and their devices usually lasted longer.

Nor do the familiar promises of a techno-future hold up to much scrutiny. Tens of thousands die every year in car crashes; how much worse would it be if the cars were moving at high speed through the sky? Even now, as tech media praise the future of self-driving cars, they show a shocking inability to consider questions like: who is held responsible when (not if) it runs someone over, or is hacked, or is used to transport a bomb?

Nor would more technological complexity lead to greater equality or freedom; in totalitarian societies like China, it does the opposite. In fact, totalitarian ideologies like Naziism and Communism were rooted in the myth of progress, in the belief they could create a better future that would justify any means to get there.

When we tapped fossil fuels we won a one-time lottery. As Greer put it, though, to believe it would continue forever means believing that tomorrow we will win two lotteries, then four, then eight. It would be like a clever but naive child realising that last year they grew an inch, and this year two inches, and calculating that by the time they are a hundred years old they will be a billion feet tall.

In the real world, though, all growth runs up against some kind of natural limit. It could be an ecological limit – fish, topsoil, water, phosphorous, nitrogen. It could be a limit of energy – we could manufacture all the oil we need in a laboratory, but it costs more to make than the energy we'd get from the oil. It could be a buildup of side effects, like the loneliness of the social media age.

More complexity requires more upkeep for fewer benefits. Most of us have sensed that our computers and software get less effective with each new patch and upgrade, in exchange for obscure features that we never use. Most "smart" technologies are giant Rube Goldberg networks to do things we did perfectly well before; we have coffee makers and toasters that can spy on us, but they don't make better coffee or toast than the ones from a century ago.

Growth also runs into Braess' Paradox: We deal with traffic jams by building more roads, but more roads draw more drivers and more residents and businesses on the road, until you have more traffic jams. Most of us spend our lives dealing with technological equivalents of this; we spend more time on housework than we did before labour-saving devices.[443] Tech writer Nick Heer found in 2018 that web sites were so laden with cookies, ads and other junk that they load more slowly than they did in the 1990s.[444] Every new invention is advertised as a "revolution" – but revolutions, by definition, bring us back where we started.

The churning of fashions creates the illusion of generational change, but our cars are no faster than they were several decades ago, and many SUVs are no more fuel efficient than Model Ts were a century ago[445] Travelling through London by car today is about as fast as it was by horse and carriage a century ago.[446] Our fastest passenger jets fly at half the speed they did in the 1970s. The biggest cargo ships today run slower than some sailing ships did.[447]

We've had a few new inventions in the last several decades, like mobile phones and the internet. Those weren't as revolutionary as we imagine, though; everything we do with them, like order by catalogue or write letters, we did before them, and with fewer mind-altering side

---

[443] "Hours Spent in Homemaking Have Changed Little This Century," *National Bureau of Economic Research*, 10 Jan 2008.

[444] "The Bullshit Web," Pixel Envy blog, 30 July 2018.

[445] Most SUVs get between 17 and 26 mpg, as opposed to the 13 – 21 mpg Ford advertised for its Model T.

[446] "London traffic means buses are 'slower than a horse and cart' *The London Standard*, 17 Oct 2016.

[447] "Fuel surcharge practices of container shipping lines: Is it about cost recovery or revenue making?." *Proceedings of the 2009 International Association of Maritime Economists (IAME) Conference,* June 2009.

effects. Men landed on the moon, but in five decades we have not returned; the Space Age ended long ago, and is passing into legend.

In most areas of life, progress has become a net detriment to our lives, and doesn't need to continue indefinitely. We don't need the length of our commutes, or the amount of spam in our e-mails, or the US national debt, or the amount of pornographic photos on the internet, or any number of other things that have been exponentially growing, to continue. It's okay for these things to slow or stop, or even reverse.

I'm not saying that progress has been uniformly terrible; again, I'm glad to have cures for diseases that once killed people, or be able to type this on a laptop. In many areas, though, we would benefit from rediscovering ways that worked better. We'd benefit from turning global financial companies back into George Bailey's Savings and Loan, or the global agribusiness system into family farms again. We'd benefit from the literacy and safety people once had.

As Carl Jung wrote, "we have plunged down a cataract of progress, which sweeps us on into the future with ever wilder violence the farther it takes us from our roots. Once the past has been breached, it is usually annihilated, and there is no stopping the forward motion ... We no longer live on what we have, but on promises, no longer in the light of the present day, but in the darkness of the future, which, we expect, will at last bring the proper sunrise. *We refuse to recognise that everything better is purchased at the price of something worse.*"[448]

---

[448] *Memories, Dreams, Reflections*, p. 287, Italics mine.

Chapter Ten

Dying

Maybe your family too did something that you always thought normal as a child, until you were much older and realised how odd it was. Maybe you were the only child in your class whose family spoke a different language at home, or hunted deer, or whose family sang along to television commercials. Something you learned not to share too widely.

In my family, anyone who reached middle age was jovially presented with a "dirt cake," a chocolate cake with half a cookie poking out to look like a tombstone. My aunts and uncles exchange almost daily e-mails about who died recently -- cousins, old friends, celebrities, anyone. We divide up the belongings of newly deceased relatives, and remember them as we hang their old paintings on our walls, put on their old clothes, or use their old tools.

I still remember the moment I mentioned this to friends, and the look of revulsion on their faces. Not amusement at someone's eccentricity, not acceptance of a different family's culture. *Revulsion.* The thought of talking openly about someone's death, or using a dead person's forks or neckties or books, struck them as sickening.

What do normal people do when someone dies, I thought? In many cases, I found, they clean out Grandma's house, loading her books, favourite mugs, and keepsakes into a dumpster -- all with the same sense of grim obligation as when they visited her in the nursing home, or listened to her stories, or handled the funeral.

That is how our lives end now. As we get closer to our own deaths we are valued less, not more. We spend our final years as an annoyance, our bodies kept alive but our experiences ignored. When our bodies give out our belongings and memories will be discarded hastily, like diseased bandages. Our fingers and feet and genitals will be left for strangers to manhandle. We will rarely be brought up in conversation, and never comfortably. It's impossible to exaggerate what monsters we would seem to any culture that came before us.

For ten thousand generations our forebears dealt with life and death every day; they hunted and fished, cared for the animals they would one day slaughter, defended their families with violence and buried their own dead. Even now, John Connelly said, "to live in the countryside is to accept death as normal; it is not removed or hidden from us, but a part of life, and for that I am thankful."[449]

Unlike any other animal, we know we will die, and every culture had its own intimate spiritual rituals for it. "Death is frightening for the unprepared," Mary Fogarty's grandmother told her, "but our religion teaches us how to live and die."[450]

The Stoics of Ancient Rome taught "memento mori," that every day we should carry with us a reminder that we will die. Here in Ireland people remembered the dead on Halloween, lit candles for the dead in church, held Masses in their memory, made the sign of the cross when they passed by burial sites. On Ash Wednesday, the priest rubbed ashes into their heads to remind them, "Remember, man, that you are dust, and into dust you shall return" – not as a morbid preoccupation, but as a way – *the* way – to make us truly live.

"As my father drove to town in the pony and trap, he would tip his cap and make the sign of the cross as he passed particular gateways and old houses," Ann Gardinier remembered. "[and] launch into reminiscences about neighbours who had passed away."[451]

Today, we can afford to hide death as we once hid sex, but at the cost of maturity. Without it we hurtle towards our end unprepared. Death reminds us that we are not our avatars or online identities, limitless and ever-changing at whim. This is not a screen, not a game, not a play, not a movie, not a fantasy. When you are gone, other people will think and feel, but they will not be you, and they will spend no more time caring about

---

[449] *The Cow Book*, 89.
[450] *The Farm by Lough Gur*, 90.
[451] *The House Remembers*, 21.

you than you spent concerned for your own forebears. You will be under the grass.

During our brief time alive, death walks behind us, a heart flutter or frayed wire or sleepy driver away. We have many things on our minds, but it has only one. We think of it as an enemy, but it spurs us to live better, to put away childish things, to turn away from the mirrors in our minds and feel the snore of a baby in our arms, observe the shafts of green light through treetops, cherish the touch of an aging hand. *This is all you will ever have. Make the most of it.*

"My father, who worked with the Earth, felt a closeness to Nature with a full acceptance of its laws and the laws of God," Alice Taylor said. "Years afterward, when he was a very old man, visiting him I would ask, 'How are you?' and he would smile serenely and say, 'Waiting.' Death was as natural to him as the seasons and he had come to terms with his God out in the fields … in old age he found an inner peace; it was as if, coming near the end of the road, he looked back and saw that all the turnings had led him in the one direction."[452]

Of course, people tell me, we live longer than most of our ancestors, and should be thankful death is so unfamiliar to us. Of course that's true to a point, although we saw earlier that human life-spans weren't as short as we imagine; adults often survived into their 70s, and outside of a few exceptional events, people were not dropping dead of starvation or plague every day anymore than we are. True, our technology has given us a few more years on average, but how do we spend those years? In the case of most elderly people I know, they will be spent sitting lonely, in front of a television.

Yet they are not usually allowed to die at home, even though 71 percent of Americans say they would like to.[453] For one thing, most people can't afford to; a nurse recently wrote about caring for her mother and finding it cost $145,000.[454] Most of us, rather, will die attached to machines in a hospital, occasionally visited by staff paid to look like they

---

[452] *To School Through the Fields,* 149.
[453] "Views and Experiences with End-of-Life Medical Care in the U.S.," KFF survey, 27 April 2017.
[454] "My grandmother died at home, just as she wanted. It cost $145,000," KBUR, 8 Feb 2023.

care about us. Death -- like birth or food or education or anything else in our culture -- has become an industry, an inconvenience we outsource to specialists.

In a village, though, you know the elderly among you. You see them every day, heard their stories, sang next to them in church, footed turf with them, sowed fields together, perhaps watched as they showed you how to deliver a calf or find the fishes' hiding places. "The old were never alone as the neighbours joined hands around them and the young, too, were included in the circle," Taylor said. "As in every group of individuals, all had their own idiosyncrasies, and we as children were educated in human awareness by the close association with many people."[455]

When elders grew close to death, friends and neighbours from all around came to visit, people who might have explored birds' nests together, helped foot the turf, accepted each other's cheques when the banks closed. People depended on each other, so a death meant a library of memories gone, a gap in the voices of the choir, an empty pew in church, a vacant seat at the pub. Only in our modern world do so many people die alone and unremembered.

Their last days were a vigil of daughters and sons and sisters, people who shared most of the same daily memories for decades, their souls intertwined into a single living thing with a memory centuries old. Together they had delivered, nursed, healed and buried many relatives before them, their joys heightened because they were shared, their grief lessened because they were shared.

As death drew nearer the family gathered around the dying in their small rooms, just as other humans did in their huts or yurts or shelters as long as we have been human. They said the rosary together, prayer after prayer. And sometimes, they tell me, a swelling rose inside them, like a wind filling sails, and their gathered bodies became its instruments, and they lifted their voices together in song.

***

---

[455] *To School Through the Fields*, 7.

Imagine, as Irish journalist Kevin Toolis put it, inviting all your neighbours to your home, only to reveal Grandma's dead body lying on the kitchen table. Imagine, in our culture, offering everyone whiskey and sandwiches while everyone sat around the body and chatted. Imagine hundreds of people coming by, not just to sit in uncomfortable silence around the corpse but to tell stories, to laugh about good times past, to sob in each other's arms. Imagine an entire party where people flirted and fought and played games around the body. Or carrying the body for miles to the graveyard by hand, or digging the grave yourself.

Most people today, of course, would call the police; exposing a body publicly can be illegal, Toolis points out, and accident victims are shrouded or pixelated. Many of us go years or decades without ever seeing a body, and never one that has not been embalmed and covered in cosmetics to feign life.

Yet in traditional Ireland people laid out their loved ones just like this – and a few still do. Virtually every traditional culture had some similar ritual where the living gather around the dead and say farewell, whether jungle tribes, desert nomads or the Greeks of the *Iliad* feasting for nine days to mourn Hector. The wake could be our species' oldest and most universal tradition – and one that has disappeared from many cultures in living memory, without anyone noticing.

When most of us today picture death, or grief – or lovemaking, or conversation, or almost anything – we are picturing actors enacting them on a screen, as part of a story written and sold for profit, designed to pound our emotional buttons and resolve in an hour or two. Real grief, though, doesn't follow the same course as movie grief; it unfolds in its own way, with our loss stabbing us at inconvenient moments, between stretches of peace and laughter. Modern funerals ask us to conceal inconvenient feelings while we sit in discomfort, but wakes give us permission to enjoy our final days with a loved one, and give grief license to come when it will.

"… a wake was like a wedding," said Nellie McCann of Dublin. "As a kid I'd go to a wake with me mother. Oh, you'd go to a wake and you'd be telling frightening stories the whole night and you'd be afraid of your life to come out then and so you'd stay till dawn. And the banshee would be around, always come for someone that'd died. The dead was there for three solid nights. And my mother'd go in and wash them and do them out and put the habit on them. At wakes you'd get everything, jokes and singing and everything!... Oh, the wakes were great."[456]

No neighbours needed to be invited to a wake, Mary Corbally said, but everyone was expected to appear. "See, the door was open and anyone could turn up," she said. "They'd go to wakes like they'd go to dances now. They might not even know the person."[457]

No wake was complete without alcohol, and according to Irish radio, it could cost more than the grave; people could judge how beloved someone was by how many empty barrels they had left over.[458] "A barrel of stout was purchased the day after our grandfather died and it was shared among friends and neighbours who called to pay their respects," Michael Curran said.[459]

After the funeral, likewise, "the women would go off together and get drunk, and not come home until late" – one of the few times women got a day off. "Oh, the women'd be looking forward to it!"[460]

If laying out a body in the middle of the house doesn't sound shocking enough to modern ears, people often played games throughout the wake, "strange ancient games ...[like] Shuffle the Brogue and the Rope Game and the Horse Fair 'and a very wicked one called the Mock Marriage.' But every half hour the gamesters stopped to pray for the soul of the dead."[461] Some of the games got surprisingly racy for the occasion, particularly kissing games between unmarried men and women; many a match was made at a wake. More than anything else, wakes are celebrations of life, of the specific life now ending and of the cycle of life continuing after them. "Live wakes," saying goodbye to a family member moving overseas, were the truly mournful occasions.

In the modern world, of course, we have an entire industry – hospitals, hospices, nursing homes, medical examiners and mortuaries, designed to

---

[456] *Dublin Voices*, 258.
[457] *Dublin Tenement Life*, 207.
[458] "House Strictly Private," RTE documentary.
[459] *Tides of Change*, 17.
[460] *Dublin Tenement Life*, 89.
[461] *The Farm by Lough Gur*, xv.

hide death and those close to it. "We don't want to see the sick, smell the decay of wizened flesh, feel the coldness of the corpse, or hear the cry of keening women," Toolis wrote. "We don't want to intrude on the dying because we don't want to look at a mirror of our death."[462]

As Toolis points out, our taboo of death is so powerful that it overrides our modern impulse to make every activity into a racket. You'd think someone would have created an UberHearse app for the best deals on funerals and graves, but our physical demise remains our last sacred subject.

It also overrides our claims of a free society. Even the most anti-government libertarian ignores the fact that once your body is cold a state official can saw off the top of your head, take out your brain, or do whatever they see fit. Our bodies' fluids are drained, replaced with toxic chemicals that will leach from our bodies slowly over centuries to come, poisoning children we will never know. Families might not be able to object, and if they do not have the right forms they might not get the body back. As Toolis puts it, when we die we enter a kind of communist state in which we need permission from governments to do anything.

"We have come to believe that this ... is our natural order," he wrote. "That the old and the sick will die happier amidst the babbling noise and alien light of a hospital ward. That the indignities inflicted upon them are necessary...that being packed off in the ambulance to die among strangers --- whoever happens to be on that night's hospital shift – is what the dying deserve, because this is how life now ends, for all of us."[463]

In most Western countries the modern death industry supplanted the old traditions in the 20th century, with few people commenting on it even at the time. Ireland, as usual, only transitioned within living memory, and a 1970s radio documentary interviewed some of the new breed of undertakers offering "American-style" pre-made coffins and mortuary homes to a sceptical Irish population. Even then, while they believed they represented a more "enlightened attitude toward death," they wanted to find a sane middle ground between tradition and modern customs.

---

[462] *My Father's Wake*, 20.
[463] *My Father's Wake*, 22.

"When they see that it's not a gimmick, that it's a service we're providing, they're happier about it," one said, "but they are very suspicious of this business of exploiting, and I feel a lot of the Americans' way of death is exploiting."

Other more traditional undertakers disagreed with anything that would detract from the Irish wake. "It's foreign to Ireland, anyway, it's an American way of life," said undertaker Michael Walsh. "It's shouldn't happen in Ireland.... It's most disrespectful to bury your person without a wake." One man said that for funeral homes were "exploiting a sad situation."[464]

"...my uncle ... Davy built a funeral parlour a few months ago," John Connelly said. "He tells me it is the way of the future – that wakes and removals, which have been part of the fabric of rural Ireland for so many centuries, perhaps since before the time of Christianity, are now a thing of the past. People no longer want to have the body of their loved one in the house for three days. We will do things the American way in the future, he says. I find this odd, for it is our rituals of death that have helped us mourn those who have passed. The three days give us, the living a chance to grieve ... When my time comes, I too shall go in the old ways."[465]

***

When the wake was done, the family of the deceased put the body into a coffin -- perhaps one they had made by hand, perhaps long ago and set aside awaiting this day – and carried the body to the church, often for miles, with the community walking behind and everyone they passed stopping and taking off their caps. "See, the way it was, if one was in sorrow, we were all in sorrow. Everybody knew everybody else. It was a *community*."[466]

I still saw this happen when I commuted by bus from my home in the countryside; occasionally the bus slowed and stopped for twenty minutes or more, waiting for dozens of people to walk down a dim country road on

---

[464] House Strictly Private, RTE documentary.
[465] *The Cow Book*, 89.
[466] *Dublin Tenement Life*, 89.

a winter night, carrying a coffin. All of us on the bus, too, got out and stood silently, caps in hand, as they passed.

After the Mass the dead was laid in the churchyard, ringed by the ancient yew trees that are the symbol of life and death. They spend eternity as they lived, surrounded by names they knew, part of something greater and older than any of us. In our modern world, too, most of us will lay in death as we were in life; surrounded by strangers in a strange land.

Around the grave, the women began to caoin (pronounced "keen"), "a loud high-pitched piercing wail without words, and for those who heard it for the first time the memory lingers on," said Mike Curran. "At that moment the voice seemed frozen in time as the sound filled the graveyard. After some minutes the sound ceased and like the calm that follows the storm, normality was soon restored. At that particular time I was nine years old and that sound will always remain with me."[467]

"It was a tradition that on that evening of the removal of the body from the house to the church, the family walked behind the hearse ..." said undertaker Joseph Fanagan. "Or sometimes they didn't want a hearse at all and they'd carry the coffin .... to the church. And you always ask the family when they go out of the church, 'Would you like to go around by the house?' That still goes on. But now, funerals in Ringsend or on City Quay, not only would they go by the house, but they'd go by the pubs he drank in!"[468] Local pubs might help pay for the funeral of their longtime patrons, as mentioned earlier.

It was a tradition that on the evening of the removal of the body from the house to the church the family walked behind the hearse, even in my time. They'd walk up to half a mile. Or sometimes they didn't want a hearse at all and they'd carry the coffin .... The next morning the Mass would be at 10 am – that's the usual time – and mourning coaches and carriages would be brought to the church. And you always ask the family when they go out of the church, "Would you like to go around by the house?" That still goes on. But now funerals in Ringsend or on City Quay,

---

[467] *Tides of Change*, 18.
[468] *Dublin Voices*, 136.

not only would they go by the house but they'd go by the pubs he drank in![469]

**

The church was at the centre of every village, and the Church of every life and death. People walked the country roads and through fields to church every Sunday, holy day, wedding, christening, first communion, funeral and memorial. Some people went every day. The only neighbours who didn't show were the sick, so it became the barometer of health. "'Is she back at Mass yet?' You might hear somebody ask," said Ann Gardinier.[470]

It was a social gathering as well as a spiritual one, with all the men sitting together on one side and all the women on the other. "The older women in the back pew had their heads together, whispering about clocking hens, egg prices and local scandals," Gardinier said. "The newly married woman, walking up the aisle, who'd put on a bit of weight, came under their scrutiny. They counted months on their fingers."[471]

Anyone could drop by a church at any time, for just like all homes, all churches were unlocked. "No one would ever think of pinching anything from a church," one old man told me. "The doors were open all the time."

Most went about once a week to confess their sins to the priest, and were sent away with a certain number of prayers to say in penitence. Christy Kennealley remembered all his schoolmates quickly figuring out which priests gave the easy assignments, and all the boys lining up only for them in church.[472]

When Declan Hassett went to an unfamiliar church one day, he went into the confessional booth, unburdened his soul and realise he'd been facing the wrong way, talking to a solid wall. Turning around to face the priest, he said, "in a panic I came up with a whopper just to get through the confession. I mumbled my act of contrition and stumbled out through the half-door of the church, red-faced and embarrassed," he said. "I had to

---

[469] *Dublin Voices*, 83.
[470] *The House Remembers*, 63.
[471] *The House Remembers*, 65.
[472] *Maura's Boy*, 119.

go back to confession the following week and tell the priest about the lie. I heard a groan and even in the dark I could see the priest's head in his hands. I did not wait for an absolution."[473]

"When I'd think of those poor men stuck in a confined space listening to a recital of our little misdemeanours for two hours, I'd have great sympathy for them," Gene Kerrigan said. "They were sorely tested as we considered confession as a reason to be out of school and we were going to make the most of it."[474]

As avuncular as most priests were, they held real authority then, and questioned loitering teenagers like a police officer; Gerry Rafferty remembers he and his friends scattering when they saw the priest coming in the distance. People tipped their caps when they passed a priest on the road, asked his advice, consulted him before getting married. The priest at Naas, near where I lived, was notoriously gruff; when a nervous couple showed up at his door one night and said, "We're thinking of getting married," he responded, "Well, come back when you've made up your minds," and closed the door on them.[475]

They also carried real responsibility. When someone was sick, the priest was called to sit with them; when fishermen prepared for the wild Atlantic waters, the priest blessed the boats. When someone in town was being disruptive, like the boy racer in the introduction, it was the priest's job to have a word with them. When the grumpy owner of Tony Carr's pub went into one of his black moods and refused to open, it was the priest who climbed a ladder to bang on his window.

For centuries of English rule in Ireland, to be a priest was to be an underground revolutionary, for the Catholic Church was effectively banned, soldiers broke up Masses, and priests were imprisoned and hanged. Yet just as the Irish organised their own schools, they organised their own Masses, holding them in the forest on special "Mass rocks." Or they gathered in people's homes, in secret. My neighbours told me stories, passed down through the generations, of British soldiers who burst in while a priest was secretly saying Mass, and all the men and women

---

[473] *The Way We Were*, 27.
[474] *Another Country*, 100.
[475] *Some Time to Kill*, 208.

formed a barrier to protect the priest while he escaped – some old houses still have the secret hiding places and passageways.

Occasionally people still do this, as when our priest held Mass in the nearby forest, shafts of green light slanting through the treetops around us like stained glass. And for centuries, even after Catholics were free to use the church, many rural parishes held Mass at people's homes, in what was called "the Stations."

"In our townland our turn for the Stations came around every six years and then it was like three Christmases rolled into one," Alice Taylor said. "The night before the Stations had a special atmosphere filled with a sense of expectancy. The whole house lay in readiness, with fires set in all the downstairs rooms. Tables were laid with fine china and shining silver while bowls of lump sugar and dishes of butter rolls lay covered in the kitchen. In front of the fire was a row of polished shoes graduating from tiny tots upwards. We were all bathed in a big timber tub in front of the bedroom fire and we young ones were the last to be washed because our chances of getting dirty again were the greatest."[476]

The next day they saw all their neighbours arrive at the door in their best clothes, along with two priests, one to hear their confessions in front of the fire, the other to say Mass in the kitchen. "There was a warm feeling about this Mass and communion, with all the neighbours gathered around the kitchen table," Taylor said. "We had worked and played together and now we were sharing something much greater with formed a different bond between us. It was like the Last Supper."[477]

Each local household got a chance to host the Stations, Taylor remembered, and everyone cleaned up their house for the occasion. When it fell to the local eccentric woman who lived alone, all the neighbours pitched in to help her clean up the place and repaint the furniture. On that occasion, though, everything went wrong; the chimney backed up, filling the house with smoke; everyone fled the house overpowered, and one of the ladies had to sit down, only to discover that the new furniture paint had not dried. Only the priest stuck it through to the end.

---

[476] *To School Through the Fields*, 13.
[477] *To School Through the Fields*, 14.

If the countryside was known for Stations, the cities had Corpus Christi processions every summer, in which the priest led thousands of parishioners behind him in a religious parade. "All the streets were decorated, and all the traffic was stopped, and the police were all on duty," my neighbour Christy said. Everyone from the Army to the Boy Scouts walked in the procession, he said, and even in Dublin's Jewish neighbourhood everyone came to watch and wave. "...There would be speakers attached to the poles all around. And all the people would decorate their houses, and all the shops would decorate their shops, with images and flowers and candles. It was massive."

It's difficult to imagine any parade shutting down a city or being treated with such reverence today, except perhaps during Pride season, where a very different priesthood perform very different acts in public. Even for religious people, church is often a weekly interruption of a modern life. For the Irish then, though, faith suffused life; people punctuated their words with blessings, crossed themselves as they passed churchyards, said the rosary before bed. Most families had priests or nuns in the family, but even laypeople were active in Catholic Confraternities or made pilgrimages to holy shrines. Everyone had a forehead mark on Ash Wednesday, everyone fasted during Lent. The radio and television paused – and still pause -- their broadcasts for the Angelus bell.

Rough dockworkers coming home stopped when they heard the Angelus bell, Ton Byrne said, and said the prayer together. They'd line up for church during Mission Week, and "and they'd sit there and some of them wouldn't have had anything to eat," he said. "And you'd look down at them, men that was after working all day, physically played out, and there they'd be going to the mission," even though "some of them was *tough* customers."[478]

When the Catholic Church held a Eucharistic Congress in Dublin in 1932, "every street and every house was decorated and you had altars outside. And holy pictures of the Pope. And you wouldn't find a piece of paper [litter] on the street where we lived."[479]

---

[478] *Dublin Voices*, 125.
[479] *Dublin Tenement Life*, 96.

Some Irish took part in regular pilgrimages to shrines of the Virgin Mary at Knock or other places where people had seen visions of her. Stephen Rynne took part in a pilgrimage up the mountain of Croagh Patrick, and saw that many around him – farmers like himself, children, old men and women -- were doing the climb in their bare feet. "Thank God that I belong to these people," he wrote. "Nothing that I have done, or read, or held, could alienate me from them. They are mine and I am theirs, I am proud not only of the grand old people, but even of the youngest and most frivolous. .... They are all of the right stuff, equally children of [St.] Patrick and fosterlings of [St.] Brigid."[480]

Today in Ireland the churches are filled with fewer grey heads every year as the country belatedly follows the same path as most of Europe. Of course, the sexual scandals revealed in the 1990s struck a blow to the Church's status, but it was already weakening. Catholicism remains recognisable from mass media, for when Central Casting needs someone to be demonically possessed or Whoopi Goldberg to wear a disguise, the Hawaiian shirts of feel-good mega-church pastors don't cut it. The Church represents all things arcane and traditional in Hollywood pop culture, yet that same culture has made those traditions difficult to maintain.

I'm focusing on the Catholic Church so intertwined with Irish culture, but of course you might be Orthodox or Jewish or Pentecostal or Mormon or Druid, or follow a Stoic code of ethics. Modern pop culture, though, doesn't respect these or any other tradition. It portrays all religion as something to escape, something stuck in the past that keeps people repressed.

Exactly. That's its purpose. Our ideology of perpetual indulgence doesn't come with a "stop" button, no star to guide us other than current fashion, no discipline to endure hardship or reason to do so.

Whatever you may think of the Catholic Church, its believers here saved classical learning for the world, even passing down mythologies they disagreed with. They fed the hungry and taught children for a millennia and a half. They worshiped in secret, blocked soldiers with their bodies, starved and died rather than give up their faith. In the millions. For centuries.

They had strength we do not. They believed in something.

---

[480] *Green Fields*, 249.

Chapter Eleven

Modern Ireland

For twenty years I lived in Ireland and talked to my neighbours, researched the lives they lived, and eventually, went to many of their wakes. In those years, though, I watched Ireland transform into a very different country.[481] The process had begun in the late 1990s, as global corporations set up headquarters in this low-tax country and started an economic "Celtic Tiger" that turned Ireland from one of Europe's poorest countries to one of its richest on paper. Global media celebrated Ireland's joining the modern world, belatedly but at a breakneck speed.

Of course many Irish not only benefitted from this wealth, but took pride in no longer being a backwater. Yet an IMF study found that three-quarters of that investment was simply corporations avoiding taxes by moving money through the country; the top 10 percent became fabulously wealthy, but little of that wealth reaches most people.[482] Between 1994 and 2001 About 60 percent of Irish people make less than 30,000 euros a year -- $32,000 -- yet Dublin is one of the most expensive cities to live in the world, and many of the old families are priced out of their own neighbourhoods. Dublin can now afford a bronze monument to the children that Christy remembered swinging from streetlamps, but no real children swing there anymore.[483]

---

[481] The details are outside the scope of this book, but have been admirably documented by journalist John Waters in his trilogy *Jiving at the Crossroads, Was it for This?* and *Give Us Back the Bad Roads.*

[482] "Almost two-thirds of Irish FDI is 'phantom' – IMF study," *Irish Times*, 9 Sept 2019.

[483] The Knight Frank Global Affordability Monitor 2019, www.knightfrank.com/blog /2019/01/28/the-knight-frank-global-affordability-monitor-2019. Also, "Our income divide will shape the election in two major ways," Irish Business Post, 26 Jan 2020.

A survey taken in 2002, as the Tiger was ramping up, found that 77 percent of Irish said the economic boom had not improved their quality of life.[484] A 2001 survey found that 73 percent of Irish found life more stressful than five years before.[485] An online survey the same year asked whether most people's stress had increased; 96 percent said yes.[486] The number of Irish who reported they were "very satisfied" with their lives dropped by a third between 1997 and 2002.[487]

Ireland is now seeing the same vivisection as most Western countries into two distinct and hostile cultures. The rural and working-class majority, whether in Missouri or County Sligo, are struggling, their formerly healthy villages and streets increasingly boarded-up and covered in graffiti, their people increasingly aging, yet still committed to the place and its people. They are "somewheres," to use David Goodheart's term, as opposed to the "anywheres" of the urban upper class.

In broad strokes, "anywheres" work for global corporations, universities, government bureaucracies and the entertainment industry. As they have the money to travel freely and the online jobs to work from anywhere, they increasingly shuttle between cities and countries, identical cubicles and coffeeshops in Dublin and Dubai, Singapore and San Francisco. The ones I've met seem to have increasingly no culture other than whatever is trending online. They are loyal to no country and no people, other than others of their class, and all share a searing contempt for all things rural, working-class or traditional.

Much chatter has been devoted to the red-blue divide in the USA, with Democratic-leaning urban dots in a red ocean. Or to Brexit in the UK, where almost all rural England favoured Brexit but London did not. Or the French elections, where almost every district backed Le Pen except for Paris. Mostly the chatter focuses on political parties or on the outdated left-right spectrum, but all these are paper reflections of a deeper split of class and culture.

---

https://www.businesspost.ie/economics/our-income-divide-will-shape-the-election-in-two-major-ways/
[484] 'Celtic tiger did not improve quality of life, study finds' *Irish Times* 9 Nov 2002.
[485] 'Three out of four report life is more stressful' *Irish Times*, 9 Oct 2001.
[486] SLAN survey Department of Health 1999.
[487] Eurobarometer surveys 47 and 57.

Nowhere does this divide become more obvious than on the issue of Third-World immigration, and here too Ireland has hurtled into modernity. Almost all political parties in Ireland have backed a flood of immigrants to Ireland, until now I can walk through crowded Dublin streets and see barely a single Irish person. They are all Muslim, Indian, Slavic, African, either part of the globetrotting elite or brought here by the elite as cheap labour.

Of course, I'm an immigrant myself, albeit someone of Irish heritage with family ties here. And the early waves of Celtic Tiger immigrants – mostly Eastern Europeans – were largely literate, monogamous, educated and eager to work. Communities mostly welcomed the new families, and aside from being a Porizkova or Singh amid the Murphys and Flanagans, their children could grow up in the parish, Irish in all but blood.

In order for immigrants to be absorbed into the community, though, there must be a community, and the rise in immigration coincided with their decline. By the time we moved to Ireland many of the rituals my neighbours described, like dancing around the Maypole, were unknown to their grandchildren. And the vanishing continues; when my daughter was grown I went back to the Wren Day festival and discovered it had been discontinued, as a gathering required insurance premiums that no one could afford.

It also matters how many immigrants arrive at once; one family per village per decade could be absorbed, but by now more than 21 percent of Ireland's population is foreign-born, most added in the last two decades.

Many claim to be refugees, and are given housing and support from the Irish government, even though many are clearly frauds. In 2015 the Irish government agreed to take in Syrian refugees, and I volunteered to spend time with them and help them adjust – but when I talked to them privately, it turned out that not all were Syrian. When Ireland agreed to take in women and children fleeing war in Ukraine, a majority of those who showed up turned out to be 70 percent fighting-age men, and clearly from Africa or the Middle East.

An astonishing 40 percent had false or no passports, yet receive government assistance anyway;[488] some migrants convicted of rape or murder recently turned out to have been living on government welfare for decades. Yet Ireland has become so expensive that many are still homeless. When I briefly lived in Dublin (my daughter was grown and I prepared to return to the USA to care for my parents) I could see the number of tents multiply along the sidewalks and in the parks, most with homeless African and Middle Eastern men inside.

Amazingly, the Irish government's response has been to ship busloads of these men to rural villages without warning, to be housed in camps or local pubs. In some formerly sleepy villages *migrants now outnumber Irish.*[489]

Yet their numbers keep increasing; in 2022 the number of migrants increased 415 percent from the year before.[490] On the rare occasion when a migrant was ordered to be deported, only 15 percent of deportation orders were carried out.[491] A 2023 poll found that 75 percent of Irish thought the country had let in too many immigrants.[492]

It also matters whether the immigrants want to embrace the culture of their new home. An increasing number of migrants are from Muslim countries, where women can be beaten or imprisoned for not wearing veils, or where men mutilate women's genitals. In the UK next door, tens of thousands of British girls were raped or sexually assaulted, largely by Muslim men.[493] After letting in millions of Islamic migrants, Sweden went from having one of the lowest rates of rape in the world to one of the highest, and a majority of rapists were foreign-born.[494] An early-2000s

---

[488] "Over 5,000 asylum seekers arrived in Ireland without valid travel documents," *Newstalk*, 2 Feb 2023.

[489] "Lisdoonvarna: the home of matchmaking where refugees now outnumber locals," *Sunday Times*, 13 August 2023.

[490] "International protection applicants rose 415% in 2022," RTE News, 29 Nov 2023.

[491] 'Ridiculous': Just 15% of those who received Deportation Orders were deported in last five years," *Gript Magazine*, 1 June 2023.

[492] "Red C poll: three out of four think Ireland has taken too many refugees," *Business Post*, 27 May 2023.

[493] "'White girls are filthy': Wives of Asian men jailed for raping vulnerable British girls reveal why they blame the victims," *Daily Mail*, 30 Sept 2017.

[494] "Sweden rape: Most convicted attackers foreign-born, says TV," BBC News, 22 August 2018.

poll in the UK showed that 40 percent of all Muslims there want to institute Muslim religious law in the country.[495]

Now Ireland, too, is seeing a surge in murder, rape and other crimes, and Dublin has gone from being one of Europe's safest cities to one of the most dangerous.[496] In 2022 a Muslim migrant stalked gay men in Ireland and killed two, beheading one,[497] and had a list of others he planned to kill. Another Muslim migrant stabbed a priest in Galway, where the most common boy's name is now Muhammad.[498] Gauging how many of these crimes are committed by migrants is difficult, as the media typically report the perpetrator only as a "Dublin man" or other place of residence, but they often turn out to not be originally from Dublin.

Since the national media covers these issues so poorly, many Irish are going on Twitter with daily stories and videos of women harassed by gangs of Muslim men, or machete fights in once-peaceful neighbourhoods – all shocking, but also all unconfirmed. In village after village, protesters have lined roads to protest busloads of migrants being dumped in their town, sometimes clashing violently with police.

Finally, on 23 November 2023, at an school in Dublin, children and staff were stabbed by an Algerian migrant.[499] Previous attacks could be swept under the rug, but this was in the heart of the shopping district near the holidays, on a square named for a national hero, at an Irish-language school, favoured by people proud of their heritage, in a neighbourhood now populated heavily by migrants.

Within hours local families marched through their neighbourhoods in force, gathering in the square near the school, and got violent when police

---

[495] "Poll reveals 40pc of Muslims want sharia law in UK," *The Telegraph*, 19 Feb 2006.

[496] "Rape, sexual assault & domestic violence on the rise in Ireland with murder up 76 per cent, shock new crime stats show," *Irish Sun*, 3 March 2023; "Dublin one of the safest cities in the world," *Irish Examiner*, 15 April 2003; "Dublin ranks among the top ten most dangerous major cities in Europe," *Sunday World*, 9 Jan 2024.

[497] "Palani jailed for life for murder of two gay men in Sligo," RTE News, 23 Oct 2023.

[498] "Teenage boy remanded in custody in connection with stabbing of priest at Army barracks," *Irish Times*, 17 Aug 2024.

[499] "Breaking News: Suspect in Dublin stabbing Algerian national, Gardai believe," RTE, 23 Nov 2023.

tried to disperse them. Then looters descended on the neighbourhood – who, eyewitnesses told me, "didn't look Irish."[500] The resulting riot smashed the windows of the shopping district and set police cars, a double-decker bus, and the city's light rail train on fire.

I was living just down the road, and when I heard the news I ran down the street, only to be blocked by legions of police in riot gear. I watched the riot from behind police lines, on usually-bustling streets gone strangely dark and silent, interviewing people escaping the chaos. I talked to police that night who had been pulled in from rural villages on the other side of the country. You'll recall that police traditionally had little to do; they weren't prepared for this.

International news agencies descended on the city, wanting to know what happened. The police commissioner blamed everything on a "hooligan faction driven by far-right ideology," and the world media ran with that angle.[501] Irish politicians seemed to compete to see who could more strongly denounce the protesters; one city councillor, originally from Bangladesh, said he wanted to see them "shot in the head."[502]

I've visited a few protests, before and after the riots, to see these extremists for myself. I've talked with them over beers in the pub afterwards. They're working-class Irish, not ordinarily political and with nothing against immigrants in general. Ireland doesn't even have a right-wing party, much less a far right.

When the media here – populated by globalist "anywheres" – mention the crimes, they blame not the perpetrators, but the Irish. After the beheading, former president Mary McAleese blamed Christian churches for being "conduits of homophobia,"[503] even though the assailant was Muslim with no connection to Christianity, and such things never happened when Ireland was overtly Christian. When 23-year-old Irish

---

[500] Photos of people sought by police show a mix of ethnicities, including some who may have been Irish and some who were not. https://www.garda.ie/en/persons_of_interest/

[501] How the rise of the far right in Ireland provoked the Dublin riots," NPR, 26 Nov 2023.

[502] 'I'd like to see them shot in the head': Councillor's hard line on Dublin riots," *Limerick Post*, 29 Nov 2023.

[503] "McAleese accuses Churches of being 'conduits for homophobia' following Sligo deaths," BreakingNews.ie, 16 April 2022.

musician Ashling Murphy was stabbed 11 times by a migrant, global media ran articles on Irish men's "culture of misogyny," even though the murderer was not an Irish man.[504]

When I walk around Dublin, not only are the people on the street no longer Irish, but neither are people in Irish advertisements for Irish companies; they tend to be African or Muslim. A recent advertising campaign for a local museum showed a red-haired man wearing an Irish jersey, with the caption, "This is not Us." Last Pride season I saw signs all over Dublin that said, "Irish history is black history. Irish history is Queer history." Other posters displayed around town claimed that "black people built Dublin." A recent government schoolbook contrasted a "good" Irish family, who travel all over the world and are part Nigerian and part Romanian, with a "bad" Irish family made up of traditional Irish people who liked Irish sports, Irish dancing and the Irish language. In other words, the bad Irish are Irish people who like anything Irish.

Since any discussion of these issues in the media – again, representing the cosmopolitan upper class – frames these issues exclusively as promoting "diversity" over "racism," I feel compelled to address the issue. No one I know in Ireland hates people of different races. Most Muslim immigrants, moreover, are from ethnic groups we call "white" as soon as they dress in Western clothes; tech guru Steve Jobs was of Syrian descent, rock singer Freddie Mercury was Iranian. The Caucasus Mountains of the Middle East give us the word "Caucasian." No one is objecting to skin colour.

Most here are also sympathetic to people genuinely interested in starting a better life in a new country, as so many Irish did; again, I and my neighbours volunteered to work with Syrian refugees. And there are moderate, Westernised Muslims; even if 40 percent of British Muslims want to impose Sharia law, that means 60 percent do not. Most Irish would not object to good neighbours of any race or religion who wanted to join their community.

Most Irish do object to armies of fighting-age men from cultures openly hostile to Western values, with no jobs or prospects, moving into

---

[504] "Ashling Murphy's killing has shocked Ireland – but will it change a culture of misogyny?," *The Guardian*, 18 Jan 2022.

their communities under false pretences and sleeping on the sidewalks. They also object to being called racist or far-right for noticing that this is happening, or being told that they are the villains of the story. They also object to paying for all this to happen. If elites want to create a genuine far-right movement in Ireland, this is the way to do it.

Meanwhile angry locals in working-class neighbourhoods continued to confront politicians when they appeared in public, until officials went around surrounded by armed guards.[505] The Christmas shopping crowds were thin that winter, and most people seemed fearful; when the city put up towers for a scheduled "winter holiday" light show, working-class locals told me they feared they were for snipers.

Shortly after the protests I talked to families protesting outside a pub in Ringsend – whose residents you might remember from previous chapters. They had heard that the pub was to house more migrants, and told me stories of women being harassed by foreign gangs in their neighbourhood. A few days later someone burned the pub to the ground. Similar arsons have been happening all over Ireland, wherever migrants were set to move in.[506]

Astonishingly – I'm trying not to overuse that word -- the Irish government's response to all this was to push for a "hate speech" bill that would allow police to enter anyone's home, seize their computer or phone and hold it "for so long as is necessary,"[507] and arrest any Irish person who refuses to give them their passwords.[508] The proposed law could imprison people for "hatred," but never defined how that would be different from criticising the government's immigration policy, or Islam. Worst of all, under the proposed bill Irish people would be guilty until proven innocent.[509] Seventy-three percent of Irish were against it, but a version of it passed anyway.[510]

---

[505] "24-hour house guard for Leo Varadkar and Micheal Martin over threat from far-right factions," Dublin Live, 2 Dec 2023.
[506] "Fire at former Dublin pub was arson," BBC, 1 Jan 2024.
[507] Section 15, subsection 3.
[508] Section 10, subsection 4.
[509] Section 10, subsection 3.
[510] "Hate speech consultation received mostly negative responses," *Gript Magazine*.

***

If Ireland wanted new blood and cultural enrichment, there was an easy group they could have turned to instead: Irish-Americans, the 90 or so percent of Irish who no longer live on the island.

When our ancestors fled the Famine and flooded into the USA, they experienced the usual ghettos and ethnic conflict that always happen when large numbers of immigrants move into a place. Irish immigrants were persecuted by the Know-Nothings, who pursued and killed Irish as the Ku Klux Klan did black people, and who murdered one of my ancestors in 1850.

Irish-Americans also journeyed back to visit their cousins here so often that tourism became Ireland's main industry – and no one was coming for the weather or the food. Sometimes they did more than visit. Eamonn De Valera, the Irish Revolutionary who became its first prime minister, was Irish-American.

Some people have asked me how I can oppose poor people from another culture moving en masse to Ireland, when my own ancestors immigrated to the USA and faced opposition as well. First, my own ancestors were families fleeing genocide, not armies of men seeking wealth. Second, my ancestors' experiences teach us that a mass of immigrants from another culture into an area, whatever the circumstances, causes conflict. Conflict will be devastating for both the indigenous Irish and people genuinely seeking a new life. My ancestors' arrival in America created enough conflict to see my ancestor and many others killed, and they were Western, literate, monogamous, Christian and English-speaking. How much worse will conflicts be with Islamists in rural Ireland.

Finally, Irish citizens should note that Irish-Americans are still proudly Irish, French-Canadians proudly French, and Chinese-Americans often still live in Chinatowns and practice their own form of Chinese culture, even if their culture and that of Communist China have long parted ways. A century from now, Arab Muslims in Ireland will still consider themselves Arab Muslims in Ireland. Even in the modern world, when so many have lost their cultures and identities, communities that remain together will endure.

Today, every year, my family and dozens of others march through my city's Irish neighbourhood, where you can still see Irish pubs with Irish music advertised in the Irish language, almost two centuries after immigration began. Of course my cousins have married Americans of many ethnic groups, so our Irish family is now part Native, Filipino, German, Black, Mexican, Polish and Japanese. Nonetheless, we are part of the same family, raised on the same stories, marching under the same banner.

Most younger Irish, though, despise Americans who call themselves Irish, and I understand; they've all been subjected to drunken American tourists in leprechaun costumes on St. Patrick's Day. I understand that most Irish-Americans know little about the actual 21st century country, with its highways and skyscrapers. For that reason, while I am in Ireland I accept being a foreigner; only in my native country do I become Irish.

Yet if you want to find people who still care about Irish culture or speak the Irish language, a majority of them will be in the USA. They are proud of their history, and rightly so. Our ancestors also experienced the Famine, were scattered like the Jews, harassed and driven out of towns like African-Americans. Many of our traditions mutated in the New World – Samhain into Halloween, Irish folk music into American country music – and were re-popularised in Ireland in their new forms.

When I mentioned my family to my elderly neighbours, I was surprised to hear them call us Irish, though I had avoided doing so. Unlike most younger and urban Irish, my neighbours still thought of Ireland as a people and a culture, and not just as an economic zone.

This country, and most European countries, gave up an extraordinary resource when they refused to acknowledge their children overseas. The French could have maintained ties with the Quebecois and Cajuns, Swedes with Minnesotans, finding people enthusiastic about their culture while also adding new blood, wealth and perspectives. European governments could have chosen this over importing millions of people from cultures that were actively hostile to their values, and threatening to imprison anyone who objected. But they made their choices.

Chapter Twelve

Conclusion

I moved here because I wanted to try a new life. I saw that most of my peers hated their jobs and tolerated their lives, spent their evenings staring at screens, and marked their days by television shows and pop-culture events. Many seemed to thrash about in life searching for something more. Some fell into charismatic churches or New Age groups that promised a more primal relationship with the divine, others plunged into crafts that allowed them to create something with their own hands. Others grew old and grey playing video games where they could be post-apocalyptic survivors or medieval warriors, and enjoy the illusion of accomplishment.

They were all searching for something most of our ancestors had, which modern world had taken away, and whose loss they felt in their bones. A tradition that made them part of an ongoing story. A discipline to direct their energies. A brotherhood in a sea of strangers. An anchor and compass in a life adrift.

As I interviewed my mentors and tried my own hapless experiments with country living, I wrote about what I learned – in a newspaper column, a blog, in magazine articles. And while most people seemed to like my writings, sometimes I'd set off a flood of hostile responses. I'd clearly touched a nerve, but wasn't sure how.

When I mentioned that people were often better educated than we imagine, people would respond with a snarky comment about smallpox. When I mentioned that people had stronger communities, I'd get comments about colonialism and genocide. Apparently many people think that if I compliment anything about any time and place, I am endorsing the worst tragedies of history.

Of course I'm glad to live in a time when we have modern medicine, when I can talk to my parents across an ocean and fly to see them once every few years. I'm grateful to live in an age and country where all men and women have human rights codified in law. The fact that some of our ancestors sometimes suffered, though, does not mean they have nothing to teach us. I am proposing that the modern world we've created has brought both advantages and disadvantages, and that we can disentangle them and – perhaps – keep the benefits of our age while restoring what we've lost.

Some people ask sarcastically if I could live the way my neighbours did. If they are asking if I could grow food, kill animals and live minimally, I tell them, I have done so happily. I didn't give up all technology – I still had a car when I needed it, and still used the internet for my day job and writing gigs – but I'm not asking anyone else to either. Reviving some aspects of traditional life – craftmanship, or community, or outdoor play – does not mean giving up medicine or living like cavemen.

Of course people endured many tragedies; many of my neighbours lived through the Irish Revolution, the Irish Civil War, the Great Depression, World War II, and the Catholic-Protestant Troubles. Their own grandparents had endured the Famine. Of course they often left to start a new life – including my own forebears. Many books have already been written about how their lives were tragic; as mentioned in the beginning, I wrote this about how they were able to maintain a safe, close, literate culture while enduring tragedy.

What surprised me was now *indignant* the responses were, and how defensive. People back then *must have been* less educated than I am, with all my student loans. Women *must have been* oppressed when they could not be interchangeable cogs in a corporate machine. Childhood *must have been* miserable before television and Ritalin. Food *must have been* dreary before chemicals. Everyone *must have been* a hateful fanatic, people have shouted at me.

I see the same on social media: Whenever anyone posts a photo of happy people in, say, the 1950s, they are flooded with comments that everyone in the crowd must have been secretly gay, or alcoholic, or molesting children, or something. The underlying assumption is that whatever vices are widespread today *must have been* even more widespread then, but since we don't hear about them much, they must have been all kept secret. Certainly that's the picture we get from *The Hours, The Shape of Water* or recent Oscar-bait portrayals of that era.

I see the same when someone posts about medieval knights, and comments pile on that those knights never bathed and lived in fear of the Inquisition. Many people can't allow any good thing to be said about any of our forebears, without insisting that everything was miserable, and all the things that seem good must have been secretly miserable.

Such attitudes seem especially concentrated in my "woke" friends, the ones most likely to see "white supremacy" everywhere – yet they have substituted a far more extreme and sweeping temporal supremacy. Everyone, of every culture who ever lived, they believe, *must have been* stupider, less healthy, less tolerant, less virtuous than we. Only we are a master race, they seem to think; everyone who came before us was subhuman.

There are two exceptions when our modern culture allows for traditional solutions. One is if it's disguised as something hip and cutting-edge.

You can see this when the young and "queer" call themselves "demi-sexual," or only attracted to people they love – which never had be justified before. You can see this in technology; a new model of ship cut fuel costs using a zero-carbon, wind-powered sustainable energy source -- what used to be called "sails." You can see this in the hipster trend for organic food and small houses, which used to be called "food" and "houses." To paraphrase Auron McIntyre, "once in a while modern people accidentally reverse-engineer some aspect of a healthy life, and act like they've discovered Atlantis."

The other striking exception is Native peoples – Americans, Africans, Aborigines and others portrayed in our media as near-nude innocents in a Garden of Eden. Most of this comes, however, not from actual history but from the 1960s counterculture, fed by con men pretending to be Native. Most real native Americans, as mentioned earlier, practiced savage violence against their neighbours. Nor are most Native sites very old; the pub down the road is almost as old as Mayan temples.

It is true that Native American peoples had many admirable qualities, lived sustainably, practiced skilled crafts or had a rich oral tradition. But *all of us* – Irish and Chinese, Ukrainians and Hawaiians, Greeks and Tamils – come from indigenous people who did the same. We all had tribal elders who passed on family stories and songs, legends and heroes, whether we remember them or not. We are all descended from people who knew ancient and sustainable folkways. They all were, at one time or another, enslaved and persecuted, yet survived. We can all take pride in our past.

Every culture until ours venerated their ancestors; in Egypt and China, Africa and Alaska, Ireland and Iceland, people built monuments to them, and their pyramids and dolmens and gravestones are usually the thing that survives when all else has crumbled. They lit candles for their ancestors, prayed to them, sung songs about them around the fire. We are the first to dismiss the generations on whose shoulders we stand, to have hacked away our identity like an unwanted limb, to flop around severed from a place in the great human story, and to call ourselves free.

* * *

Most of our images of our own past come from Hollywood movies and television, and most are nonsense. Early humans looked nothing like the cavemen we picture from cartoons; they built homes, wore coats, buried their dead with religious rituals and made musical instruments. They had less to work with than we do, but they weren't dumber; geneticist Gerald Crabtree argues they were smarter, and we've been losing intelligence for thousands of years.[511]

Or take the Middle Ages: we know from many records and illustrations that people bathed, and as mentioned earlier, cities like London had regulations against throwing waste into streets. Most of the torture devices we now see in museums were invented recently to wow the tourists. Medieval people knew the world was round; there might be more flat-earthers today than a thousand years ago. About half the population could read and write, as mentioned, and if everyone who could read did read, they read more than modern people.

---

[511] "Are People Getting Dumber? One Geneticist Thinks So," *Popular Science*, 19 Nov 2012.

The Spanish Inquisition deserves a special mention in these myths, as it has become our byword for fundamentalist tyranny. Aside from the fact that they appeared after the Middle Ages, though, they were a much more rational and civilised organisation than we imagine. It was simply Spain's legal court system, and most trials were for real crimes, like murder or robbery. They stopped most witch hysterias by demanding proof of witchcraft – which people could not usually provide – and executed less than two percent of accused. They executed fewer people per year on average than the state of Texas does today, even adjusting for population.[512] Of course they did things differently in the 1400s, including some things we would not agree with – but again, they were people like ourselves and not cartoons.

We could take similar myths in every other era up to our own. Feminists didn't burn any bras in the 1960s. There were few bloody gunfights in the Old West. Stockbrokers didn't actually jump out of windows when the Great Depression hit. Few people actually panicked during the War of the Worlds broadcast in 1938. Turns out, most people in any era just aren't that stupid.

Of course people in the Stone Age or Middle Ages or Victorian Europe had some thoughts and habits that would seem brutal or alien to us, but they lived in very different circumstances. As sick and dependent as we are in the modern world, and as much damage as we have done to our own land, we should not assume we have a monopoly on wisdom.

Of course we can compare our lives to anyone in history and say that ours are better, because we are inevitably comparing the victims of history's worst plagues and famines to our privileged lives as First-World professionals. No one does the opposite and compares, say, Edwardian lords to modern African cobalt miners.

Of course we can say that the past had more horror and tragedy than the present does, because the past outnumbers the present by something like a million to one. Medieval Europe seems like it saw a great deal of turmoil, from barbarian invasions to plagues, but we forget that those things took place here and there across a continent over a thousand years.

---

512 Parker, 1982. See also *The Spanish Inquisition: A Historical Revision* by Henry Kamen, p. 198-199.

It would be like picturing all the world wars and dictatorships of the last century taking place in a single year, to the same people.

Of course human history is full of tragedy and injustice, for these things are literally *what history records*.

Yet most of the time, life wasn't like that. "Civilization is a stream with banks," historian Will Durant once said. "The stream is sometimes filled with blood from people killing, stealing, shouting and doing the things historians usually record, while on the banks, unnoticed, people build homes, make love, raise children, sing songs, write poetry and even whittle statues. The story of civilization is the story of what happened on the banks. Historians ... ignore the banks for the river."[513]

***

If people today can entertain only one monstrous image of the past, they also do the same for the future.

When people agree with me about modern problems -- with children, or the environment, or immigration, or anything -- the conversation nearly always jumps to an imminent apocalypse. The world can't go on much longer this way, people tell me, and they talk about what will tip us over the edge. I want to steer people away from this, for two reasons.

The first is that post-apocalyptic futures are not fears, but fantasies. They flatter us by saying that our prime years were civilisation's height, that we see the world clearly but are surrounded by brainwashed idiots, that the event will destroy everything we don't like, and that everyone will wish they had listened to us. And since there is nothing we can do, these fantasies forgive our doing nothing.

What's more, as strange as it sounds, an apocalypse is not the worst that could happen. A people with a culture, who band together in times of hardship, have a *why* to endure any *how*. They can carry their songs and stories inside them and rebound quickly, and stronger. We know this because one of the closest things the world has ever seen to an apocalypse has already happened, in one of the unusual events mentioned earlier. It happened here in Ireland, almost two centuries ago.

---

[513] *Life* magazine, 18 Oct 1963, p. 92.

The Famine – you can still hear the capital F – wiped out the potato crop, which provided almost all the calories of poor farmers who had been forced off their lands by English conquerors. Writers of the time described the pale, skeletal figures wandering the roads, even pulling the corpses of their loved ones behind them, refusing to abandon them. In fields all over Ireland, graves of hundreds of skeletons, mothers and fathers with clusters of tiny skeletons all around them lay just beneath the sod. Before the Famine this island held at least eight million Irish – some estimates run higher – and within a few decades the population had been reduced to four million. All the rest died, or fled to America, including some of my own family.

The British authorities used the Famine as an opportunity to evict many of the farmers who could no longer pay rent, and cast them onto the roads. Astonishingly, the plantations continued to export food crops to England while the people starved around them. It was genocide, the largest in European history until the Nazi Holocaust.

The Famine helps explain why Ireland was so late in modernising. In the last 200 years Britain's population increased eight-fold, America's population 36-fold. Ireland's fell by more than half, and only recently began to recover. It explains Ireland's stark landscape of empty fields and ruined castles, the template for the entire medieval fantasy genre today. In real life, those fields and castles used to be full of people. The traditional Ireland that my neighbours grew up in, of rural villages and a close, safe, literate society, *was a post-apocalyptic world*.

The Irish, like the Jews, came through the crucible with a fierce sense of shared solidarity and a desire to regain what they had lost. Those who left for America multiplied their numbers tenfold and prospered despite persecution and poverty. Those who still remained on this island, only a few generations later, overthrew the world's most powerful empire. The Famine also proved that for a people with a culture, even near-extinction is not the end.

The second reason I want to steer people away from apocalyptic thinking is that civilisations do end, but not that way. As mentioned, the decline of Rome took centuries, and while people played, grew up, fell in love, did daily chores and raised children, they were concerned with the burning usual of daily life. Civilisations decline as they rise, too slowly for most people to notice.

We are declining as well, and you can see it clearly if you come back to the USA as I did. Everything is much more expensive, but no one is making more money. Fewer people are getting married or having children, as the costs and risks of both have increased. People drive around town in golf carts that cost a fraction as much as a car. More homes have been broken into, and more people are buying guns. While I was away a race riot broke out, making Ferguson, Missouri unexpectedly infamous.

Life expectancy, IQ, height, savings, social trust – every indicator of prosperity is falling. Happiness peaked in the early 1960s, and depression has doubled every generation. Over the rest of the 20th century the divorce rate doubled, violent crime trebled, illiteracy trebled and the prison population increased eight-fold. In economy and health, most of the USA is a Third World country, and many Western countries can say the same.

Since I left America suicide has increased 50 percent, and those are just the obvious ones. Drug overdoses have increased *500 percent*, something that's not happening in other countries where opiates are more freely available. Mass shootings have become a normal feature of life, something that didn't happen even in the 1950s when guns were also freely available. We can debate the details of these trends and the solutions, but they are not happening in spite of progress. They are progress, in the wrong direction.

Compare pictures of St. Louis or Detroit several decades ago with today, and you'd wonder what year Armageddon happened. The decades between, though, did not see a science fiction doomsday, but a baseline that crept down over generations, until no one is bothered by what they see around them, because no one remembers what normal looks like.

All the survivalists are preparing for the wrong thing. A decline in the economy doesn't mean Doomsday. Instead, it becomes normal again to forgo college, to move in with relatives, to declare bankruptcy, to keep student loans at bay forever, to work multiple jobs. A decline in food production doesn't create mass graves; instead it becomes common to buy cheaper and worse food, or to grow gardens or keep chickens. A decline in democracy doesn't bring stormtroopers smashing windows, but a co-worker getting fired, ostracised, perhaps arrested for having an unpopular opinion, and everyone quietly keeping their head down and moving on.

Even invasions don't play out in real life as we imagine, with Mad Max survivors fighting off axe-wielding Visigoths. Instead, a foreigner moves into your neighbourhood, and then another and another. Over the years it becomes filled with people who talk only to each other and not to you, and you learn not to say the wrong thing in their presence. Teenage girls disappear, or learn to cover themselves, or walk outside only with male escorts. All the adults around you pretend this is normal, and the children don't believe it was ever any other way.

You might notice that all these things are already happening, just not all in the same places, and perhaps not where you live. Yet.

***

Even decline doesn't have to be terrible. For most people in history – and as recently as the 1970s for my neighbours – the banks could fail and the world would go on. The same was true when Ireland was isolated by the Second World War. When people live together in self-sufficient communities, as most of our ancestors did through history, the elite infrastructure can crumble and might affect them little.

Our problem is more than decline. Nor is it a doomsday – in many ways it is the opposite. We are saturated with material things – for now – but a loss of community, of faith, of singing, of skills, of literacy, of tradition, of play, of any of the things that any other culture had in abundance. It is a great forgetting, a cultural apocalypse.

We are the first humans to live mostly indoors, not knowing all the people in the homes and offices around us. We are the first to be unfamiliar with the plants and animals around us, and to be incapable of feeding ourselves. We are the first people in history whose employment, child care, mediation, transportation, nursing, funerals and burial have all been made into transactions, given over to unseen authorities. We are the first to be unable to make or repair any of our own possessions.

We are the first whose children are raised by strangers and screens. We are the first to have no stories or songs of our own other than what was handed to us from corporations. We are the first to be unfamiliar with our own past, and to despise it. We are the first to be told that men are interchangeable with women, and that we can turn from one to the other. We are the first people to mostly die alone, tended by people who don't care about us. We might be the first to have astronomical rates of mental illness, addiction and suicide.

We have all been guinea pigs in the largest experiment ever devised, resulting in vast populations sick and dependent as caged animals. And like caged animals, we live in a world that gives us everything we could possibly want, and as much as we want, but nothing we need.

When I tell people things used to be different, though, they don't believe me. Most younger people in Ireland have never heard of sennachai or rambling houses, bank strikes or Corpus Christi processions, May day dances or Wren Day chases. They don't believe that children roamed miles from home, that farm-hands eagerly read Plutarch and St. Augustine, that houses took in all visitors. Most Westerners, in any country, would say the same about their own forebears.

They feel no sense of loss, for they do not believe these things could be real. They would more easily believe in a lost civilisation of Atlantis or a vast conspiracy of lizard-people than look up the actual lost civilisation whose ruins are all around us, whose citizens are only recently under the grass, and whose books might still be in your local library.

***

It doesn't have to be this way. We could begin to undo the disturbing trends of the modern world, one life at a time. It doesn't mean giving up on progress in the sense of improvement, for there is much to improve around us. It doesn't mean going Amish, and you don't have to move to a bog in Ireland. Wherever we live, many of our problems could be solved, however slowly and incrementally, if we stopped trying to create ever-more extreme versions of our present, and again tried to restore what our grandparents or great-grandparents had.

Letting children play freely, growing a garden, making meals from scratch, learning hand crafts, reading classic books, spending less time in front of screens and more time with friends and family – anything old-fashioned will probably be healthier, cheaper, better for the environment, and allow you to live more independently of governments and corporations. It also means that if our nations erupt into civil war, or if the governments become more authoritarian, or if our culture becomes more insane, your household or community can be the place to get water, or food, or education, or sanity.

It would satisfy many desires on the left and right alike, but both factions today might have to overcome a few of their prejudices. Most environmentalists I know appreciate my neighbours' respect for nature, but bristle when I suggest that they also lived in harmony with male and female natures. Most conservatives I know appreciate their religious devotion or independence, but bristle when I tell them those values were part of an old-fashioned economy, not a throwaway one.

It would mean changing our own stories first. Instead of being someone struggling in a declining power, or being oppressed by vast conspiracies, we could think of ourselves as people who study our ancestors' lives decades or centuries ago, and carry the torch of their civilisation to our children and grandchildren, as monks did after the fall of Rome.

The modern world can make some of these things more difficult than they used to be – in high-crime areas, of course, parents might not want their children wandering far. In some jurisdictions simple things like growing a garden or hanging clothes out to dry or teaching your own children can be illegal. You have to pick and choose ways to embrace a traditional life, depending on your circumstances.

Whatever your situation, start small, but start now. Measure the amount of time you spend on video games or social media or television in a day, and tomorrow reduce it by ten percent, then ten percent again, until it is near zero. Estimate the amount of time you spend listening to other people sing on loudspeakers or playlists, versus the amount of time you spend singing. Start simple; look up old folk songs meant to be sung by normal human voices, and learn how to sing properly. Do the same with storytelling, cooking, gardening, anything.

Learn to read prose again, instead of scanning text. Read books written more than a century ago, starting with children's books and working your way up. Read to your children, and make it normal to read to each other as you garden or cook. Try reading the Greek and Roman classics; I re-wrote the often-stilted translations of Plutarch and Aristophanes into punchier, more modern language to read them to my daughter. Try reading Stoics like Epictetus and Seneca, whose wisdom is timeless.

Seek simple physical solutions, rather than buying or downloading something. Instead of buying a car that promises to boost efficiency by 10 percent, you can boost your own car's efficiency by 500 percent for free by putting four more people in it.

Meet your neighbours, and try to find other people interested in the same journey, from your church, a local club, or the internet. Some will have different political or religious leanings than you do, but that's not as much of a barrier as you might think; again, I've worked with environmentalists and Christian conservatives alike, and the real people are better than the cartoons you see on social media.

If enough are interested, you can create a neighbourhood watch, an emergency network, a community garden, a carpool, a lending library. We use libraries only for books, but you could create one for anything; instead of 12 houses each having 12 drills, 12 barbecue pits and 12 VeggieTales videos, each of which gets used for minutes every year, a neighbourhood could have a general shed in which everyone pays for a share.

When you find others around you with the same values, help raise and home-school each others' children, with a common agreement not to raise them with television or mobile phones. Give them a chance to grow up with other children living the same kind of life, so that it seems normal to them.

Join the Hibernians or Knights of Columbus or some other surviving fraternal lodge. Consider starting a mutual improvement society, as the British and Irish had in the 1800s, where people practice speaking in front of others, telling stories, debating issues and sharing tips on saving money or gardening. Start rebuilding communities one reliable neighbour at a time.

All of these sound ridiculously tiny compared to the problems that we face, but when you do them, you're doing something tangible and likely to improve your life. It doesn't change the world, but it changes your world.

You don't have to move with your toddler to a bog in rural Ireland. As someone who did that and wrote about it, I got a lot of e-mails from people who wanted a similar escape, and I had to disillusion them; You don't escape life. You don't leave your problems behind and start over somewhere pure, as a new person. Wherever you go, you will bring yourself and your own problems along for the ride, and the world follows you.

A traditional life will not be a place you escape to, but a life you build in baby steps over years. You will not be able to change anything but yourself and your own surroundings and habits, and then only in tiny increments, with many false starts and failures.

You make your choices, and for a long time nothing will seem to change ... until one day, you look behind you at the path your life has taken, and see how much you've changed, and how strange the rest of the world appears in the distance.

Sources

Memoirs of Ireland:

And the Band Played On, by G. Rafferty. Friar's Bush Press (January 1, 1990) ISBN: 978-0946872374.

Another Country – Growing Up In '50s Ireland: Memoirs of a Dublin Childhood, by Gene Kerrigan. Gill Books (April 1, 1998).

The Aran Islands, by J.M. Synge. Independently published (August 19, 2022). ISBN: 979-8847259286.

Around the Farm Gate, edited by PJ Cunningham. Ballpoint Press Limited (September 17, 2015) ISBN: 978-0993289255.

Back Through the Fields: Memories of Rural Life, by Maurice MacAleese. Appletree Press Ltd (October 14, 2005) ISBN: 978-0862819859.

Barnacle Soup and Other Stories from the West of Ireland, by Josie Gray and Tess Gallagher, Blackstaff Press (September 1, 2007) ISBN: 978-0856408144.

Books from the Attic: Treasures from an Irish Childhood, by Alice Taylor. Brandon (December 5, 2020) ISBN: 978-1788492140.

The Boy's Country-Book: Being the Real Life of a Country Boy, by William Howitt, Wentworth Press (February 22, 2019) ISBN: 978-0469418363.

Country Days, by Alice Taylor, St. Martin's Griffin; Reprint edition (February 15, 1996) ISBN: 978-0312141028.

Do You Remember? by Alice Taylor, Brandon; Reprint edition (December 27, 2014) ISBN: 978-1847176844.

Dublin Tenement Life: An Oral History by Kevin Kearns. Gill Books; (March 7, 2006) ISBN: 978-0717140749.

Dublin Voices, by Kevin Kearns, Gill & Macmillan Ltd. (January 1, 1998). ISBN: 978-0717126507.

The Farm by Lough Gur, by Mary Carberry. Longmans, Green & Co. (January 1, 1940).

Fifty Years Behind the Counter, by Kevin Duffy. Self-published. (March 1, 2001) ISBN: 978-0954003401.

Give us Back the Bad Roads, by John Waters. Currach Books (October 19, 2018). ISBN: 978-1782189015.

Green Fields : a Journal of Irish Country Life, by Stehen Rynne. London: Macmillan Co, 1938, London; First Edition. (January 1, 1938).

Growing Up with Ireland: A Century of Memories from Our Oldest and Wisest Citizens, by Valerie Cox. Hachette Ireland (November 3, 2020). ISBN: 978-1529337389.

Hearthlands: A Memoir of the White City housing estate in Belfast, by Marianne Elliot. Blackstaff Press (November 2, 2017). ISBN: 978-0856409974.

High Shelves and Long Counters: Stories of Irish Shops, by Winifred McNulty, Heike Theile and Dermot Healy. THP Ireland (July 1, 2012). ISBN: 978-1845887520.

The House Remembers, by Ann Gardinier. Self-published (January 1, 2009) ISBN: 978-0956708403.

Inishkillane: change and decline in the west of Ireland, by Hugh Brody. Allen Lane; F edition (January 1, 1973). ISBN: 978-0713903188.

An Irish Country Childhood: A Bygone Age Remembered, by Marrie Walsh. Metro Books (March 5, 2010). ISBN: 978-1844548927.

Irish Women's Letters, by Laurence Flanagan. Sutton Pub Ltd (January 1, 1997), ISBN: 978-0750912570.

Island Cross-Talk: Pages From a Diary, by Tomas O'Crohan and Tim Enright. Oxford University Press; First Edition (January 23, 1986). ISBN: 978-0192819093.

The Islander: Complete and Unabridged, Tomas O'Crohan, David Sowby and Garry Bannister. Gill Books; Unabridged edition (July 15, 2013). ISBN: 978-0717157945.

Jaysus Wept! By the Midland Tribune, 1984.

The Joy of Boyhood Years, by John Lyons, North Kerry Literary Trust (2008). ISBN: 978-09544505-3-3.

Land of My Cradle Days, by Martin Morissey. The O'Brien Press (January 1, 1991). ISBN: 978-0862782290.

Malachi Horan Remembers, by George Little. M.H. Gill & Son, Dublin; First Edition. (January 1, 1943).

Maura's Boy, by Christy Kenneally. Irish Amer Book Co (January 1, 1997) ISBN: 978-1856351515.

Me and Nu: childhood at Coole, by Anne Gregory. Smythe; First Edition (January 1, 1970). ISBN: 978-0900675485.

My Fathers Wake, by Kevin Toolis. Weidenfeld & Nicolson (August 23, 2018). ISBN: 978-1474605243.

No Shoes in Summer, Mary Ryan, Sean Browne and Kevin Gilmour. Irish Amer Book Co (January 1, 1995) ISBN: 978-0863274879.

An Old Woman's Reflections, by Peig Sayers, Seamus Ennis and W.R. Rodgers. ISBN: Oxford University Press; First Edition. (January 1, 1962).

Quench the Lamp, by Alice Taylor. St. Martin's Griffin (February 15, 1994). ISBN: 978-0312105280.

Skelligs Calling, by Michael Kirby. Lilliput Pr Ltd (May 24, 2004). ISBN: 978-1843510260.

Some Time to Kill: Memories of Kill Village, by Tony Carr. Trafford Publishing (July 6, 2006) ISBN: 978-1412024334.

Tales from the Blue Stacks, by Bob Bernen. Poolbeg Press Ltd (January 1, 1980). ISBN: 978-0905169279.

Tales from a City Farmyard, by Patrick Boland. Self-published.

Then There Was Light, by P.J. Cunningham. Ballpoint Press Limited (September 17, 2016). ISBN: 978-0995479319.
Those Days are Gone Away, by Michael Taafe. Hutchinson; First Edition. (January 1, 1959).
Tides of Change, by John Curran. Curran Publishing (January 1, 2004). ISBN: 978-0954702601.
The Times of Our Lives, by Walter Love. Appletree Press, 1990.
To School Through the Fields, by Alice Taylor. Brandon; 2nd edition (August 6, 2016). ISBN: 978-1847178237.
Twenty Years A-Growing, by Maurice O'Sullivan. Oxford University Press; New Ed edition (April 17, 1983). ISBN: 978-0192813251.
The Way We Were, by Declan Hassett. Mercier Press (1999).
The Western Island, by Robin Flower. Oxford Univ Pr; First Edition (January 1, 1946).
Where We Sported and Played, by Teddy Delaney. Irish Amer Book Co (January 1, 1991). ISBN: 978-0853429647.
Would They Were With Us Again! By Ultan Brady. Kells Publishing (1992).
Your Dinner's Poured Out: Memoirs of a Dublin that has Disappeared, by Paddie Crosbie. The O'Brien Press; 2nd edition (May 26, 2012). ISBN: 978-1847173041.

Other books:

Amusing Ourselves to Death: Public Discourse in the Age of Show Business, by Neil Postman. Penguin Books; Anniversary edition (December 27, 2005). ISBN: 978-0143036531.
Child's Play: Rediscovering the Joy of Play in Our Families and Communities, by Silken Laumann, Random House Canada; First Edition (April 18, 2006). ISBN: 978-0679314066.
A Description of Killarney, by David G. Dunn. J. Dodsley, in Pall-Mall, 1776.
The Disappearance of Childhood, by Neil Postman. Vintage/Random House (August 2, 1994). ISBN: 978-0679751663.
Eating on the Wild Side: The Missing Link to Optimum Health, by Jo Robinson. Little, Brown Spark; Reprint edition (May 20, 2014) ISBN: 978-0316227933.
Free to Learn: Why Unleashing the Instinct to Play Will Make Our Children Happier, More Self-Reliant, and Better Students for Life, by Peter Gray. Basic Books; 1st edition (March 5, 2013). ISBN: 978-0465025992.
The Hedge Schools of Ireland, by P.J. Dowling. Mercier Press; Revised edition (June 1, 1997). ISBN: 978-1856351812.
A Hunter-Gatherer's Guide to the 21st Century: Evolution and the Challenges of Modern Life, by Heather Heying and Bret Weinstein. Portfolio; First Edition (September 14, 2021). ISBN: 978-0593086889.
The Intellectual Life of the British Working Classes, by Jonathan Rose. Yale University Press; Second edition (July 6, 2010). ISBN: 978-0300153651.

Jiving at the Crossroads, by John Waters. Transworld Ireland; New edition (January 1, 2011). ISBN: 978-1848271272.

The Land and its People, by R. E. Prothero, later Lord Ernle. 'Women on the land, 1917-19,' *The Land and its People* (London, 1925).

Last Child in the Woods: Saving Our Children From Nature-Deficit Disorder, by Richard Louv. Algonquin Books; Updated and Expanded edition (April 10, 2008). ISBN: 978-1565126053.

The Light Ages: The Surprising Story of Medieval Science, by Seb Falk. W. W. Norton & Company (November 30, 2021). ISBN: 978-0393868401.

London Street Games, by Norman Douglas. Chatto And Windus; Second Edition (January 1, 1931).

The Lore and Language of Schoolchildren, Iona and Peter Opie. NYRB Classics (April 9, 2001). ISBN: 978-0940322691.

Nation of Rebels: Why Counterculture Became Consumer Culture, by Joseph Heath and Andrew Potter. Harper Business; First U.S. Edition, Later Printing (December 14, 2004) ISBN: 978-0060745868.

Out of the Ashes: Rebuilding American Culture, by Anthony Esolen. Regnery Gateway (September 13, 2022). ISBN: 978-1684514090.

Philanthropic Giving, by F. Emerson Andrews. December, 1950 ISBN:978-0-87154-022-5.

The Paradox of Choice: Why More Is Less, Revised Edition, by Barry Schwartz. Ecco; Revised edition (May 17, 2016) ISBN: 978-0062449924.

The Political Anatomy of Ireland, with the Establishment for that Kingdom when the late Duke of Ormond was Lord Lieutenant, by William Petty, 1691.

Radical Hollywood: The Untold Story Behind America's Favorite Movies, by Paul Buhle and David Wagner. The New Press (August 1, 2003) ISBN: 978-1565848191.

Reinventing Collapse: The Soviet Experience and American Prospects-Revised & Updated, by Dmitry Orlov. New Society Publishers; Revised and Updated edition (June 1, 2011).

Rural Rides: Early 19th Travelogue of England, by William Cobbett. Independently published (October 20, 2023) ISBN: 979-8864916834.

The Scythe Book: Mowing Hay, Cutting Weeds, and Harvesting Small Grains with Hand Tools, by David Tresemer. Stackpole Books; 2021st edition (May 1, 2021). ISBN: 978-0811739795.

Smart Moves: Why Learning Is Not All in Your Head, by Carla Hannaford. Great River Books; 2nd edition (September 18, 2007). ISBN: 978-0915556373.

A Statistical Account, or Parochial Survey of Ireland: drawn up from the communications of the clergy, by William Shaw Mason. Published 1814.

The Technological Society, by Jacques Ellul. Vintage Books (January 1, 1964). ISBN: 978-0394703909.

War Before Civilization: The Myth of the Peaceful Savage by Lawrence Keeley, Oxford University Press; Reprint edition (December 18, 1997) ISBN: 978-0195119121.

The World Beyond Your Head: On Becoming an Individual in an Age of Distraction, by Matthew Crawford. Farrar, Straus and Giroux; Reprint edition (April 5, 2016). ISBN: 978-0374535919.

Who Killed Homer?: The Demise of Classical Education and the Recovery of Greek Wisdom, by Victor Davis Hanson and John Heath. Encounter Books; First Edition (April 1, 2001) ISBN: 978-1893554269.

War Before Civilization: The Myth of the Peaceful Savage, by Lawrence Keeley. Oxford University Press; Reprint edition (December 18, 1997). ISBN: 978-0195119121.

Articles:

Childhood

Bixler, Floyd, Hammitt, (2002). "Environmental Socialization: Quantitative Tests of the Childhood Play Hypothesis," *Environment and Behavior, 34*(6), 795-818.

Blair S.N., Clark D.G., Cureton K.J. & Powell K.F. (1989) "Exercise and Fitness in Childhood: Implications for a lifetime of health" in Gisolfi C.V. & Lamb D.R. (Eds) *Perspectives in Exercise Science and Sports Medicine,* vol. 2. *Youth, Exercise, and Sports,* pp. 401–430. Indianapolis: Benchmark Press.

Ellis, Michael J., "Play, Novelty, and Stimulus Seeking," *Child's Play,* Routledge 1984.

Gabbard, Carl. (1998). "Windows of Opportunity for Early Brain and Motor Development. Journal of Physical Education," *Recreation & Dance.* 69. 54-55.

Hillman, Adams and Whitelegg, "ONE FALSE MOVE...A Study of Children's Independent Mobility" January 1990, PSI Publishing.

Hirsh-Pasek, Kathy; Golinkoff, Roberta Minchik; *A Mandate for Playful Learning in Preschool,* 2009 Oxford University Press.

Hughes, C. (1998). "Finding your marbles: Does preschoolers' strategic behavior predict later understanding of mind?" *Developmental Psychology, 34*(6), 1326–1339.

Lorraine Maxwell, Gary Evans, "The effects of noise on pre-school children's pre-reading skills," *Journal of Environmental Psychology,* Volume 20, Issue 1, 2000, Pages 91-97.

Maynard, Waters, Clement: "Child-initiated learning, the outdoor environment and the "underachieving" child," *Early Years,* 33 (2013).

Pyle. "Eden in a Vacant Lot: Special Places, Species,and Kids in the Neighborhood of Life," *Children and Nature,* Chapter 12, 305-327. MIT Press 2002.

Shaw, Ben; Fagan-Watson, Ben; Redecker, Andreas: *Children's independent Mobility: a comparative study in England and Germany (1971-2010),* Policy Studies Institute (Jan 2013) ISBN: 9780853748557.

Soucise, A., Vaughn, C., Thompson, C.L. *et al.* "Sleep quality, duration, and breast cancer aggressiveness," *Breast Cancer Res Treat* 164, 169–178 (2017).

M I Wallhagen, W J Strawbridge, R D Cohen, and G A Kaplan, 1997: "An increasing prevalence of hearing impairment and associated risk factors over three decades of the Alameda County Study," *American Journal of Public Health* **87**, 440-442.

American Journal of Public Health **87**, 440_442Wells and Leskies, "Nature and the Life Course: Pathways from Childhood Nature Experiences to Adult Environmentalism," *Children, Youth and Environment* Vol. 16:1 (2006).

Worpole, Ken. *No Particular Place to Go: children, young people and public space,* Groundwork UK, 2003.

Keeping Animals

Smedbol and Wroblewski, "Metapopulation theory and northern cod population structure: interdependency of subpopulations in recovery of a groundfish population," *Fisheries Research,* Volume 55, Issues 1–3, 2002, Pages 161-174.

Foraging

Anderson, M.K. – "The fire, pruning and coppice management of temperate ecosystems for basketry material by Californian Indian tribes," *Human Ecology* 27(I) 79-113. 1999.

Brandenburg WE, Ward KJ. Mushroom poisoning epidemiology in the United States. *Mycologia.* 2018 Jul-Aug;110(4):637-641.

Elsen, J. "Microscopy of historic mortars — a review," *Cement and Concrete Research*, July 2005.

Elsen, J. "Chemistry and Technology of Lime and Limestone," *Cement and Concrete Research,* December 2005.

Landberg, T.; Greger, M. "Phytoremediation Using Willow in Industrial Contaminated Soil," *Sustainability* 2022, *14*, 8449.

Farming

Bekleyen, A. "The dovecotes of Diyarbakır: the surviving examples of a fading tradition." The Journal of Architecture, 14(4), 451-464. 2009.

Clayton, P.; Rowbotham, J. "How the Mid-Victorians Worked, Ate and Died," *Int. J. Environ. Res. Public Health* 2009, *6*, 1235-1253.

Cordain L, Lindeberg S, Hurtado M, Hill K, Eaton SB, Brand-Miller J. Acne Vulgaris: A Disease of Western Civilization. *Arch Dermatol.* 2002;138(12): 1584–1590.

Cordell D, Drangert J, and White S (2009), 'The story of phosphorus: global food security and food for thought,' *Global Environmental Change*, 19, p292–305.

Philippe Corsenac, Isabella Annesi-Maesano, Damian Hoy, Adam Roth, Bernard Rouchon, Isabelle Capart, Richard Taylor.

Corsenac et al, "Overweight and obesity in New Caledonian adults: Results from measured and adjusted self-reported anthropometric data," *Diabetes Research and Clinical Practice*, Volume 133, 2017, Pages 193-203.

Irimia, A, et al, "The Indigenous South American Tsimane Exhibit Relatively Modest Decrease in Brain Volume With Age Despite High Systemic Inflammation," *The Journals of Gerontology: Series A*, Volume 76, Issue 12, December 2021, Pages 2147–2155.

Jackson M. et al, "Unlocking the secrets of Al-tobermorite in Roman seawater concrete," *American Mineralogist* 2013; 98 (10): 1669–1687.

Jackson M, et al, "Material and elastic properties of Al-tobermorite in ancient Roman seawater concrete," *Journal of the American Ceramic Society*, Volume 96, Issue 8 p. 2598-2606, 28 May 2013.

McGregor, P. "Demographic Pressure and the Irish Famine: Malthus after Mokyr," Land Economics, Vol. 65, No. 3. (Aug., 1989), pp. 228-238.

Pop, R.-M.; Tenenboum, A.; Pop, M. "Secular Trends in Height, Body Mass and Mean Menarche Age in Romanian Children and Adolescents," 1936–2016. *Int. J. Environ. Res. Public Health* 2021, *18*, 490.

Rowbotham J, Clayton P. "An Unsuitable and Degraded Diet? Part I: Public Health Lessons from the Mid-Victorian Working-class Diet," *Journal of the Royal Society of Medicine*, 2008;101:282–9.

Stushnoff, C., McSay, A.E., Luby, J. and Forsline, P.L. (2003). "Diversity of Phenolic and Antioxidant Content and Radical Scavenging Capacity in the USDA Apple Germplasm Core Collection," *Acta Hortic.* 623, 305-312.

Crafting

Knoop, Douglas and Jones, G.P. and Cheney C.R., "Rules for the observance of feast-days in medieval England," *Bulletin of the Institute of Historical Research* 34, 90, 117-29 (1961).

Ritchie, Nora "Labour conditions in Essex in the reign of Richard II," in E.M. Carus-Wilson, ed., *Essays in Economic History, vol. II*, London: Edward Arnold, 1962.

Rogers, J. *Six Centuries of Work and Wages* (London: Allen and Unwin, 1949), 542-43.

Walker, Robert S.; Bailey, Drew H. "Body counts in lowland South American violence," *Evolution and Human Behavior,* Volume 34, Issue 1, 2013, Pages 29-34.

Wrzesniewski, Amy; Dutton, Jane; Debebe, Gelaye "Interpersonal Sensemaking and the Meaning of Work," *Research in Organizational Behavior,* Volume 25, 2003, Pages 93-135.

Schooling

Goodman et al, U.S. Department of Education, "Literacy, Numeracy, and Problem Solving in Technology-Rich Environments Among U.S. Adults," 2012.

Laurie O'Higgins, "(In)Felix Paupertas: Scholarship of the Eighteenth-century Irish Poor," *Arethusa*, Vol. 40, No. 2 (Fall 2007) p. 421-450.

M. Quane, 1954 "Banna School, Ardfert, with a Preparatory Survey of Classical Education in Kerry in the Eighteenth Century," *Journal of the Royal Society of Antiquaries of Ireland* 84.156-72.

Visiting

Dworkin, R "The Rise of the Caring Industry," *Policy Review*, 161 (Jun/Jul 2010): 45-49.

Robert Epstein, Mayuri Pandit and Mansi Thakar, "How Love Emerges in Arranged Marriages: Two Cross-cultural Studies," *Journal of Comparative Family Studies*, Volume 44 Issue 3, May–June 2013, pp. 341-360.

Gupta, U., & Singh, P. (1982). An exploratory study of love and liking and type of marriages. *Indian Journal of Applied Psychology, 19*(2), 92–97.

Paull Yelsma and Kuriakose Athappilly, "Marital Satisfaction and Communication Practices: Comparisons Among Indian and American Couples," *Journal of Comparative Family Studies,* Volume 19 Issue 1, Spring 1988, pp. 37-54.

"Generation Z and the Transformation of American Adolescence: How Gen Z's Formative Experiences Shape Its Politics, Priorities, and Future," *Survey Centre on American Life*, 9 Nov 2023.

"The Paradox of Declining Female Happiness," *National Bureau of Economic Research*, May 2009.

"Adult Psychiatric Morbidity Survey: Survey of Mental Health and Wellbeing," NHS, Sept 2016.

Storytelling

Baumer, E. P. S., Guha, S., Quan, E., Mimno, D., & Gay, G. K. (2015). Missing Photos, Suffering Withdrawal, or Finding Freedom? How Experiences of Social Media Non-Use Influence the Likelihood of Reversion. *Social Media + Society, 1*(2).

Roberts, J., Yaya, L., & Manolis, C. (2014). The invisible addiction: Cell-phone activities and addiction among male and female college students. *Journal of Behavioral Addictions, 3*(4), 254-265.

Trading

Iyengar, Sheena S., and Mark R. Lepper. "When choice is demotivating: Can one desire too much of a good thing?." *Journal of personality and social psychology* 79.6 (2000): 995.

Murphy, Antoin "Money in an Economy Without Banks: The Case of Ireland," Murphy, Murphy, *The Manchester School* 46.1 (1978): 41-50.

Read, Daniel, and George Loewenstein. "Diversification bias: Explaining the discrepancy in variety seeking between combined and separated choices." *Journal of Experimental Psychology: Applied* 1.1 (1995): 34.

Redden, Joseph P., Kelly L. Haws, and Jinjie Chen. "The ability to choose can increase satiation." *Journal of Personality and Social Psychology* 112.2 (2017): 186.

Simonson, Itamar. "The effect of purchase quantity and timing on variety-seeking behavior." *Journal of Marketing research* 27.2 (1990): 150-162.

Conclusion

Parker, Geoffrey. "Some recent work on the Inquisition in Spain and Italy." *The Journal of Modern History* 54.3 (1982).